THE YALE GERTRUDE STEIN

THE YALE
GERTRUDE STEIN

Selections, with an Introduction
by Richard Kostelanetz

NEW HAVEN AND LONDON

YALE UNIVERSITY PRESS

For Edward Burns
—a friendship initiated and
continued through Stein

The Introduction originally appeared in slightly different form in *The Hollins Critic*,
under the title "Gertrude Stein: The New Literature," copyright © 1975 by Hollins
College.
  The selections for this edition are reprinted from the following works by Gertrude
Stein: *Two: Gertrude Stein and Her Brother, and Other Early Portraits (1908–12)*, copyright
1951 by Alice B. Toklas, renewed 1979 by Calman A. Levin; *Mrs. Reynolds and Five
Earlier Novelettes*, copyright 1952 by Alice B. Toklas; *Bee Time Vine and Other Pieces
(1913–1927)*, copyright 1953 by Alice B. Toklas; *As Fine as Melanctha (1914–1930)*,
copyright 1954 by Alice B. Toklas; *Painted Lace and Other Pieces (1914–1937)*, copyright
© 1955 by Alice B. Toklas; *Stanzas in Meditation and Other Poems (1929–1933)*, copyright
© 1956 by Alice B. Toklas; *Alphabets and Birthdays*, copyright © 1957 by Alice B.
Toklas; *A Novel of Thank You*, copyright © 1958 by Alice B. Toklas.
Set in Janson type.
Printed in the United States of America by Vail-Ballou Press, Inc.,
Binghamton, N.Y.

Library of Congress Cataloging in Publication Data

Stein, Gertrude, 1874–1946.
  The Yale Gertrude Stein.

  Selected from The Yale edition of the unpublished
writings of Gertrude Stein.
  I. Kostelanetz, Richard. II. Title.
PS3537.T323A6 1980   818'.5209   80-5398
ISBN 0-300-02574-2
ISBN 0-300-02609-9 (pbk.)

10 9 8 7 6 5 4 3 2 1

CONTENTS

Alice B. Toklas is always forethoughtful which is what is pleasant for me so she said she would make copies of all my writing not yet published and send it to Carl Van Vechten for safe keeping. In spite of everything and everything means a fair amount printed there still is a good deal unpublished. . . .

Besides I said I wanted them to go ahead and print everything, it has always been my hope that some day someone would print everything, it does not bother me so much now, well partly because it does not and partly because if it is not printed someone will discover it later and that will be much more exciting or they will not and that will be so much more disturbing.

Gertrude Stein, *Everybody's Autobiography* (1937)

Every Gertrude Stein enthusiast who has ever seen or even heard about the eight Yale University Press volumes of "The Unpublished Writings of Gertrude Stein" has regretted that they were not readily available. Initially published between 1951 and 1958, they went completely out of print in the mid sixties, to be revived several years later by hardback reprinters whose prices only libraries could afford. Since these Yale volumes contain some of Stein's most extraordinary work—particularly her best poems—it seemed appropriate to greet the 1980s with a one-volume selection of *The Yale Gertrude Stein*.

Though Bennett Cerf of Random House agreed to publish all her *new* work in the wake of the success of both *The Autobiography of Alice B. Toklas* (1933) and her 1934 American tour, Gertrude Stein died with a large cache of works that had never been printed. As Carl Van Vechten tells it in his preface to the last of the Yale volumes, *A Novel of Thank You*, "She had made me, in some of her last conscious moments, her literary executor, with instructions to publish what material of hers still re-

mained unpublished, for which purpose she instructed her at-
torney to provide me with the essential sums of money." As
Stein's oldest and most loyal American friend, Van Vechten
had already received copies of these manuscripts and had
turned them over to the Yale University Library. Thus it was
arranged that Yale University Press would publish the volumes, one each year for eight years; friends of Stein were re-
cruited to write the prefaces—Janet Flanner, Lloyd Frank-
enberg, Virgil Thomson, Natalie Barney, Daniel-Henry
Kahnweiler, Donald Sutherland, Donald Gallup, and, of
course, Van Vechten. Just as Stein had subsidized the original
editions of not only her earliest books but the middle ones too
(the Plain Edition of 1931–33), so it became inevitable that she
contributed to the publication of the original editions of her
final ones as well.

My introduction to this selection is drawn from an essay that
initially appeared in *The Hollins Critic* (Summer 1975) and that
will become part of a projected critical book on experimental
literature in America. This introduction is general, it is true,
scarcely mentioning the individual selections; for in my judgment, once Stein's particular developments are understood,
there is no need for didactic guidance through individual
pieces. In making selections I have tended to favor Stein's more
experimental works, in part because it is these, rather than,
say, *Three Lives* or *The Autobiography of Alice B. Toklas*, that make
her a major writer. Thus, this book includes Stein's major long
poems—"Stanzas in Meditation," largely an extended abstrac-
tion; "Patriarchal Poetry," a mixture of poetry and prose; and
"Lifting Belly," a lesbian classic—along with shorter poems;
and it includes compressed novels, such as "Brim Beauvais" and
the three-page "What Does She See When She Shuts Her
Eyes," along with abstract prose, such as "A Sonatina Followed
by Another," and extended stories, such as "Subject-Cases:
The Background of a Detective Story," which also reflects
Stein's personal enthusiasm for detective fiction. I have included examples of what we would now call sound poetry
("New," "Go in Green"), abstract poetry ("Dates"), and minimal poetry ("One or Two. I've Finished"), in addition to a

Steinian tongue-twister ("Tillie") and "Emp Lace," which
mixes a variety of characteristic devices of both prose and poetry within ten pages. There are also plays, such as the skit
"Yet Dish," and essays, such as the extrinsically structured "A
Birthday Book," the minimal "Mark Twain Centenary," and
"More Grammar for a Sentence," which presages *How to Write*
(1931). The one selection I regret losing, because of limitations
in space, is "Two: Gertrude Stein and Her Brother," which
contains some of Stein's most spectacular writing (around pages
83–88 in the original edition) and would have represented her
interest in extended prose repetition. Otherwise, examples of
all the technical devices mentioned in the introduction are included in the book.

For advice in reconsidering these selections, I am indebted to
my friends Edward Burns and Dick Higgins.

RICHARD KOSTELANETZ

New York City
14 May 1980

INTRODUCTION

That they have nothing outside of themselves to say should not
be disturbing, even in literary plays, because no literature, once
you are out of school and have heard everything, is interesting for
what it has to say.

Donald Sutherland, *Gertrude Stein* (1951)

What distinguishes Gertrude Stein (1874–1946) from her chro-
nological contemporaries in American literature (e.g., Dreiser,
Stephen Crane, Vachel Lindsay, and others) is that even today
most of her works are commonly misunderstood. The principal
reason for such continued incomprehension is that her experiments in writing were conducted apart from the major developments in modern literature. Neither a naturalist nor a sur-
realist, she had no interest in either the representation of social
reality or the weaving of symbols, no interest at all in myth,
metaphor, allegory, literary allusions, uncommon vocabulary,
synoptic cultural critiques, shifts in point of view, or much else
that preoccupied writers such as James Joyce, Thomas Mann,
and Marcel Proust. Unlike them, she was an empiricist, who
preferred to write about observable realities and personally familiar subjects; the titles of her books were typically declarative
and descriptive, rather than symbolic and allusive. Not unlike
other modern writers, she was influenced by developments in
the nonliterary arts; but Stein feasted upon a fertile aesthetic
idea that her literary colleagues neglected—to emphasize prop-
erties peculiar to one's chosen medium and it alone. As her art
was writing, rather than painting, Stein's primary interest was
language—more specifically, American English and how *else* its
words might be used. Indicatively, the same aesthetic idea that
became so quickly acceptable in modernist painting and music
was for so long heretical, if not unthinkable, in literature.

From nearly the beginnings of her creative career, Stein experimented with language in several ways. Starting from scratch, she neglects the arsenal of devices that authors had traditionally used to enhance their prose. Though she was personally literate, her language is kept intentionally unliterary and unconnotative. Her diction is mundane, though her sentence structure is not, for it was her particular achievement to build a complex style out of purposely limited vocabulary. An early device, already evident in *Three Lives* (drafted in 1904), is the shifting of syntax, so that parts of a sentence appear in unusual places. Adverbs that customarily come before a verb now follow it, and what might normally be the object of a sentence either becomes its subject or precedes it. These shifts not only repudiate the conventions of syntactical causality, but they also introduce dimensions of subtlety and accuracy. Instead of saying "someone is alive," Stein writes, "Anyone can be a living one." As the critic Norman Weinstein points out, the present participle indicates "the *process* of living." Some parts of speech are omitted, while others are duplicated; and nouns, say, are used in ways that obscure their traditional functions within the structure of a sentence.

Especially in *The Making of Americans*, which was begun in 1902 and revised in 1908–11, Stein inserts extra gerunds into otherwise normal clauses. Around this time she also began to remove adjectives, adverbs, and internal punctuation, thereby increasing the suggestions of ambiguity. Because parts of speech are scrambled and individual words are functioning in multiple ways, it is impossible to diagram even this superficially simple sentence: "Any one being one being in any family living is being one having been saying something." And paraphrase is similarly futile. Such devices not only tend to make her sentences more prolix than normal (in Stein's idiosyncratic heresy), but they are invariably more striking as well. Even rather commonplace perceptions become in her words more witty and, in ways, more elegant:

Everybody called Gertrude Stein Gertrude, or at most Mademoiselle Gertrude, everybody called Picasso Pablo and Fernande Fernande and everybody called Guillaume Apollinaire Guillaume and Max Jacob Max but everybody called Marie Laurencin Marie Laurencin.

The subjects of Stein's books tended to be personally familiar—that of *The Making of Americans*, say, is the saga of her own family in America; for instead of "making up" plots and characters, she concentrated on inventing linguistic structures.

In that 925-page milestone, her longest single book, Stein broached what subsequently became her initial notorious device—the use of linguistic repetition. To be precise, she repeats certain key words or phrases within otherwise different clauses and sentences; so that even though the repetitions are never exact, this repeated material comes to dominate the entire paragraph or section. The effect is initially wearisome—the reader's eye wants to leap ahead to something else, because he can quickly discern, by looking at the entire paragraph, which words will be emphasized. (And experienced readers, like experienced hikers, invariably short-cut by instinct.) However, it would be wise to linger, or even to read the passage aloud, because what makes Stein's repetitions so interesting is precisely the varying relationships that the repeated elements have to their surrounding frames. As phrases are rarely repeated exactly, what initially seems identical is, upon closer inspection, seen to be quite various, for one theme of Stein's repetitions (and near-repetitions) is the endless differences amid recurring sameness. Sometimes the repetition becomes a modifier, introducing degrees of reconsideration apart from punctuation (e.g., "not necessary not really necessary," "the story must be told will be told can be told"). As Kenneth Rexroth observed, "Gertrude Stein showed, among other things, that if you focus your attention on 'please pass the butter,' and put it through enough permutations and combinations, it begins to take on a kind of glow, the splendor of what is called an 'aesthetic object.' "

By dominating the reader's attention, repetitions become a device for focusing and emphasis; a passage is remembered in terms of this repeated material. (One aesthetic truth that Stein probably learned from painting is the importance of an "after-image.") She also believed that repetitions could be a tool for penetrating beneath the surface of character:

> I began to get enormously interested in hearing how every-body said the same thing over and over again with infinite variations but over and over again until finally if you lis-tened with great intensity you could hear it rise and fall and tell all that there was inside them.

This kind of comprehension was, in Stein's view, as much im-plicit as explicit: "Not so much by the actual words they said or the thoughts they had but by movement of their thoughts and words endlessly the same and endlessly different." By empha-sizing not what was said but how, Stein paradoxically aimed to communicate, in the course of repetition, human dimensions that were ultimately beyond the capacities of language. (Docu-menting this last claim remains, in my opinion, beyond the capacities of empirical criticism.)

In reading Stein, one finds that the reapplication of attention, especially after a lapse or rebuff, can produce a range of un-usual effects, because the reader's mind is forced out of its cus-tomary perceptual procedures. While talking about something else, the composer John Cage once suggested, perspicaciously, "In Zen they say: If something is boring after two minutes, try it for four. If still boring, try it for eight, sixteen, thirty-two and so on. Eventually one discovers that it's not boring but very interesting." A similar experience is possible reading Stein. Though she personally abjured both alcohol and mind-changing drugs, both her work and Cage's rationale prophet-ically precede a certain kind of art that became particularly prevalent around the psychedelic apex of 1967—works both vi-sual and aural in which certain motifs are repeated to excess, transcending themselves to initiate a different kind of experi-ence.

Because of its audacious exploration of repetition as a device, not only of style but of understanding, *The Making of Americans*

seems "contemporary" and "innovative" and "incredible" long
after it was written. Originally drafted in the first decade of this
century, well before the innovative novels of James Joyce and
William Faulkner, it represents the first giant step beyond nine-
teenth-century fiction, and other prose works written around
1910 are no less advanced—"Many Many Women," "A Long
Gay Book," and "Two." Stein's biggest book also stands as an
epitome of that colossal, uneven, digressive, excessive, eccentric
masterpiece that every great American innovative artist seems
to produce at least once. Its peers in this respect are Walt Whit-
man's *Leaves of Grass*, Ezra Pound's *Cantos*, Faulkner's *Absalom,
Absalom!*, and Charles Ives's Fourth Symphony. Not unlike
other American geniuses, Stein walked the swampy field between brilliance and looniness; and even today, as in her own
time, her works are perceived as extraordinary or mad or, more
precisely, both.

In addition to defining emphasis, Stein's linguistic repetitions
also serve as a structural device, for the repeated word becomes
the primary cohering force within a passage. Consequently, expository units, such as the paragraph, are reorganized. Instead
of proceeding from a topic sentence through various examples,
the paragraph is now filled with clauses that have equal weight
within the whole:

> Not and now, now and not, not and now, by and by not
> and now, as not, as soon as not not and now, now as soon
> now now as soon, now as soon as soon as now. Just as soon
> just now just now just as soon just as soon as now. Just as
> soon as now. ["As a Wife Has a Cow: A Love Story" (1926)]

In Stein's view, the repetition of a single word can also evoke
connotations, not only by assuming different meanings in varying contexts but also through the suggestions of secondary qualities. In explaining her most famous repetition of "rose is a rose
is a rose is a rose," she once told a university audience: "I'm no
fool. I know that in daily life we don't go around saying [that],
but I think that in that line the rose is red for the first time in

English poetry for a hundred years." Readers struck by the simplicities of much Stein prose tend to forget how intelligent, conscious, and literate she actually was, for only an assuredly smart author would risk such semblances of stupidity. In his classic *Seven Types of Ambiguity* (1929), William Empson places Stein with Dryden among those authors who "write with the whole weight of the [English] language, to remind one always of the latent assumptions of [English]." Nonetheless, her writing reveals her literacy paradoxically—not through echoes and allusions, but through the scrupulous avoidance of them.

These innovations, simple at base, had radical and complex effects. As she neglected subject, setting, anecdote, conflict, analysis, and many other conventional elements, *style* became the dominant factor in Stein's writing. It became more important than "theme" or "character"; so that from *The Making of Americans* onward, her books could be characterized as a succession of experiments in particular styles, other dimensions being merely incidental. (Even within *Americans*, her style becomes progressively more experimental.) Secondly, since language is primary, climactic structures become secondary; thus, narrative elements tend to be as flat and uninflected as Stein's language. To put it differently, the kind of structural flattening to which Stein subjected the paragraph was extended to longer forms in her exposition and narrative; so that even in the family history of *The Making of Americans*, no event is more important than any other. In this respect in particular, Stein clearly precedes the formally uninflected, counter-hierarchical prose of, say, Samuel Beckett and Alain Robbe-Grillet.

This emphasis upon style also diminishes the importance of representational concerns, and that in turn contributes to an entirely different kind of flattening—the elimination of both temporal and spatial perspectives. Stein defined this effect when she said that her books take place in the "continuous present." All these changes brought the abolition of linear causality in the portrayal of character and activity; they also enabled Stein to introduce an event at one point of *The Making of Americans* and then postpone further consideration of it for several hundred pages. Historically, we can see that the use of such forms

placed her among the first imaginative writers to represent the
modern awareness of discontinuous experience. In the nineteenth century, as Donald Sutherland defined it, "Something
belongs to everything automatically. But nothing now is really
convincingly a part of anything else; anything stands by itself if
at all and its connections are chance encounters." In *The Making
of Americans*, as well as other works of hers, I find a sense of indefinite space where characters are perceived apart from their
surroundings and each other, where environment is not a for-
mative factor, where the sense of time is more spatial than
sequential. In her *Lectures in America* (1935), Stein justifies not
only her own penchant for fragmentary perception but that of
others as a distinctly American style of literary representation:
"A disembodied way of disconnecting something from anything
and anything from something."

All of these experiments in style progressively freed Stein
from the restrictions of conventional syntax (and the Aris-
totelian assumptions informing it); so that in future works she
was able to explore the possibilities of not just one but several
kinds of alternative language. Having worked with accretion
and explicitness, as well as syntactical transposition, she then
experimented with ellipses and economy; having written about
something with many more words than usual, she also tried to
write with far, far fewer. In *Tender Buttons*, which was begun in
1911 and finished the following year, her aim was the creation
of texts that described a thing without mentioning it by name.
She would approach a subject from various perspectives, just as
a cubist painter would; and like them she was interested in dis-
covering the limits of reorganized representation. Each of the
prose sections of that early book has a subtitle or opening words
that provide a context for otherwise unexplicit language. This
passage is prefaced by the subtitle "A Box":

> Out of kindness comes redness and out of rudeness comes
> rapid same question, out of an eye comes research, out of
> selection comes painful cattle. So then the order is that a
> white way of being round is something suggesting a pin
> and is it disappointing, it is not, it is so rudimentary to be

analysed and see a fine substance strangely, it is so earnest
to have a green point not to red but to point again.

What distinguishes this passage is a scrupulous disregard for ev-
eryday linguistic functions—not only conventional transitions
but any definitions of extrinsic experience; and though this language scarcely resembles verse, it could be called "poetic" precisely because it is not prosaic.

Though critics commonly suggest that Stein's language has
some implicit relation to one's experience of the ostensible subject, the prose can be (and often is) perceived apart from any
content. For instance, in the following passage from "Precio-
silla," which appeared in *Composition as Explanation* (1926), Carl
Van Vechten found "an attempt to recapture the rhythm of [a]
flamenco dancer":

> Not so dots large dressed dots, big sizes, less laced, less
> laced diamonds, diamonds white, diamonds bright, dia-
> monds in the in the light, diamonds light diamonds door
> diamonds hanging to be four, two four, all before, this
> bean, lessly, all most, a best, willow, vest, a green guest,
> guest, go go go go go go, go. Go go. Not guessed. Go go.

While this passage does indeed capture the blatant percus-
siveness of flamenco dancing, it is nonetheless astonishing, un-
precedented prose that realizes its peculiar charms and coherences *apart from* the reader's knowledge of any ulterior subject
or content. As E. E. Cummings, then an undergraduate, observed in reviewing *Tender Buttons* for the *Harvard Advocate*,
"Gertrude Stein subordinates the meaning of words to the
beauty of the words themselves." Sherwood Anderson more
precisely perceived, "She is laying word against word, relating
sound to sound, feeling for the taste, the smell, the rhythm of
the individual word." Her writings represent, at their human
base, an extended celebration of the possibilities of American
English.

II

One may, and Gertrude Stein did, write as if every instant of writing were complete in itself, as if in the act of writing something were continually coming true and completing itself, not as if it were leading to something.

Donald Sutherland, *Gertrude Stein* (1951)

Certain other prose pieces, composed mostly in the post–World War I decade, are yet more extraordinary, having no apparent subject or other semantic content at all, because their real theme—their major concern—is the kinds of coherences that can be established within language itself:

Able there to ball bawl able to call and seat a tin a tin whip with a collar. The least licence is in the eyes which make strange the less sighed hole which is nodded and leaves the bent tender.

This passage comes from "A Sweet Tale (Gypsies)," where another passage reads:

Appeal, a peal, laugh, hurry merry, good in night, rest stole. Rest stole to bestow candle electricity in surface. The best header is nearly peek.

Here and elsewhere in Stein, words become autonomous objects, rather than symbols of something else, for they are themselves, rather than windows onto other terrain. They cohere in terms of stressed sounds, rhythms, alliterations, rhymes, textures, and consistencies in diction—linguistic qualities other than subject and syntax; and even when entirely divorced from semantics, these dimensions of prose have their own powers of effect. She also discovered that disconnection enhances language, precisely because the process of transcending mundane sentences makes every word important. "You use the glasses as a magnifying glass and so read word by word reading word by

word makes the writing that is not anything be something."
Elsewhere she explains how this discovery was exploited: "I
took individual words and thought about them until I got their
weight and volume complete and put them next to another
word and at this same time I found very soon that there is no
such thing as putting them together without sense." Indeed,
especially in the articulation of these linguistic qualities, Stein's
language at times approaches the density of *Finnegans Wake*.

Having abandoned prolix paragraphs, she then made fictions
out of abbreviated notations, such as these from "The King or
Something" in *Geography and Plays:*

PAGE XV.

We didn't
Allow me to differ.

PAGE XVI.

Did you say it did.

PAGE XVIII.

Very likely I missed it.

PAGE XIX.

Turn turn.

PAGE XX.

You must never hurry yourself.
No indeed
Now I understand.

PAGE XXI.

Think a minute think a minute there.

Not only does such compression (along with the telling omis-
sion of page XVII) represent a radical reconsideration of fictional
scale, but writings like these also represent, in Sutherland's
judgment, "the first uncompromising attempt to create [in liter-
ature] a thing existing in itself." Though working apart from
the French symbolists, she realized their theoretical ideal of a
completely autonomous language—creating a verbal reality
apart from extrinsic reality. However, whereas the symbolists
regarded language as the tip of the iceberg, revealing only part
of the underlying meaning, Stein was primarily concerned with

literature's surfaces, asking her readers to pay particular attention to words, rather than to the content and motives that
might lie behind them. There are few, if any, purposely ulterior subjects in her writing after 1910. What you read is most of
what there is.

Such prose is frequently called "musical," because of its distance from expository language; but since words divorced from
the demands of syntax and semantics are still words, that metaphor is inaccurate. Actually, it is more appropriate to regard
such writing as an accurate analogy to atonality in music.
Whereas composers such as Debussy and Schoenberg were
abandoning the tonality of tonics and dominants—the standard
musical syntax since the Renaissance—in order to emphasize
the cohering capabilities of other dimensions of musical material, Stein had similarly eschewed conventional syntax for alternative emphases. By neglecting semantics as well, she was free
to emphasize elements strictly indigenous to language. What
initially attracted the composer Virgil Thomson to Stein's texts
was this absence of extrinsic references. "There was no tempta-
tion toward tonal illustration," he explained. "If a text were set
correctly for the sound of it, then meaning will take care of itself."

Stein also recapitulated in literature the evolution of modernist painting. Her earliest works could be considered "cubist" in
their syntactical radicalism, the redistribution of traditional emphases, and the distortion of space-time representation, in addition to the twofold attempt not only to abstract the most important elements from a mass of detail but also to depict an
underlying reality that was beyond exterior surfaces. Many of
her later, post–World War I writings, by contrast, strike me as
decidedly nonrepresentational, lacking even the suggestion of
anything outside themselves.* To put it differently, as purely
abstract paintings represented nothing more than color and

---

*Edward Burns claims, to the contrary, that even in these works "Stein never leaves
the object. It is just harder to get the key." Impressed though I am by the research informing Burns's identifications, I find that unless the reader has the key in advance, he
must confront the writing on the door without it. And that door need not be opened for
the writing to be appreciated, if not understood.

shape on two-dimensional canvases, so abstract writing is based exclusively upon materials indigenous to the medium of language: words that are unified by elements other than syntax and semantics. Thus, just as each new abstract painting is largely indebted to previous paintings, so Stein's prose refers largely to previous works of language. At these formal levels, painting-as-painting resembles writing-as-writing. Passages like those quoted before could also be characterized as "acoherent" with respect to traditional kinds of linguistic coherence, much as the epithet "atonal music" has been used to distinguish new ways of organizing sound from traditional diatonic tonalities. As the "meaning" of such passages lies wholly within language, rather than beyond it, this prose need not be "interpreted" in terms of other meanings. What you read is all there is.

Abandoning certain constraints upon language, she looked for other rules to guide her propensities for linguistic invention. By regarding language as a technology that existed apart from herself, she could subject it to various experimental modifications. Viewing herself as a disciplined intermediary, she would write passages with words of only one syllable and others with consistently abrupt sentences. An entire book was written in the voice of her lifetime companion, Alice B. Toklas. Attuned to the linguistic possibilities of nonverbal experience, she wrote nonsyntactical prose whose rhythms echoed those made by her dog's lapping and yet other passages that imitated the sounds heard on a Parisian street; she drafted "A Comedy Like That" to the sound of running water and a whole novel, *Lucy Church Amiably* (1931), in close proximity to a waterfall. Stylistic ideas, coupled with her immediate experience, were the root inspirations of her most extraordinary works. "Language as a real thing," she wrote in *Lectures in America*, "is not imitation either of sounds or colors or emotions it is an intellectual recreation." All her experimenting with the technology of language produced not just one original style but several, some of which are quite different from the others, all of which seem, nonetheless, to be distinctly Steinian. Perhaps the most extraordinary quality of these inventions is their continuing contemporaneity; a reader today can scarcely believe that all the passages quoted in this essay were written over fifty years ago.

Although Stein initially regarded herself as a novelist, descending not only from Henry James and Gustave Flaubert but also from the classic tradition of British fiction, she must have recognized that her emphasis upon verbal style was applicable to other genres as well. In sharp contrast to those modernist poets whose works in other genres were fairly conventional (e.g., T. S. Eliot's plays, Ezra Pound's essays), Stein let her artistic predilections transcend the demands of genre, rather than the reverse. Her plays, for instance, consist primarily of a series of prose passages, which are sometimes connected to particular characters and other times not. Only occasionally are characters identified at the beginning, while her texts rarely include stage directions of any kind. In a Stein play, there is typically nothing about tone, pace, costumes, decor, or any other theatrical specifics, all of which are thus left to the interpretation of the plays' directors. Instead of explicitly bothering with these dimensions, Stein customarily created concise verbal texts that are so distinctive that their style informs every aspect of a theatrical production. Their sections are also cavalierly scrambled, as "act III" (or "page III") does not necessarily follow "act II" (or "page II"), and reordering the parts into a conventional chronology is no more apt either. As Edward Burns suggests, "Like a landscape they can be viewed from any duration at any speed." Since scripts like these are simply not conducive to conventional realistic staging, directors like Lawrence Kornfeld have favored highly spectacular, sensorily abundant productions that incorporate music and dance, in sum exemplifying not only Stein's concept of theater as an art of sight and sound but also the most valid kind of "opera" America has yet seen.

These texts are, in essence, verbal settings for generating a live performance, and in crucial stylistic respects they are clearly unlike anything ever written for earlier theater. They should be considered plays, rather than stories or poems, because, as Donald Sutherland perceives, they portray "movement in space, or in a landscape. . . . A number of people or

things or even ideas presenting themselves together, as exis-
tences in space constituted a play." Many of these plays seem
nonrepresentational, because they do not refer to anything spe-
cific outside of language and the performers speaking it. Lacking any attempt at illusionism, they take place in a second nature that exists apart from mundane nature. As Van Vechten
perceived, their aim was "without telling what happened to
make a play the essence of what happened." What you see is
most, if not all, of what there is.

Another dimension that separates them from traditional plays
is the emphasis upon each line, or upon each moment, primarily for itself, rather than for its contribution to a larger
structure; and as in Stein's fiction, this redistribution of emphasis brings an elimination not only of climaxes but also of sharp
beginnings and decisive ends—in sum, a general flattening of
theatrical form. Sutherland suggested in 1951 that those "plays"
written before 1920 were not intended to be performed, but
even by the sixties such abstruse texts as "What Happened"
(1913) and "In Circles" (1920) were successfully staged. What is
most remarkable about Stein's plays is that they were written at
a time when varieties of realism dominated the American stage.
Her more prominent contemporaries included such forgotten
names as Percy MacKaye (1875–1956) and Eugene Walter
(1875–1941); Eugene O'Neill (1888–1953) was fourteen years
Stein's junior. While *The Making of Americans* was much longer
than a standard novel, these plays are shorter and more skeletal
than standard plays, for Stein foreshadowed the contemporary
avant-garde principle of making art that is either much more *or*
much less than before.

Her essays also were unlike anything written in that genre
before. In discussing a particular subject, she avoided the conventions of exposition, such as example and elaboration, in
favor of accumulating disconnected details and miscellaneous
insights, which were invariably subjected to her favorite device
of repetition. As in her plays and prose, the result is an overall
flattening of expository form, so that an essay's themes are not
concentrated at the beginning and at the end but scattered
throughout the piece. The absence of linear focus also accounts

for the penchants for digression and non sequitur. Like the cubist painters, she endeavored, as she put it, "to describe the inside as seen from the outside." Because her essays are structured as a succession of detached moments, they are remembered not in terms of their opening sentences or even their choicest aphorisms but by what is repeated, whether words or phrases (e.g., Matisse is "struggling").

In doing a portrait of "Monsieur Vollard et Cézanne" (1912), she learned that perceptions could be organized vertically as well:

> This is truth.
> Trust
> Thrust to be
> Actually.

In an essay entitled "We Came: A History" (1930), she used equal signs as internal punctuation, suggesting that each part of a single paragraph is as important as any other. The mechanical device of a mathematical symbol becomes a means toward qualitative ends:

> History there = Is no disaster because = Those who make history = Cannot be overtaken = As they will make = History which they do = Because it is necessary = That every one will = Begin to know that = They must know that = History is what it is = Which it is as they do =. . . .

She frequently claimed that in writing she was "telling what she knew," but most of her knowledge concerned writing. It is probably significant that the principal theme of her essays, reiterated as much by example as by explanation, is the autonomy of language. It was, I think, her greatest ambition to be as inventive and fecund in her arts as Picasso was in his.

Works that Stein meant to publish as poems, such as *Before the Flowers of Friendship Faded Friendship Faded* (1931) and the pieces posthumously collected in *Bee Time Vine* (1953) and in

Stanzas in Meditation (1956), resemble her most abstract writing in entirely eschewing subjects in order to explore alternative linguistic coherence—diction, alliteration, rhythm, rhyme, timbre, repetition, and other similarly nonsemantic qualities:

> A clock in the eye ticks in the eye a clock ticks in the eye.
> A number with that and large as a hat which makes rims think quicker than I.
> A clock in the eye ticks in the eye a clock ticks ticks in the eye.

Another passage from *Before the Flowers* is yet more exemplary:

> It is always just as well
> That there is a better bell
> Than that with which a half is a whole
> Than that with which they went away to stay
> Than that with which after any way,
> Needed to be gay to-day.

A poem like "One or Two. I've Finished" (1914) not only eschewed conventional linear syntax; it pioneered the format of horizontal minimalism (e.g., the poems of Robert Lax and Kenneth Gangemi), as it has only one word to a line for its entirety:

> There
> Why
> There
> Why
> There
> Able
> Idle

That Stein's poems are in English seems merely a convenience, perhaps testifying to her abiding love for her native language; for she did not follow Lewis Carroll's "Jabberwocky" (or precede James Joyce's *Finnegans Wake*) in creating an artificial language. Not until recently have critics begun to examine Stein's remarkable poetic styles, and no dimension of her oeuvre illustrates as well Sutherland's suggestion, back in 1951, that "Sooner or later criticism will have to get used to thinking in terms of forces, tensions, movements, speeds, attractions, etc."

Largely because Stein's writings were so unconventional, even in terms of the developments of literary modernism, it took her long, far too long, to get them into public print. She subsidized the publication of two of her first three books; she and Alice Toklas sold a Picasso to finance the Plain Edition publication of five more volumes in the early thirties (one of these containing texts that had *all* been written more than two decades before); and her will provided for subsidizing the posthumous publication of previously unpublished writings. Though she had been writing steadily from the age of twenty-nine, she was thirty-eight before any editor, on his own volition, accepted her work for publication (and that was Alfred Stieglitz of *Camera Work*); not until she was fifty-nine (and one of the most respected writers in the English language) did any major American publishing firm invest its own name and money in a book of hers. Though other commercial publishers wanted to capitalize on the success of *The Autobiography of Alice B. Toklas* (1933), most of the books issued after then were pale echoes of her previous achievements. (Virgil Thomson suggests that around 1926 she became attracted to a neo-romanticism that fired her incipient egotism, as well as undermining the anti-expressionistic premises of her earlier writing.) Typically, nearly all her poetry first appeared in print after her death, and its excellences are still rarely acknowledged by poetry critics and anthologies. (Stein's poetry is absent from Donald Barlow Stauffer's otherwise compendious *A Short History of American Poetry*, 1974, and Richard Ellmann's mammoth *The New Oxford Book of American Verse*, 1976, among other comparable repositories.) Since many of her greatest books—the unabridged edition of *The Making of Americans* and *Geography and Plays*, for two—were unavailable for more than two decades after her death, their active life with both literate readers and literary critics was, to say the least, belated.

The enterprise of American literary criticism has scarcely no-

ticed Stein's work, and too many literary professionals honor
and teach the simpler books, such as *Three Lives* and *The Autobiography of Alice B. Toklas*, to the neglect of the more extraordinary ones—those whose special qualities have never been ex-
ceeded. (Even Edmund Wilson preferred *Three Lives*, which he
praised for its mimeticism: "caught the very rhythms and ac-
cents of the minds of her heroines.") Remarkably little percep-
tive criticism of her work appeared during her lifetime, and
prior to Donald Sutherland in 1951 her best "critics" were other
writers. Indeed, this default with Stein is an index of the more
general failure of American criticism to acknowledge its native
experimental tradition. (The default over E. E. Cummings is
another index.) Furthermore, this failure partly accounts for
why Stein never felt obliged to make more precise statements
about her purposes. Her essays and speeches on her own work
tended to be suggestive and formally interesting but, by critical
standards, evasive and incomplete; and I am scarcely alone in
regarding *How to Write* (1931) as misleadingly labeled. This
elusiveness in turn accounts for the sense that I have in 1980: I
think I know what she was doing—the techniques and qualities
defined in this essay—because I am familiar with the history of
experimental literature since Stein (and see her thus as a precur-
sor of contemporary concerns); but I am not at all sure what she
ultimately thought she was doing.

Though her work as a whole was commonly dismissed, we
can see, by now, that no other twentieth-century American author had as much influence as Stein; and none influenced his or
her successors in as many ways. There are echoes of Stein's
writings in her friends Sherwood Anderson, Thornton Wilder,
and Ernest Hemingway, as well as in William Faulkner's extended sentences, E. E. Cummings's syntactical playfulness,
John Dos Passos's ellipses, Allen Ginsberg's attempt to use
mantra-like language to escalate into unusual mental states, and
any narrative that is structurally uninflected, as well as much
else—for current examples, the indefinite poetry of John Ash-
bery's middle period (the 1960s) and the nonsyntactic writing of
Clark Coolidge, John Cage, bp Nichol, and myself. Because of
her influence on Hemingway, Stein's preference for denotative

language had an indirect effect upon American newspaper writing and upon crime fiction. One curious fact that I will let others explain is the absence of visible influence upon subsequent women writers.

In his imperceptive biography of Stein, *The Third Rose* (1959), John Malcolm Brinnin declares, "If Gertrude Stein had never lived, sooner or later works very much like those she produced would have been written by someone else." However, quite the opposite is more likely true, precisely because most of her innovations went against the dominant grain of literary modernism and her originality was so multifarious. Had she not existed—had she not pursued her experimental proclivities—her inventions probably would not have happened and, thus, subsequent literature would have been quite different. What is more extraordinary is that this influence continues, not only through her imitators but directly through her own works—not only with her experiments in literary alternatives but in her general attitudes toward language and literary art.

THE YALE GERTRUDE STEIN

Fourteen people have been known to come again. One came. They asked her name. One after one another. Fourteen is not very many and fourteen came. One after another. Six were known to be at once. Welcomed. How do you do. Who is pleasant. How often do they think kindly. May they be earnest.

What is the wish.

They have fourteen. One is in a way troubled may he succeed. They asked his name. It is very often a habit in mentioning a name to mention his name. He mentioned his name.

Earnest is partly their habit.

She is without doubt welcome.

Once or twice four or five there are many which is admirable.

May I ask politely that they are well and wishes.

Cleanly and orderly.

Benjamin Charles may amount to it he is wounded by their doubt.

Or for or fortunately.

No blame is a blemish.

Once upon a time a dog intended to be mended. He would be vainly thought to be pleasant. Or just or join or clearly. Or with or mind or flowery. Or should or be a value.

Benjamin James was troubled. He had been certain. He had perused. He had learned. To labor and to wait.

Or why should he be rich. He was. He was lamentable and discovered. He had tried to sin. Or with perplexity.

She may be judicious.

Many will be led in hope.

He was conveniently placed for observation. They will. They may well

3

Be happy.

Any and every one is an authority.

Does it make any difference who comes first.

She neglected to ask it of him. Will he like gardening. She neglected to ask her to be very often. Made pleasantly happy. They were never strange. It is unnecessary never to know them. And they

LIFTING BELLY

I have been heavy and had much selecting. I saw a star which was low. It was so low it twinkled. Breath was in it. Little pieces are stupid.

I want to tell about fire. Fire is that which we have when we have olive. Olive is a wood. We like linen. Linen is ordered. We are going to order linen.

All belly belly well.

Bed of coals made out of wood.

I think this one may be an expression. We can understand heating and burning composition. Heating with wood.

Sometimes we readily decide upon wind we decide that there will be stars and perhaps thunder and perhaps rain and perhaps no moon. Sometimes we decide that there will be a storm and rain. Sometimes we look at the boats. When we read about a boat we know that it has been sunk. Not by the waves but by the sails. Any one knows that rowing is dangerous. Be alright. Be careful. Be angry. Say what you think. Believe in there being the same kind of a dog. Jerk. Jerk him away. Answer that you do not care to think so.

We quarreled with him. We quarreled with him then. Do not forget that I showed you the road. Do not forget that I showed you the road. We will forget it because he does not oblige himself to thank me. Ask him to thank me.

The next time that he came we offered him something to read. There is a great difference of opinion as to whether cooking in oil is or is not healthful.

I don't pardon him. I find him objectionable.

What is it when it's upset. It isn't in the room. Moonlight and darkness. Sleep and not sleep. We sleep every night.

What was it.

I said lifting belly.

You didn't say it.

I said it I mean lifting belly.

Don't misunderstand me.

Do you.

Do you lift everybody in that way.

No.

You are to say No.

Lifting belly.

How are you.

Lifting belly how are you lifting belly.

We like a fire and we don't mind if it smokes.

Do you.

How do you do. The Englishmen are coming. Not here. No an Englishwoman. An Englishman and an Englishwoman.

What did you say lifting belly. I did not understand you correctly. It is not well said. For lifting belly. For lifting belly not to lifting belly.

Did you say, oh lifting belly.

What is my another name.

Representative.

Of what.

Of the evils of eating.

What are they then.

They are sweet and figs.

Do not send them.

Yes we will it will be very easy.

PART II

Lifting belly. Are you. Lifting.

Oh dear I said I was tender, fierce and tender.

Do it. What a splendid example of carelessness.

It gives me a great deal of pleasure to say yes.

Why do I always smile.

I don't know.

It pleases me.
You are easily pleased.
I am very pleased.
Thank you I am scarcely sunny.
I wish the sun would come out.
Yes.
Do you lift it.
High.
Yes sir I helped to do it.
Did you.
Yes.
Do you lift it.
We cut strangely.
What.
That's it.
Address it say to it that we will never repent.
A great many people come together.
Come together.
I don't think this has anything to do with it.
What I believe in is what I mean.
Lifting belly and roses.
We get a great many roses.
I always smile.
Yes.
And I am happy.
With what.
With what I said.
This evening.
Not pretty.
Beautiful.
Yes beautiful.
Why don't you prettily bow.
Because it shows thought.
It does.
Lifting belly is so strong.
A great many things are weaknesses. You are pleased to so.
I say because I am so well pleased. With what. With what I said.
There are a great many weaknesses.

Lifting belly.
What was it I said.
I can add that.
It's not an excuse.
I do not like bites.
How lift it.
Not so high.
What a question.
I do not understand about ducks.
Do not you.
I don't mean to close.
No of course not.
Dear me. Lifting belly.
Dear me. Lifting belly.
Oh yes.
Alright.
Sing.
Do you hear.
Yes I hear.
Lifting belly is amiss.
This is not the way.
I see.
Lifting belly is alright.
Is it a name.
Yes it's a name.
We were right.
 So you weren't pleased.
I see that we are pleased.
It is a great way.
To go.
No not to go.
But to lift.
Not light.
Paint.
No not paint.
All the time we are very happy.
All loud voices are seen. By whom. By the best.
Lifting belly is so erroneous.

I don't like to be teased and worried.
Lifting belly is so accurate.
Yes indeed.
She was educated.
And pleased.
Yes indeed.
Lifting belly is so strong.
I said that to mean that I was very glad.
Why are you very glad.
Because that pleased me.
Baby love.
A great many people are in the war.
I will go there and back again.
What did you say about Lifting belly.
I said lifting belly is so strong.
Yes indeed it is and agreeable and grateful.
We have gratitude.
No one can say we haven't.
Lifting belly is so cold. Not in summer. No nor in winter
either.
All of it is a joke.
Lifting belly is no joke. Not after all.
I am so discouraged about it. About lifting belly. I question.
I am so discouraged about lifting belly.
The other day there was a good deal of sunlight.
There often is.
There often is here.
We are very well satisfied at present.
So enthusiastic.
Lifting belly has charm.
Charming.
Alright.
Lifting belly is not very interesting.
To you.
To me.
Say did you see that the wind was from the east.
It usually is from the South.
We like rain.

Sneeze. This is the way to say it.
You meant a pressure.
Indeed yes.
All the time there is a chance to see me. I don't wish it to be
said so.
The skirt.
And water.
You mean ocean water.
Not exactly an ocean a sea.
A success.
Was it a success.
Lifting belly is all there.
Lifting belly high.
It is not necessary to repeat the word.
How do you do I forgive you everything and there is nothing
to forgive.
Lifting belly is so high.
Do you like lilies.
Do you like lilies.
Use the word lifting belly is so high.
In place of that.
A special case to-day.
Of peaches.
Lifting belly is delightful.
Lifting belly is so high.
To-day.
Yes to-day.
Do you think that said yesterday.
Yes to-day.
Don't be silly.
In that we see that we can please me.
I don't see how you can write on the wall about roses.
Lifting belly a terminus.
What is there to please me.
Alright.
A pocket.
Lifting belly is good.
Rest.

Arrest.

Do you please m.

I do more than that.

When are you most proud of me.

Dare I ask you to be satisfied.

Dear me.

Lifting belly is anxious.

Not about Verdun.

Oh dear no.

The wind whistles that means it whistles just like any one. I thought it was a whistle.

Lifting belly together.

Do you like that there.

There are not mistakes made.

Not here at any rate.

Not here at any rate.

There are no mistakes made. Not here at any rate.

When do I see the lightning. Every night.

Lifting belly again.

It is a credit to me.

There was an instant of lifting belly.

Lifting belly is an occasion. An occasion to please me. Oh yes. Mention it.

Lifting belly is courteous.

Lifting belly is hilarious, gay and favorable.

Oh yes it is.

Indeed it is not a disappointment.

Not to me.

Lifting belly is such an incident. In one's life.

Lifting belly is such an incident in one's life.

I don't mean to be reasonable.

Shall I say thin.

This makes me smile.

Lifting belly is so kind.

A great many clouds for the sun. You mean the sun on high.

Leave me.

See me.

Lifting belly is no joke.

I appreciate that.
Do not show kindness.
Why not.
Because it ruffles me.
Do not say that it is unexpected.
Lifting belly is so scarce.
Not to-day.
Lifting belly is so kind.
To me there are many exceptional cases.
What did you say. I said I had not been disturbed. Neither had we. Lifting belly is so necessary.
Lifting belly is so kind.
I can't say it too often.
Pleasing me.
Lifting belly.
Extraordinary.
Lifting belly is such exercise.
You mean altogether.
Lifting belly is so kind to me.
Lifting belly is so kind to many.
Don't say that please.
If you please.
Lifting belly is right.
And we were right.
Now I say again. I say now again.
What is a whistle.
Miracle you don't know about the miracle.
You mean a meteor.
No I don't I mean everything away.
Away where.
Away here.
Oh yes.
Lifting belly is so strong.
You said that before.
Lifting belly is so strong and willing.
Lifting belly is so strong and yet waiting.
Lifting belly is so soothing. Yes indeed.
It gives me greater pleasure.

Does it.

It gives me great pleasure.

What do you mean by St. John.

A great many churches are visited.

Lifting belly try again.

I will not say what I think about lifting belly. Oh yes you will.

Well then please have it understood that I can't be responsible
for doubts. Nobody doubts.

Nobody doubts.

I have no use for lifting belly.

Do you say that to me.

No I don't.

Anybody who is wisely urged to go to Inca goes to the hill.

What hill. The hill above lifting belly.

Is it all hill.

Not very well.

Not very well hill.

Lifting belly is so strong.

And clear.

Why do you say feeding.

Lifting belly is such a windmill.

Do you stare.

Lifting belly to me.

What did he say.

He didn't say that he was waiting.

I have been adequately entertained.

Some when they sigh by accident say poor country she is
betrayed.

I didn't say that to-day. No indeed you didn't.

Mixing belly is so kind.

Lifting belly is so a measure of it all.

Lifting belly is a picnic.

On a fine day.

We like the weather it is very beautiful.

Lifting belly is so able.

Lifting belly is so able to be praised.

The act.

The action.

A great many people are excitable.
Mixing belly is so strange.
Lifting belly is so satisfying.
Do not speak to me.
Of it.
Lifting belly is so sweet.
That is the way to separate yourself from the water.
Lifting belly is so kind.
Loud voices discuss pigeons.
Do loud voices discuss pigeons.
Remember me to the hill. What hill. The hill in back of
Genova.
Lifting belly is so kind. So very kind.
Lifting belly is so kind.
I never mean to insist to-day.
Lifting belly is so consecutive.
With all of us.
Lifting belly is so clear.
Very clear.
And there is lots of water.
Lifting belly is so impatient.
So impatient to-day.
Lifting belly is all there.
Do I doubt it.
Lifting belly.
What are my plans.
There are some she don't mention.
There are some she doesn't mention. Some others she doesn't
mention.
Lifting belly is so careful. Full of care for me. Lifting belly
is mean. I see. You mean lifting belly is all right.
Lifting belly is so simple.
Listen to me to-day.
Lifting belly is so warm.
Leave it to me.
Leave what to me.
Lifting belly is such an experiment.
We were thoroughly brilliant.

If I were a postman I would deliver letters. We call them letter carriers.

Lifting belly is so strong. And so judicious.

Lifting belly is an exercise.

Exercise is very good for me.

Lifting belly necessarily pleases the latter.

Lifting belly is necessary.

Do believe me.

Lifting belly quietly.

It is very exciting.

Stand.

Why do you stand.

Did you say you thought it would make any difference.

Lifting belly is not so kind.

Little places to sting.

We used to play star spangled banner.

Lifting belly is so near.

Lifting belly is so dear.

Lifting belly all around.

Lifting belly makes a sound.

Keep still.

Lifting belly is gratifying.

I can't express the hauntingness of Dugny.

I can't express either the obligation I have to say say it.

Lifting belly is so kind.

Dear me lifting belly is so kind.

Am I in it.

That doesn't affect it.

How do you mean.

Lifting belly and a resemblance.

There is no resemblance.

A plain case of misdeed.

Lifting belly is peacable.

The Cataluna has come home.

Lifting belly is a success.

So is tenderness.

Lifting belly is kind and good and beautiful.

Lifting belly is my joy.

Do you believe in singling. Singing do you mean.
Lifting belly is a special pleasure.
Who can be convinced of this measure.
Lifting belly is perfect.
I know what you mean.
Lifting belly was very fatiguing.
Did you make a note of it of the two donkeys and the three
dogs. The smaller one is the mother of the other two.
Lifting belly
Exactly.
Lifting belly all the time.
Do be careful of me.
Remarkably so.
Remarkably a recreation.
Lifting belly is so satisfying.
Lifting belly to me.
Large quantities of it.
Say that you see that you are praised.
Lifting belly.
See that.
You have entertained me.
Hurry up.
Hurry up with it.
Lifting belly does that astonish you.
Excuse me.
Why do you wish to hear me.
I wish to hear you because it pleases me.
Yesterday and to-day.
Yesterday and to-day we managed it altogether.
Lifting belly is so long.
It is an expression of opinion.
Conquistador. James I.
It is exceptional.
Lifting belly is current rolling. Lifting belly is so strong.
Lifting belly is so strong.
That is what I say.
I say it to please me.
Please yourself with thunder.

Lifting belly is famous.
So are many celebrations.
Lifting belly is so.
We mean lifting belly.
We mean it and do we care.
We keep all the letters.
Lifting belly is so seen..
You mean here.
Not with spy glasses.
Lifting belly is an expression.
Explain it explain it to me.
Lifting belly is cautious.
Of course these words are said.
To be strong.
Lifting belly.
Yes orchids.
Lifting belly is so adaptable.
That will amuse my baby.
Lifting belly is a way of sitting.
I don't mean to laugh.
Lifting belly is such a reason.
Lifting belly is such a reason.
Why do I say bench.
Because it is laughable.
Lifting belly is so droll.
We have met to-day with every kind of consideration.
Not very good. Of course it is very good.
Lifting belly is so kind.
Why do you say that.
Bouncing belly.
Did you say bouncing belly.
We asked here for a sister.
Lifting belly is not noisy.
We go to Barcelona to-morrow.
Lifting belly is an acquisition.
I forgot to put in a special cake. Love to be.
Very well.
Lifting belly is the understanding.

Sleepy.
Why do you wake up.
Lifting belly keep it.
We will send it off.
She should.
Nothing pleases me except dinner.
I have done as I wished and I do not feel any responsibility
to you.
Are you there.
Lifting belly.
What do I say.
Pussy how pretty you are.
That goes very quickly unless you have been there too long.
I told him I would send him Mildred's book. He seemed very
pleased at the prospect.
Lifting belly is so strong.
Lifting belly together.
Lifting belly oh yes.
Lifting belly.
Oh yes.
Remember what I say.
I have no occasion to deliberate.
He has no heart but that you can supply.
The fan goes alright.
Lifting belly what is earnest. Expecting an arena to be mon-
umental.
Lifting belly is recognised to be the only spectacle present.
Do you mean that.
Lifting belly is a language. It says island. Island a strata. Lift-
ing belly is a repetition.
Lifting belly means me.
I do love roses and carnations.
A mistake. There can be no mistakes.
I do not say a mother.
Lifting belly.
Lifting belly.
Cry.
Lifting belly.

Lifting belly. Splendid.
Jack Johnson Henry.
Henry is his name sir.
Jack Johnson Henry is an especially eloquent curtain.
We see a splendid force in mirrors.
Angry we are not angry.
Pleasing.
Lifting belly raining.
I am good looking.
A magazine of lifting belly. Excitement sisters.
Did we see the bird jelly I call it. I call it something religious.
You mean beautiful. I do not know that I like large rocks. Sarsen
land we call it. Oh yes. Lifting belly is a persuasion. You are
satisfied. With it. With it and with you. I am satisfied with your
behavior. I call it astonishing. Lifting belly is so exact and audible
and Spanish curses. You know I prefer a bird. What bird. Why
a yellow bird. I saw it first. That was an accident. You mean by
accident. I mean exactly what I said. Lifting belly is a great
luxury. Can you imitate a cow.
Lifting belly is so kind.
And so cold.
Lifting belly is a rare instance. I am fond of it. I am attached to
the accentuation.
Lifting belly is a third.
Did you say third. No I said Avila.
Listen to him sing.
She is so sweet and thrilling.
Listen to me as yet I have no color. Red white and blue all
out but you.
This is the best thing I have ever said. Lifting belly and it, it
is not startling. Lifting belly until to-morrow. Lifting belly to-
morrow.
I would not be surprised surprised if I added that yet.
Lifting belly to me.
I am fondest of all of lifting belly.
Lifting belly careful don't say anything about lifting belly.
I did not change my mind.
Neither did you carefully.

Lifting belly and again lifting belly.

I have changed my mind about the country.

Lifting belly and action and voices and care to be taken.

Does it make any difference if you pay for paper or not.

Listen to me. Using old automobile tires as sandals is singularly interesting. It is done in Avila.

What did I tell. Lifting belly is so kind.

What kind of a noise does it make. Like the man at night. The man that calls out. We hear him.

Lifting belly is so strong. I love cherish idolise adore and worship you. You are so sweet so tender and so perfect.

Did you believe in sandals. When they are made of old automobile tire. I wish I knew the history of it.

Lifting belly is notorious.

A great many people wish to salute. The general does. So does the leader of the battalion. In spanish. I understand that.

I understand everything.

Lifting belly is to jelly.

Holy most is in the sky.

We see it in three.

Yes we see it every night near the hills. This is so natural. Birds do it. We do not know their name.

Lifting belly or all I can never be pleased with this. Listen to me. Lifting belly is so kind.

Lifting belly is so dear.

Lifting belly is here.

Did we not hear and we were walking leave it to me and say come quickly now. He is not sleepy. At last I know why he laughs. Do you.

I will not imitate colors. From the stand point of white yellow is colored. Do you mean bushes. No I mean acacias. Lilacs do fade. What did you say for lifting belly. Extra. Extra thunder. I can so easily be fastidious.

II

Kiss my lips. She did.

Kiss my lips again she did.

Kiss my lips over and over and over again she did.

I have feathers.

Gentle fishes.

Do you think about apricots. We find them very beautiful. It is not alone their color it is their seeds that charm us. We find it a change.

Lifting belly is so strange.

I came to speak about it.

Selected raisins well their grapes grapes are good.

Change your name.

Question and garden.

It's raining. Don't speak about it.

My baby is a dumpling. I want to tell her something.

Wax candles. We have bought a great many wax candles. Some are decorated. They have not been lighted.

I do not mention roses.

Exactly.

Actually.

Question and butter.

I find the butter very good.

Lifting belly is so kind.

Lifting belly fattily.

Doesn't that astonish you.

You did want me.

Say it again.

Strawberry.

Lifting beside belly.

Lifting kindly belly.

Sing to me I say.

Some are wives not heroes.

Lifting belly merely.

Sing to me I say.

Lifting belly. A reflection.

Lifting belly adjoins more prizes.

Fit to be.

I have fit on a hat.

Have you.

What did you say to excuse me. Difficult paper and scattered.

Lifting belly is so kind.

What shall you say about that. Lifting belly is so kind.

What is a veteran.

A veteran is one who has fought.

Who is the best.

The king and the queen and the mistress.

Nobody has a mistress.

Lifting belly is so kind.

To-day we decided to forgive Nellie.

Anybody can describe dresses.

How do you do what is the news.

Lifting belly is so kind.

Lifting belly exactly.

The king and the prince of Montenegro.

Lifting belly is so kind.

Lifting belly to please me.

Excited.

Excited are you.

I can whistle, the train can whistle whistle we can hear the whistle, the boat whistle. The train is not running to-day. Mary whistle whistle for the whim.

Didn't you say you'd write it better.

Mrs. Vettie. It is necessary to have a Ford.

Yes sir.

Dear Mrs. Vettie. Smile to me.

I am.

Dear Mrs. Vettie never better.

Yes indeed so.

Lifting belly is most kind.

What did I say, that I was a great poet like the English only sweeter.

When I think of this afternoon and the garden I see what you mean.

You are not thinking of the pleasure.

Lifting belly again.

What did I mention when I drew a pansy that pansy and petunia both begin with p.

Lifting belly splendidly.

We have wishes.

Let us say we know it.

Did I say anything about it. I know the tittle. We know the
title.

Lifting belly is so kind.

We have made no mistake.

The Montenegrin family.

A condition to a wide admiration.

Lifting belly after all.

You don't mean disobedience.

Lifting belly all around.

Eat the little girl I say.

Listen to me. Did you expect it to go back. Why do you do
to stop.

What do you do to stop.

What do you do to go on.

I do the same.

Yes wishes. Oh yes wishes.

What do you do to turn a corner.

What do you do to sing.

We don't mention singing.

What do you do to be reformed.

You know.

Yes wishes.

What do you do to measure.

I do it in such a way.

I hope to see them come.

Lifting belly go around.

I was sorry to be blistered.

We were such company.

Did she say jelly.

Jelly my jelly.

Lifting belly is so round.

Big Caesars.

Two Caesars.

Little seize her.

Too.

Did I do my duty.

Did I wet my knife.

No I don't mean whet.
Exactly four teeth.
Little belly is so kind.
What did you say about accepting.
Yes.
Lifting belly another lifting belly.
I question the weather.
It is not necessary.
Lifting belly oh lifting belly in time.
Yes indeed.
Be to me.
Did you say this was this.
Mr. Louis.
Do not mention Mr. Louis.
Little axes.
Yes indeed little axes and rubbers.
This is a description of an automobile.
I understand all about them.
Lifting belly is so kind.
So is whistling.
A great many whistles are shrill.
Lifting belly connects.
Lifting belly again.
Sympathetic blessing.
Not curls.
Plenty of wishes.
All of them fulfilled.
Lifting belly you don't say so.
Climb trees.
Lifting belly has sparks.
Sparks of anger and money.
Lifting belly naturally celebrates
We naturally celebrate.
Connect me in places.
Lifting belly.
No no don't say that.
Lifting belly oh yes.
Tax this.

Running behind a mountain.
I fly to thee.
Lifting belly.
Shall I chat.
I mean pugilists.
Oh yes trainer.
Oh yes yes.
Say it again to study.
It has been perfectly fed.
Oh yes I do.
Belly alright.
Lifting belly very well.
Lifting belly this.
So sweet.
To me.
Say anything a mudding made of Caesars.
Lobster. Baby is so good to baby.
I correct blushes. You mean wishes.
I collect pearls. Yes and colors.
All colors are gods. Oh yes Beddlington.
Now I collect songs.
Lifting belly is so nice.
I wrote about it to him.
I wrote about it to her.
Not likely not very likely that they will seize rubber. Not
very likely that they will seize rubber.
Lifting belly yesterday.
And to-day.
And to-morrow.
A train to-morrow.
Lifting belly is so exciting.
Lifting belly asks any more.
Lifting belly captures.
Seating.
Have a swim.
Lifting belly excuses.
Can you swim.
Lifting belly for me.

When this you see remember me.
Oh yes.
Yes.
Researches and a cab.
A cab right.
Lifting belly phlegmatically.
Bathing bathing in bliss.
I am very well satisfied with meat.
Kindness to my wife.
Lifting belly to a throne.
Search it for me.
Yes wishes.
I say it again I am perfection in behavior and circumstance.
Oh yes alright.
Levelheaded fattuski.
I do not wish to be Polish.
Quite right in singing.
Lifting belly is so recherché.
Lifting belly.
Up.
Correct me.
I believe he makes together of pieces.
Lifting belly.
Not that.
Think of me.
Oh yes.
Lifting belly for me.
Right there.
Not that yesterday.
Fetch missions.
Lifting belly or Dora.
Lifting belly.
Yes Misses.
Lifting belly separately all day.
I say lifting belly.
An example.
A good example.
Cut me a slice.

You see what I wish.
I wish a seat and Caesar.
Caesar is plural.
I can think.
And so can I.
And argue.
Oh yes you see.
What I see.
You see me.
Yes stretches.
Stretches and stretches of happiness.
Should you have put it away.
Yes you should have put it away.
Do not think so much.
I do not.
Have you a new title.
Lifting belly articulately.
It is not a problem.
Kissing and singing.
We have the habit when we wash.
In singing we say how do you do how do you like the war.
Little dumps of it.
Did you hear that man. What did he say close it.
Lifting belly lifting pleasure.
What can we say about wings.
Wings and refinement.
Come to me.
Sleepy.
Sleepily we think.
Wings after lunch.
I don't think.
No don't I regret a silver sugar.
And I platinum knitting needles.
And I sherry glasses.
I do not care for sherry I used to use for castor-oil.
You mean licorice.
He is so fond of coffee.
Let me tell you about kissing. We saw a piece of mistletoe.

We exchanged a pillow. We murmured training and we were asleep.

This is what happened Saturday.

Another day we said sour grass it grows in fields. So do daisies and green flowers.

I have never noticed green flowers.

Lifting belly is my joy.

What did I tell Caesars.

That I recognised them.

It is the custom to answer swimming.

Catch a call.

Does the moonlight make any difference to you.

Lifting belly yes Miss.

I can lean upon a pencil.

Lifting belly yes address me.

I address you.

Lifting belly magnetically.

Did you make a mistake.

Wave to me.

Lifting belly permanently.

What did the Caesars.

What did they all say.

They said that they were not deceived.

Lifting belly such a good example. And is so readily watchful.

What do you think of watches.

Collect lobsters.

And sweetbreads.

And a melon.

And salad.

Do not have a term.

You mean what do you call it.

Yes sir.

Sing to me.

Lifting belly is neglected.

The Caesar.

Oh yes the Caesar.

Oh yes the Caesar.

Lifting belly pencils to me.

And pens.
Lifting belly and the intention.
I particularly like what I know.
Lifting belly sublimely.
We made a fire this evening.
Cooking is cheap.
I do not care for Ethel.
That's a very good one. I say that's a very good one.
Yes and we think.
A rhyme, I understand nectarine. I also understand egg.
A special case you are.
Lifting belly and Caesar.
Did I explain it.
Have I explained it to you.
Have I explained it to you in season. Have I perplexed you.
You have not perplexed me nor mixed me. You have addressed
me as Caesar. This is the answer that I expected. When I said do
not mention any words I meant no indifference. I meant do your
duty and do not forget that I establish myself.
You establish yourself.
When this you see believe me.
Lifting belly etcetera.
Lifting belly and a hand. A hand is black and not by toil. I do
not like fat resemblances. There are none such.
Lifting belly and kind.
This is the pencil for me.
Lifting belly squeezes.
Remember what I said about a rhyme.
Don't call it again.
Say white spots.
Do not mention disappointment in cups.
Oh you are so sweet.
Lifting belly believe me.
Believe it is for pleasure that I do it.
Not foreign pleasure.
Oh no.
My pleasure in Susie.
Lifting belly so kind.

So kindly.
Lifting belly gratuitously.
Lifting belly increase.
Do this to me.
Lifting belly famously.
When did I say I thought it.
When you heard it.
Oh yes.
Bright eyes I make you ties.
No mockings.
This is to say I knit woolen stockings for you. And I understand it and I am very grateful.
Making a spectacle.
Drinking prepared water.
Laughing together.
Asking lifting belly to be particular.
Lifting belly is so kind.
She was like that.
Star spangled banner, story of Savannah.
She left because she was going to have the child with her.
Lifting belly don't think of it.
Believe me in truth and marriage.
Believe that I use the best paper that I can get.
Do you believe me.
Lifting belly is not an invitation.
Call me semblances.
I call you a cab sir.
That's the way she tells it.
Lifting belly is so accurate.
I congratulate you in being respectable and respectably married.
Call me Helen.
Not at all.
You may call me Helen.
That's what we said.
Lifting belly with firmness and pride.
Lifting belly with industry beside.
Heated heated with cold.

Some people are heated with linen.
Lifting belly comes extra.
This is a picture of lifting belly having a cow.
Oh yes you can say it of me.
When this you see remember me.
Lifting belly says pardon.
Pardon for what.
For having made a mistake.
Can you imagine what I say.
I say impossible.
Lifting belly is recognised.
Lifting belly presumably.
Do we run together.
I say do we run together.
I do not like stubbornness.
Come and sing.
Lifting belly.
I sing lifting belly.
I say lifting belly and then I say lifting belly and Caesars. I
say lifting belly gently and Caesars gently. I say lifting belly again
and Caesars again. I say lifting belly and I say Caesars and I say
lifting belly Caesars and cow come out. I say lifting belly and
Caesars and cow come out.
Can you read my print.
Lifting belly say can you see the Caesars. I can see what I kiss.
Of course you can.
Lifting belly high.
That is what I adore always more and more.
Come out cow.
Little connections.
Yes oh yes cow come out.
Lifting belly unerringly.
A wonderful book.
Baby my baby I backhand for thee.
She is a sweet baby and well baby and me.
This is the way I see it.
Lifting belly can you say it.
Lifting belly persuade me.

Lifting belly persuade me.
You'll find it a very easy to sing to me.
What can you say.
Lifting belly set.
I can not pass a door.
You mean odor.
I smell sweetly.
So do you.
Lifting belly plainly.
Can you sing.
Can you sing for me.
Lifting belly settled.
Can you excuse money.
Lifting belly has a dress.
Lifting belly in a mess.
Lifting belly in order.
Complain I don't complain.
She is my sweetheart.
Why doesn't she resemble an other.
This I cannot say here.
Full of love and echoes. Lifting belly is full of love.
Can you.
Can you can you.
Can you buy a Ford.
Did you expect that.
Lifting belly hungrily.
Not lonesomely.
But enthusiastically.
Lifting belly altogether.
Were you wise.
Were you wise to do so.
Can you say winking.
Can you say Francis Ferdinand has gone to the West.
Can you neglect me.
Can you establish the clock.
Yes I can when I am good.
Lifting belly precariously.
Lifting belly is noted.

Are you noted with me.
Come to sing and sit.
This is not the time for discussion.
A splendid table little table.
A splendid little table.
Can you be fortunate.
Yes sir.
What is a man.
What is a woman.
What is a bird.
Lifting belly must please me.
Yes can you think so.
Lifting belly cherished and flattered.
Lifting belly naturally.
Can you extract.
Can you be through so quickly.
No I cannot get through so quickly.
Are you afraid of Negro sculpture.
I have my feelings.
Lifting belly is so exact.
Lifting belly is favored by me.
Lifting belly cautiously.
I lift it in place of the music.
You mean it is the same.
I mean everything.
Can you not whistle.
Call me for that.
And sing.
I sing too.
Lifting belly counts.
My idea is.
Yes I know what your idea is.
Lifting belly knows all about the wind.
Yes indeed Miss.
Yes indeed.
Can you suspect me.
We are glad that we do not deceive.
Lifting belly regular.

Lifted belly behind.
Candidly.
Can you say that there is a mistake.
In the wash.
No in respect to the woman.
Can you say we meant to send her away.
Lifting belly is so orderly.
She makes no mistake.
She does not indeed.
Lifting belly heroically.
Can you think of that.
Can you guess what I mean.
Yes I can.
Lovely sweet.
Calville cow.
And that is it.
Lifting belly resignedly.
Now you laugh.
Lifting belly for me.
When this you see remember me.
Can you be sweet.
You are.
We are so likely.
We are so likely to be sweet.
Lifting belly handy.
Can you mention lifting belly. I can.
Yes indeed I know what I say.
Do you.
Lifting belly is so much.
Lifting belly grandly.
You can be sweet.
We see it.
We are tall.
We are wellbred.
We can say we do like what we have.
Lifting belly is more.
I am more than ever inclined to how do you do. That's the
way to wish it.

Lifting belly is so good.
That is natural.
Lifting belly exactly.
Calville cow is all to me.
Don't excite me.
Lifting belly exactly.
That's respectable.
Lifting belly is all to me.
Pretty Caesars yes they do.
Can you spell mixing.
I hear you.
How do you do.
Can you tell me about imposing.
When are you careful to speak.
Lifting belly categorically.
Think of it.
Lifting belly in the mind.
The Honorable Graham Murray.
My honorable Graham Murray.
What can you say.
I can say that I find it most useful and very warm, yet light.
Lifting belly astonishingly.
Can you mention her brother.
Yes.
Her father.
Yes.
A married couple.
Yes.
Lifting belly names it.
Look at that.
Yes that's what I said.
I put down something on lifting belly.
Humph.
Lifting belly bells.
Can you think of singing. In the little while in which I say
stop it you are not spoiled.
Can you be spoiled. I do not think so.
I think not.

I think everything of you.
Lifting belly is rich.
Chickens are rich.
I cannot disguise nice.
Don't you need to.
I think not.
Lifting belly exactly.
Why can lifting belly please me.
Lifting belly can please me because it is an occupation I enjoy.
Rose is a rose is a rose is a rose.
In print on top.
What can you do.
I can answer my question.
Very well answer this.
Who is Mr. Mc Bride.
In the way of laughing.
Lifting belly is an intention.
You are sure you know the meaning of any word.
Leave me to see.
Pink.
My pink.
Hear me to-day.
It is after noon.
I mean that literally.
It is after noon.
Little lifting belly is a quotation.
Frankly what do you say to me.
I say that I need protection.
You shall have it.
After that what do you wish.
I want you to mean a great deal to me.
Exactly.
And then.
And then blandishment.
We can see that very clearly.
Lifting belly is perfect.
Do you stretch farther.
Come eat it.

What did I say.
To whom.
Calville or a cow.
We were in a fashion deceived in Calville but not in a cow.
I understand when they say they mean something by it.
Lifting belly grandly.
Lifting belly sufficiently.
Come and be awake.
Certainly this morning.
Lifting belly very much.
I do not feel that I will be deceived.
Lifting belly fairly.
You mean follow.
I mean I follow.

Need you wish me to say lifting belly is recognised. No it is not necessary lifting belly is not peculiar. It is recognised. Can you recognise it. In a flash.

Thank you for me.

Can you excuse any one for loving its dearest. I said from. That is eaten.

Can you excuse any one from loving its dearest.
No I cannot.
A special fabric.
Can you begin a new thing.
Can I begin.
We have a dress.
You have a dress.
A dress by him.
Feel me.
I feel you.
Then it is fair to me.
Let me sing.
Certainly.
And you too Miss Polly.
What can you say.
I can say that there is no need of regretting a ball.
Mount Fatty.
That is a tremendous way.

Leave me to sing about it to-day.

And then there was a cake. Please give it to me. She did.

When can there be glasses. We are so pleased with it.

Go on to-morrow.

He cannot understand women. I can.

Believe me in this way.

I can understand the woman.

Lifting belly carelessly. I do not lift baby carelessly.

Lifting belly because there is no mistake. I planned to flourish.
Of course you do.

Lifting belly is exacting. You mean exact. I mean exacting.
Lifting belly is exacting.

Can you say see me.

Lifting belly is exciting.

Can you explain a mistake.

There is no mistake.

You have mentioned the flour.

Lifting belly is full of charm.

They are very nice candles.

Lifting belly is resourceful.

What can lifting belly say.

Oh yes I was not mistaken. Were not you indeed.

Lifting belly lifting belly lifting belly oh then lifting belly.

Can you make an expression. Thanks for the cigarette. How
pretty.

How fast. What. How fast the cow comes out.

Lifting belly a permanent caress.

Lifting belly bored.

You don't say so.

Lifting belly now.

Cow.

Lifting belly exactly.

I have often been pleased with this thing.

Lifting belly is necessarily venturesome.

You mean by that that you are collected. I hope I am.

What is an evening dress. What is a cape. What is a suit. What
is a fur collar.

Lifting belly needs to speak.

Land Rising next time.
Lifting belly has no choice.
Lifting belly seems to me to be remarkably kind.
Can you hear me witness that I was wolfish. I can. And that
I do not interfere with you. No I cannot countenance you here.
Countenance what do you mean by that. I mean that it is a pleas-
ure to prepare you. Thank you my dear.
Lifting belly is so kind.
Can you recollect this for me.
Lifting belly naturally.
Can you believe the truth.
Fredericks or Frederica.
Can you give me permission.
The Loves.
I never forget the Caesars.
Or the dears.
Lifting belly casually.
Where the head gets thin.
Lifting belly never mind.
You do please me.
Lifting belly restless.
Not at all.
Lifting belly there.
Expand my chest endlessly.
You did not do so.
Lifting belly is loved.
You know I am always ready to please you.
Lifting belly in a breath.
Lifting belly.
You do speak kindly.
We speak very kindly.
Lifting belly is so bold.

III

Lifting belly in here.
Able to state whimsies.
Can you recollect mistakes.
I hope not.

Bless you.
Lifting belly the best and only seat.
Lifting belly the reminder of present duties.
Lifting belly the charm.
Lifting belly is easy to me.
Lifting belly naturally.
Of course you lift belly naturally.
I lift belly naturally together.
Lifting belly answers.
Can you think for me.
I can.
Lifting belly endears me.
Lifting belly cleanly. With a wood fire. With a good fire.
Say how do you do to the lady. Which lady. The jew lady.
How do you do. She is my wife.
Can you accuse lifting belly of extras.
Salmon is salmon. Smoked and the most nourishing.
Pink salmon is my favorite color.
To be sure.
We are so necessary.
Can you wish for me.
I never mention it.
You need not resemble me.
But you do.
Of course you do.
That is very well said.
And meant.
And explained.
I explain too much.
And then I say.
She knows everything.
And she does.
Lifting belly beneficently.
I can go on with lifting belly forever. And you do.
I said it first. Lifting belly to engage. And then wishes. I wish
to be whimsied. I do that.
A worldly system.
A humorous example.

Lindo see me.
Whimsy see me.
See me.
Lifting belly exaggerates. Lifting belly is reproachful.
Oh can you see.
Yes sir.
Lifting belly mentions the bee.
Can you imagine the noise.
Can you whisper to me.
Lifting belly pronouncedly.
Can you imagine me thinking lifting belly.
Safety first.
That's the trimming.
I hear her snore
On through the door.
I can say that it is my delight.
Lifting belly fairly well.
Lifting belly visibly.
Yes I say visibly.
Lifting belly behind me.
The room is so pretty and clean.
Do you know the rest.
Yes I know the rest.
She knows the rest and will do it.
Lifting belly in eclipse.
There is no such moon for me.
Eclipse indeed can lifting belly be methodical.
In lifting belly yes.
In lifting belly yes.
Can you think of me.
I can and do.
Lifting belly encourages plenty.
Do not speak of San Francisco he is a saint.
Lifting belly shines.
Lifting belly nattily.
Lifting belly to fly.
Not to-day.
Motor.

Lifting belly for wind.
We do not like wind.
We do not mind snow.
Lifting belly partially.
Can you spell for me.
Spell bottle.
Lifting belly remarks.
Can we have the hill.
Of course we can have the hill.
Lifting belly patiently.
Can you see me rise.
Lifting belly says she can.
Lifting belly soundly.
Here is a bun for my bunny.
Every little bun is of honey.
On the little bun is my oney.
My little bun is so funny.
Sweet little bun for my money.
Dear little bun I'm her sunny.
Sweet little bun dear little bun good little bun for my bunny.
Lifting belly merry Christmas.
Lifting belly has wishes.
And then we please her.
What is the name of that pin.
Not a hat pin.
We use elastic.
As garters.
We are never blamed.
Thank you and see me.
How can I swim.
By not being surprised.
Lifting belly is so kind.
Lifting belly is harmonious.
Can you smile to me.
Lifting belly is prepared.
Can you imagine what I say.
Lifting belly can.
To be remarkable.

To be remarkably so.
Lifting belly and emergencies.
Lifting belly in reading.
Can you say effectiveness.
Lifting belly in reserve.
Lifting belly marches.
There is no song.
Lifting belly marry.
Lifting belly can see the condition.
How do you spell Lindo.
Not to displease.
The dears.
When can I.
When can I.
To-morrow if you like.
Thank you so much.
See you.
We were pleased to receive notes.
In there.
To there.
Can you see spelling.
Anybody can see lines.
Lifting belly is arrogant.
Not with oranges.
Lifting belly inclines me.
To see clearly.
Lifting belly is for me.
I can say truthfully never better.
Believe me lifting belly is not nervous.
Lifting belly is a miracle.
I am with her.
Lifting belly to me.
Very nicely done.
Poetry is very nicely done.
Can you say pleasure.
I can easily say please me.
You do.
Lifting belly is precious.

Then you can sing.
We do not encourage a nightingale.
Do you really mean that.
We literally do.
Then it is an intention.
Not the smell.
Lifting baby is a chance.
Certainly sir.
I please myself.
Can we convince Morlet.
We can.
Then see the way.
We can have a pleasant ford.
And we do.
We will.
See my baby cheerily.
I am celebrated by the lady.
Indeed you are.
I can rhyme
In English.
In loving.
In preparing.
Do not be rough.
I can sustain conversation.
Do you like a title for you.
Do you like a title.
Do you like my title.
Can you agree.
We do.
In that way have candles.
And dirt.
Not dirt.
There are two Caesars and there are four Caesars.
Caesars do their duty.
I never make a mistake.
We will be very happy and boastful and we will celebrate
Sunday.
How do you like your Aunt Pauline.

She is worthy of a queen.
Will she go as we do dream.
She will do satisfactorily.
And so will we.
Thank you so much.
Smiling to me.
Then we can see him.
Yes we can.
Can we always go.
I think so.
You will be secure.
We are secure.
Then we see.
We see the way.
This is very good for me.
In this way we play.
Then we are pleasing.
We are pleasing to him.
We have gone together.
We are in our Ford.
Please me please me.
We go then.
We go when.
In a minute.
Next week.
Yes indeed oh yes indeed.
I can tell you she is charming in a coat.
Yes and we are full of her praises.
Yes indeed.
This is the way to worry. Not it.
Can you smile.
Yes indeed oh yes indeed.
And so can I.
Can we think.
Wrist leading.
Wrist leading.
A kind of exercise.
A brilliant station.

Do you remember its name.
Yes Morlet.
Can you say wishes.
I can.
Winning baby.
Theoretically and practically.
Can we explain a season.
We can when we are right.
Two is too many.
To be right.
One is right and so we mount and have what we want.
We will remember.
Can you mix birthdays.
Certainly I can.
Then do so.
I do so.
Do I remember to write.
Can he paint.
Not after he has driven a car.
I can write.
There you are.
Lifting belly with me.
You inquire.
What you do then.
Pushing.
Thank you so much.
And lend a hand.
What is lifting belly now.
My baby.
Always sincerely.
Lifting belly says it there.
Thank you for the cream.
Lifting belly tenderly.
A remarkable piece of intuition.
I have forgotten all about it.
Have you forgotten all about it.
Little nature which is mine.
Fairy ham

Is a clam.
Of chowder
Kiss him Louder.
Can you be especially proud of me.
Lifting belly a queen.
In that way I can think.
Thank you so much.
I have,
Lifting belly for me.
I can not forget the name.
Lifting belly for me.
Lifting belly again.
Can you be proud of me.
I am.
Then we say it.
In miracles.
Can we say it and then sing. You mean drive.
I mean to drive.
We are full of pride.
Lifting belly is proud.
Lifting belly my queen.
Lifting belly happy.
Lifting belly see.
Lifting belly.
Lifting belly address.
Little washers.
Lifting belly how do you do.
Lifting belly is famous for recipes.
You mean Genevieve.
I mean I never ask for potatoes.
But you liked them then.
And now.
Now we know about water.
Lifting belly is a miracle.
And the Caesars.
The Caesars are docile.
Not more docile than is right.
No beautifully right.

And in relation to a cow.
And in relation to a cow.
Do believe me when I incline.
You mean obey.
I mean obey.
Obey me.
Husband obey your wife.
Lifting belly is so dear.
To me.
Lifting belly is smooth,
Tell lifting belly about matches.
Matches can be struck with the thumb.
Not by us.
No indeed.
What is it I say about letters.
Twenty six.
And counted.
And counted deliberately.
This is not as difficult as it seems.
Lifting belly is so strange
And quick.
Lifting belly in a minute.
Lifting belly in a minute now.
In a minute.
Not to-day.
No not to-day.
Can you swim.
Lifting belly can perform aquatics.
Lifting belly is astonishing.
Lifting belly for me.
Come together.
Lifting belly near.
I credit you with repetition.
Believe me I will not say it.
And retirement.
I celebrate something.
Do you.
Lifting belly extraordinarily in haste.

I am so sorry I said it.
Lifting belly is a credit. Do you care about poetry.
Lifting belly in spots.
Do you like ink.
Better than butter.
Better than anything.
Any letter is an alphabet.
When this you see you will kiss me.
Lifting belly is so generous.
Shoes.
Servant.
And Florence.
Then we can sing.
We do among.
I like among.
Lifting belly keeps.
Thank you in lifting belly.
Can you wonder that they don't make preserves.
We ask the question and they answer you give us help.
Lifting belly is so successful.
Is she indeed.
I wish you would not be disobliging.
In that way I am.
But in giving.
In giving you always win.
You mean in effect.
In mean in essence.
Thank you so much we are so much obliged.
This may be a case
Have no fear.
Then we can be indeed.
You are and you must.
Thank you so much.
In kindness you excel.
You have obliged me too.
I have done what is necessary.
Then can I say thank you may I say thank you very much.
Thank you again.

Because lifting belly is about baby.
Three eggs in lifting belly.
Éclair.
Think of it.
Think of that.
We think of that.
We produce music.
And in sleeping.
Noises.
Can that be she.
Lifting belly is so kind
Darling wifie is so good.
Little husband would.
Be as good.
If he could.
This was said.
Now we know how to differ.
From that.
Certainly.
Now we say.
Little hubbie is good.
Every Day.
She did want a photograph.
Lifting belly changed her mind.
Lifting belly changed her mind.
Do I look fat.
Do I look fat and thin.
Blue eyes and windows.
You mean Vera.
Lifting belly can guess.
Quickly.
Lifting belly is so pleased.
Lifting belly seeks pleasure.
And she finds it altogether.
Lifting belly is my love.
Can you say meritorious.
Yes camellia.
Why do you complain.

Postal cards.
And then.
The Louvre.
After that.
After that Francine.
You don't mean by that name.
What is Spain.
Listen lightly.
But you do.
Don't tell me what you call me.
But he is pleased.
But he is pleased.
That is the way it sounds.
In the morning.
By that bright light.
Will you exchange purses.
You know I like to please you.
Lifting belly is so kind.
Then sign.
I sign the bulletin.
Do the boys remember that nicely
To-morrow we go there.
And the photographs
The photographs will come.
When
You will see.
Will it please me.
Not suddenly
But soon
Very soon.
But you will hear first.
That will take some time.
Not very long.
What do you mean by long.
A few days.
How few days.
One or two days.
Thank you for saying so.

Thank you so much.
Lifting belly waits splendidly.
For essence.
For essence too.
Can you assure me.
I can and do.
Very well it will come
And I will be happy.
You are happy.
And I will be
You always will be.
Lifting belly sings nicely.
Not nervously.
No not nervously.
Nicely and forcefully.
Lifting belly is so sweet.
Can you say you say.
In this thought.
I do think lifting belly.
Little love lifting
Little love light.
Little love heavy.
Lifting belly tight.
Thank you.
Can you turn over.
Rapidly.
Lifting belly so meaningly.
Yes indeed the dog.
He watches.
The little boys.
They whistle on their legs,
Little boys have meadows,
Then they are well.
Very well.
Please be the man.
I am the man.
Lifting belly praises.
And she gives

Health.
And fragrance.
And words.
Lifting belly is in bed.
And the bed has been made comfortable.
Lifting belly knows this.
Spain and torn
Whistling.
Can she whistle to me.
Lifting belly in a flash.
You know the word.
Strawberries grown in Perpignan are not particularly good.
These are inferior kinds.
Kind are a kind.
Lifting belly is sugar.
Lifting belly to me.
In this way I can see.
What
Lifting belly dictate.
Daisy dear.
Lifting belly
Lifting belly carelessly.
I didn't.
I see why you are careful
Can you stick a stick. In what In the carpet.
Can you be careful of the corner.
Mrs. the Mrs. indeed yes.
Lifting belly is charming.
Often to-morrow
I'll try again.
This time I will sin
Not by a prophecy.
That is the truth.
Very well.
When will they change.
They have changed.
Then they are coming
Yes.

Soon.
On the way.
I like the smell of gloves.
Lifting belly has money.
Do you mean cuckoo.
A funny noise.
In the meantime there was lots of singing.
And then and then.
We have a new game
Can you fill it.
Alone.
And is it good
And useful
And has it a name
Lifting belly can change to filling petunia.
But not the same.
It is not the same.
It is the same.
Lifting belly.
So high.
And aiming.
Exactly.
And making
A cow
Come out.
Indeed I was not mistaken.
Come do not have a cow.
He has.
Well then.
Dear Daisy.
She is a dish.
A dish of good.
Perfect.
Pleasure.
In the way of dishes.
Willy.
And Milly.
In words.

So loud.
Lifting belly the dear.
Protection.
Protection
Protection
Speculation
Protection
Protection.
Can the furniture shine.
Ask me.
What is my answer.
Beautifully.
Is there a way of being careful
Of what.
Of the South.
By going to it.
We will go.
For them.
For them again.
And is there any likelihood of butter.
We do not need butter.
Lifting belly enormously and with song.
Can you sing about a cow.
Yes.
And about signs.
Yes.
And also about Aunt Pauline.
Yes.
Can you sing at your work.
Yes.
In the meantime listen to Miss Cheatham.
In the midst of writing.
In the midst of writing there is merriment.

YET DISH

I

Put a sun in Sunday, Sunday.
Eleven please ten hoop. Hoop.
Cousin coarse in coarse in soap.
Cousin coarse in soap sew up. soap.
Cousin coarse in sew up soap.

II

A lea ender stow sole lightly.
Not a bet beggar.
Nearer a true set jump hum,
A lamp lander so seen poor lip.

III

Never so round.
A is a guess and a piece.
A is a sweet cent sender.
A is a kiss slow cheese.
A is for age jet.

IV

New deck stairs.
Little in den little in dear den.

V

Polar pole.
Dust winder.
Core see.
A bale a bale o a bale.

VI

Extravagant new or noise peal extravagant.

VII
S a glass.
Roll ups.

VIII
Powder in wails, powder in sails, powder is all next to it is does
wait sack rate all goals like chain in clear.

IX
Negligible old star.
Pour even.
It was a sad per cent.
Does on sun day.
Watch or water.
So soon a moon or a old heavy press.

X
Pearl cat or cat or pill or pour check.
New sit or little.
New sat or little not a wad yet.
Heavy toe heavy sit on head.

XI
Ex, ex, ex.
Bull it bull it bull it bull it.
Ex Ex Ex.

XII
Cousin plates pour a y shawl hood hair.
No see eat.

XIII
They are getting, bad left log lope, should a court say stream, not
a dare long beat a soon port.

XIV
Colored will he.
Calamity.
Colored will he
Is it a soon. Is it a soon. Is it a soon. soon. Is it a soon. soon.

XV

Nobody's ice.
Nobody's ice to be knuckles.
Nobody's nut soon.
Nobody's seven picks.
Picks soap stacks.
Six in set on seven in seven told, to top.

XVI

A spread chin shone.
A set spread chin shone.

XVII

No people so sat.
Not an eider.
Not either. Not either either.

XVIII

Neglect, neglect use such.
Use such a man.
Neglect use such a man.
Such some here.

XIX

Note tie a stem bone single pair so itching.

XX

Little lane in lay in a circular crest.

XXI

eace while peace while toast.
ıper eight paper eight or, paper eight ore white.

XXII

Coop pour.
Never a single ham.
Charlie. Charlie.

XXIII

Neglect or.
A be wade.

Earnest care lease.
Least ball sup.

XXIV

Meal dread.
Meal dread so or.
Meal dread so or bounce.
Meal dread so or bounce two sales. Meal dread so or bounce two
   sails. Not a rice. No nor a pray seat, not a little muscle, not a
   nor noble, not a cool right more than a song in every period
   of nails and pieces pieces places of places.

XXV

Neat know.
Play in horizontal pet soap.

XXVI

Nice pose.
Supper bell.
Pull a rope pressed.
Color glass.

XXVII

Nice oil pail.
No gold go at.
Nice oil pail.
Near a paper lag sought.
What is an astonishing won door. A please spoon.

XXVIII

Nice knee nick ear.
Not a well pair in day.
Nice knee neck core.
What is a skin pour in day.

XXIX

Climb climb max.
Hundred in wait.
Paper cat or deliver.

xxx

Little drawers of center.
Neighbor of dot light.
Shorter place to make a boom set.
Marches to be bright.

xxxi

Suppose a do sat.
Suppose a negligence.
Suppose a cold character.

xxxii

Suppose a negligence.
Suppose a sell.
Suppose a neck tie.

xxxiii

Suppose a cloth cape.
Suppose letter suppose let a paper.
Suppose soon.

xxxiv

A prim a prim prize.
A sea pin.
A prim a prim prize
A sea pin.

xxxv

Witness a way go.
Witness a way go. Witness a way go. Wetness.
Wetness.

xxxvi

Lessons lettuce.
Let us peer let us polite let us pour, let us polite. Let us polite.

xxxvii

Neither is blessings bean.

xxxviii

Dew Dew Drops.

Leaves kindly Lasts.
Dew Dew Drops.

XXXIX

A R. nuisance.
Not a regular plate.
Are, not a regular plate.

XL

Lock out sandy.
Lock out sandy boot trees.
Lock out sandy boot trees knit glass.
Lock out sandy boot trees knit glass.

XLI

A R not new since.
New since.
Are new since bows less.

XLII

A jell cake.
A jelly cake.
A jelly cake.

XLIII

Peace say ray comb pomp
Peace say ray comb pump
Peace say ray comb pomp
Peace say ray comb pomp.

XLIV

Lean over not a coat low.
Lean over not a coat low by stand.
Lean over net. Lean over net a coat low hour stemmed
Lean over a coat low a great send. Lean over coat low extra extend.

XLV

Copying Copying it in.

XLVI

Never second scent never second scent in stand. Never second

scent in stand box or show. Or show me sales. Or show me
sales oak. Oak pet. Oak pet stall.

XLVII

Not a mixed stick or not a mixed stick or glass. Not a mend stone
bender, not a mend stone bender or stain.

XLVIII

Polish polish is it a hand, polish is it a hand or all, or all poles sick,
or all poles sick.

XLIX

Rush in rush in slice.

L

Little gem in little gem in an. Extra.

LI

In the between egg in, in the between egg or on.

LII

Leaves of gas, leaves of get a towel louder.

LIII

Not stretch.

LIV

Tea Fulls.
Pit it pit it little saddle pear say.

LV

Let me see wheat air blossom.
Let me see tea.

LVI

Nestle in glass, nestle in walk, nestle in fur a lining.

LVII

Pale eaten best seek.
Pale eaten best seek, neither has met is a glance.

LVIII

Suppose it is a s. Suppose it is a seal. Suppose it is a recognised
opera.

LIX

Not a sell inch, not a boil not a never seeking cellar.

LX

Little gem in in little gem in an. Extra.

LXI

Catch as catch as coal up.

LXII

Necklaces, neck laces, necklaces, neck laces.

LXIII

Little in in in in.

LXIV

Next or Sunday, next or sunday check.

LXV

Wide in swim, wide in swim pansy.

LXVI

Next to hear next to hear old boat seak, old boat seak next to hear.

LXVII

Ape pail ape pail to glow.

LXVIII

It was in on an each tuck. It was in on an each tuck.

LXIX

Wire lean string, wire lean string excellent miss on one pepper cute. Open so mister soil in to close not a see wind not seat glass.

WHAT DOES SHE SEE WHEN SHE SHUTS HER EYES   A NOVEL (1936)

IT IS VERY MERITORIOUS TO WORK VERY HARD IN A GARDEN equally so when there is good weather and something grows or when there is very bad weather and nothing grows.

When she shuts her eyes she sees the green things among which she has been working and then as she falls asleep she sees them a little different. The green things then have black roots and the black roots have red stems and then she is exhausted.

Naturally as she works in the garden she grows strawberries and raspberries and she eats them and sometimes the dog eats them and for days after he is not well and finally he is so weak he cannot stand but in a little while he is ready to eat again.

And so a day is not really a day because each day is like another day and they begin to have nothing. She herself was in mourning because her mother had died, her grandmother was dead before her mother died and her father had curly hair and took off his hat so that his eyes could see that somebody had stopped to talk with him.

It is a pleasure to be afraid of nothing. If they have no children they are not afraid of anything.

A good many of them only have one child and that is not the same as not having any children. If they are married and have no children then they are afraid. But if they are not married and have no child then they are not afraid.

Never having seen him before he becomes your servant and lives in the house and just as intimate as if he had been a father or children. It is funny that, there seems to be so much need of having always known anybody and he comes to answer an advertisement and you never saw him before and there you live in the house with him.

After all nothing changes but the weather and when she shuts her eyes she does not see clouds or sky but she sees woods and green things growing.

So the characters in this novel are the ones who walk in the fields and lose their dog and the ones who do not walk in the fields because they have no cows.

But everybody likes to know their name. Their name is Gabrielle and Therese and Bertha and Henry Maximilian Arthur and Genevieve and at any time they have happened to be happy.

Chapter I

How often could they be afraid.

Gabrielle said to any one, I like to say sleep well to each one, and he does like to say it.

He likes to do one thing at a time a long time.

More sky in why why do they not like to have clouds be that color.

Remember anything being atrocious.

And then once in a while it rains. If it rains at the wrong time there is no fruit if it rains at the right time there are no roses. But if it rains at the wrong time then the wild roses last a long time and are dark in color darker than white.

And this makes Henry Maximilian Arthur smile. It is just like the weather to be agreeable because it can be hot enough and so it might just as well not be hot yet. Which it is not.

And therefore Henry Maximilian Arthur is not restless nor is he turned around.

Chapter II

She grew sweet peas and carrots and beets. She grew tomatoes and roses and pinks and she grew pumpkins and corn and beans. She did not grow salad or turnips nor camelias nor nasturtiums but nasturtiums do grow and so do hortensias and heliotrope and fuchsias and peonies. After she was very careful she refused to pay more than they were worth and this brings Henry Maximilian Arthur to the contemplation of money. He might even not then throw it away. He might. After all he clings very tightly to what he has. But not to money because about there is no need. Money is needful those who can move about. And as yet Henry Maximilian Arthur does not do so.

No matter who has left him where he is no matter no matter who has left him where he is no matter. There he is.

No matter. It does not matter that no one has left any one where he is. It does not matter.

All birds look as if they enjoyed themselves and all birds look as if they looked as if they enjoyed themselves.

Better is not different than does it matter. It is better even if it does not matter.

Once in a while Henry Maximilian Arthur was caressed by Theresa. When Theresa caressed Henry Maximilian Arthur Henry Maximilian Arthur liked it as well as he liked it better. That is what is the way in which it was that it did as well as it did not matter.

Grasses grow and they make a shadow so just as grasses grow.

Henry Maximilian Arthur could be tickled by grasses as they grow and he could not caress but he could be caressed by Theresa as well as be tickled by grasses as they grow, when grass is cut it is called hay.

A year of grass is a year of alas. When grass grows that is all that grows but grass is grass and alas is alas.

One evening morning Henry Maximilian Arthur was awake. Once every morning he was awake and Theresa was not there and when Theresa came Henry Maximilian Arthur was there just the same.

That is what adding means and a cow. Henry Maximilian Arthur had no need of a cow. Theresa did Theresa had need of a cow, but a cow died and that was a loss a loss of a cow and the loss of the value of the cow and to replace the cow there had to be a medium-sized cow and a very small cow. But Henry Maximilian Arthur did not share the anxiety.

MARRY NETTIE

Alright make it a series and call it Marry Nettie.

Principle calling.
They don't marry.
Land or storm.
This is a chance.
A Negress.
Nurse.
Three years.
For three years.
By the time.
He had heard.
He didn't eat.
Well.
What does it cost to sew much.

A cane dropped out of the window. It was sometime before it was searched for. In the meantime the Negress had gotten it. It had no value. It was one that did bend. We asked every one. No one would be intended or contented. We gave no peace. At last the day before we left I passed the door. I saw a bamboo cane but I thought the joints were closer together. I said this. Miss Thaddeus looked in. It was my cane. We told the woman who was serving. She said she would get it. She waited and was reasonable. She asked if they found it below as it was the cane of Miss Thaddeus. It was and plain. So there. We leave.

There is no such thing as being good to your wife.

She asked for tissue paper. She wanted to use it as a respirator. I don't understand how so many people can stand the mosquitoes.

It seems unnecessary to have it last two years. We would be so pleased.

We are good.

We are energetic.

We will get the little bowls we saw to-day.

The little bowls we saw to-day are quite pretty.

They will do nicely.

We will also get a fan. We will have an electric one. Everything is so reasonable.

It was very interesting to find a sugar bowl with the United States seal on one side and the emblem of liberty on the other.

If you care to talk to the servant do not talk to her while she is serving at table. This does not make me angry nor annoy me. I like salad. I am losing my individuality.

It is a noise.

Plan.

All languages.

By means of swimming.

They see English spoken.

They are dark to-day very easily by the sun.

We will go out in the morning. We will go and bring home fish. We will also bring note-books and also three cups. We will see Palma. Shoes are necessary. Shoes with cord at the bottom are white. How can I plan everything.

Sometimes I don't mind putting on iodine and sometimes I do.

This is not the way to be pleasant. I am very careful.

To describe tube-roses.

This is the day.

Pressing.

John.

Eating garlic. Do be careful. Do be careful in eating garlic particularly on an island. There is a fish a devil fish an ink fish which is good to eat. It is prepared with pepper and sauce and we eat it nicely. It is very edible.

How did we please her. A bottle of wine not that doesn't do it.

Oil.

Oil.

To make her shine.

We entwine.

So that.

How do you do.

We don't think highly of Jenny.

SPANISH NEWSPAPER.

A spanish newspaper says that the king went to a place and addressed the artillery officer who was there and told him, artillery is very important in war.

THE COUNT.

Somebody does sleep next door.

The count went to bathe, the little boy had amber beads around him. He went.

I made a mistake.

That's it.

He wanted the towel dried.

They refused.

Towels do not dry down here.

They do up at my place, said the Count.

SHE WAS.

NOT ASTONISHING.

She came upstairs having been sick. It was the effect of the crab.

Was I lost in the market or was she lost in the market.

We were not. We thought that thirty nine was a case of say it. Please try. I could find her. A large piece. Beets. Figs. Egg plants. Fish. We walked up and down. They sold pencils. The soldier what is a soldier. A soldier is readily given a paper. He does not like that pencil. He does not try another. We were so happy. She ought to be a very happy woman. Now we are able to recognise a photograph. We are able to get what we want.

A NEW SUGAR BOWL WITH A CROSS ON TOP.

We said we had it. We will take it to Paris. Please let us take everything.

The sugar bowl with a cross on top now has sugar in it. Not soft sugar but the sugar used in coffee. It is put on the table for that.

It is very pretty. We have not seen many things. We want to be careful. We don't really have to bother about it.

ANOTHER CHANCE.

That's it. Beds. How glad I am. What was I worried about. Was it the weather, was it the sun, was it fatigue was it being tired. It was none of these. It was that wood was used and we did not know.

We blamed each other.

WE BLAMED EACH OTHER.

She said I was nervous. I said I knew she wasn't nervous. The dear of course I wasn't nervous. I said I wasn't nervous. We were sure that steam was coming out of the water. It makes that noise. Our neighbours have a small telescope. They can see the water with it. They can not see the names of ships. They can tell that their little boy is lonesome which he is. He stands there and calls out once in a while to the others. I am so annoyed.

Do we believe the germans.

We do not.

SPANISH PENS.

Spanish pens are falling. They fall there. That makes it rich. That makes Spain richer than ever. Spanish pens are in places. They are in the places which we see. We read everything. This is by no means an ordeal. A charity is true.

WHY ARE WE PLEASED.

We are pleased because we have an electrical fan.

May the gods of Moses and of Mars help the allies. They do they will.

WE WILL WALK AFTER SUPPER.

We will not have tea. We will rest all day with the electric fan. We will have supper. We can perspire. After supper. This is so humorous.

WE HAD AN EXCITING DAY.

We took a fan out of a man's hand. We complained to the mother of Richard. Not knowing her we went there. They all said it. It was useful. We went to the ball room where there was billiard playing and reading. Then we accepted it. He said it was changed from five to seven and a half.

NOT VERY LIKELY.

We were frightened. We are so brave and we never allow it. We do not allow anything at last. That's the way to say we like ours best.

PAPERS.

Buy me some cheese even if we must throw it away. Buy me some beets. Do not ask them to save any of these things. There will be plenty of them. One reason why we are careful is that carrots are indifferent. They are so and we forgot to say Tuesday. How do you do. Will you give me some of the fruit. It is thoughtless of me to be displeased.

HOT WEATHER.

I don't care for it. Why not. Because it makes me careless. Careless of what. Of the example of church. What is church. Church is not a question. So there is strength and truth and rocking.

PLEASE BE QUICK.

Why do they unload at night. Or is it that one hears it then. Perhaps it has just come. I am not suspicious.

WHY DO YOU LIKE IT.

Because it is all about you. Whom do you marry. Nettie.

WHOM DO YOU SAY YOU SEE.

You see plenty of french people. You see some foolish people. You hear one boasting. What is he saying. He says it takes a hundred men to make a steam boat landing. I am going to say you missed it. Do be still. We are awkward. Not in swimming. We are very strong. We have small touches and we do see our pride. We have earned plates. We are looking for a bell.

YOU LIKE THIS BEST.

Lock me in nearly.
Unlock me sweetly.
I love my baby with a rush rushingly.

SOMETIMES THEY CAN FINISH A BUGLE CALL.

Sometimes they can finish a bugle call when they know it.
They have a very good ear. They are not quick to learn. They
do not application.

MARRY NETTIE.

Marry who. Marry Nettie. Which Nettie. My Nettie. Marry
whom. Marry Nettie. Marry my Nettie.

I was distinguished by knowing about the flower pot. It was
one that had tuberoses. I put the others down below. That one
will be fixed.

I was also credited with having partiality for the sun. I am
not particular. I do not like to have it said that it is so necessary
to hear the next letter. We all wish to go now. Do be certain
that we are cool.

Oh shut up.

TILLIE

Tillie labor Tillie labor eye sheds or sheds, Tillie labor Tillie
labor late in shells ear shells oil shells, Tillie labor Tillie labor shave
in sew up ups ups, Tillie Tillie like what white like white where,
like, Tillie labor like where open so or Tillie labor. Tillie lay Tillie
laying Tillie laying, Tillie lime, Tillie Tillie, next to a sour bridge
next to a pan wiper next to ascent assent, next to, assent, assent.

Who was born January first.
Who was born in January first.
Who was born and believe me who was born and believe me,
who was born who was born and believe me.
At that rate.
Let us sell the bell.

Who was born and believe me for this reason, this reason the
reason is that the second of January as the second or January,
February or the second or January, he was born and believe me
the second of January. The second of January as the second of
January.

The third.
The third.
The third might be might it might it be might the third be
the third of January.
Might it be the third anyway, might it be the third of Jan-
uary anyway.
Run so might it be the third might it run so that it would be
January and the third and the third and January and run so. The
third of January.

Fourth of January reminds one of something reminds one of
the fourth. The fourth of January reminds one the fourth of
January and so forth, and so fourth and January. More January.
More slowly. More slowly fourth more slowly January fourth.

Fifth no one born.

Sixth no one born.
Sixth no one born.
Fifth no one born.

Fifth and sixth no one born.
No one born fifth and sixth no one born.
January fifth and sixth no one born.

January seventh.
As well known as January seventh.
And approach.

January eighth and an approach. Such an approach.

January ninth and nicely.
Approach.

January tenth just the same. It is just the same.

January eleventh respectively.

January twelfth may be yes.
In January can't they in January they can.

In January they can can't they.
Understood thirteen.

January fourteenth and just at noon.
How early in the day can any one be born.

January fifteenth and can they.

January sixteenth and the rest a day.

January seventeenth any day. Any day and dressed a day.
Any day and undoubtedly as it may be.

January eighteenth more easily used to be it.

January nineteenth merely in the meantime. In the meantime
and they will anyway.
January nineteenth celebrated on the seventeenth.

January twentieth has to go as prepared. Prepared as it is. All of it integrally shown and as to the hearing.

January twenty-first and to it. Do not forget birthdays. This is in no way a propaganda for a larger population.

January twenty-second and twenty-second. January twenty-second and twenty-second. January twenty-second and twenty-second.

January twenty-third not as wanted. January twenty-third as wanted not as wanted. January twenty-third for January the twenty-third.

January the twenty-fourth makes it as late, as late as that.

January the twenty-fifth ordinarily.

January the twenty-sixth as ordinarily.

January the twenty-seventh January twenty-seventh signed January the twenty-seventh.

January the twenty-eighth and August.

January the twenty-ninth as loudly.

January the thirtieth to agree, to agree to January the thirtieth.

January the thirty-first usually. Used. Usually. Usually. Used.

Thirty-one won.
Thirty-one won.
Thirty and one and won one.
Thirty-one won thirty-one won thirty-one thirty-one thirty-one won. Won. One. Thirty-one.

February first. First. At first.

February second this second.

February third Ulysses. Who Ulysses. Who Ulysses. Who Ulysses.
February third. February third heard word purred shirred heard. Heard word. Who.

February fourth. Get in, oh get in.

February fifth. Any and many, many and any. Any more.

February sixth, a mixed and mixed.

February seventh and so forth.
February seventh and so forth.
February seventh and so forth and February seventh.

February eighth oh how do you do.

February ninth collectedly, so collectedly, as collectedly.

February tenth makes eating easy, or easily. As February tenth makes it easy or easily.

February eleventh. Not is dishes. Dishes are named Emanuel or Rosita.

February twelfth consider it at all.

February thirteenth, more difference.

February fourteenth, when this you see remember me and you will anyway.

February fifteenth. Have you had it have you had it have you had it as you had it as you had it have you had it have you had it as you had it have you had it.

February sixteenth. So much so.

February seventeenth has a married lady. Married. Lady.

February eighteenth. Has it.

February twentieth. Excuse me.

February nineteenth. I agree you agree you agree I agree I agree you agree lily agree lily or three.

February twenty-first, pronounce as at first pronounce and as at first or at first, pronounce it first.

February twenty-second was mentioned.

February twenty-third. A chicken lies in or win or what it lies in.

February twenty-fourth, for a four, four leaf for or four, four leaf four leaf for four leaf or four leaf for for a leaf. Four leaf. For four leaf.
February twenty-fourth. As a wife has a cow entitled.

February twenty-fifth. Twenty days as days.

February twenty-sixth. Twenty days also twenty days.

February twenty-seventh has a place in history. Historical and so near.

On the twenty-eighth of February in and win always so prettily.

Washing away, every day.
Equally an undiscovered country so.
Every other day they may say pay.

March at one march at once march at one march for once.

March the second wedding march march or rain, and do march, march marble, marbles march.

March the third or church.

March the fourth or churches.

March the fifth or powder.

March the sixth or giggling.

March the seventh patently, patently see, patently saw, she saw he saw patently see to see. He would be.

March the eighth, jumping and picking up the purse, jumping up and picking up the purse.

March the ninth. Does it weigh.

March the tenth. Successively stay.

March the eleventh. The door.

March the twelfth. Some more.

March the thirteenth. Some more explore some more, as before as explore some more.

March the fourteenth. The weather otherwise.

March the fifteenth. Did the rest.

March the sixteenth and many.

March the seventeenth added addition.

March the eighteenth may we blame no one and in this way reconcile ourselves to every obligation.

March the nineteenth formerly not at all and now nearly as contentedly nearly as candidly nearly as swimmingly nearly as neglected, not as neglected as at all and so forth.

March the twentieth melodrama.

On March the twenty-first it is our duty to call a halt.

On March the twenty-second likewise.

And on March the twenty-third witnesses.

March the twenty-fourth able to be able to be able very able he is very able he is a very able man.

March the twenty-fifth makes it up.

On March the twenty-sixth it is made up to them everything is made up to them it is made up to them for everything.

March the twenty-seventh to declare and is it so. March the twenty-sixth declare and is it so. Is it so and March the twenty-sixth and declare and is it so.

March the twenty-seventh ordinarily. Ordinarily on March the twenty-seventh an added restraint likewise makes itself felt.

March the twenty-eighth ordinarily on March the twenty-eighth ordinarily as added as an objection.

March the twenty-ninth for instance.

March the thirtieth makes March the thirtieth makes March the thirtieth and makes, makes March the thirtieth and makes March and makes March the thirtieth.

March the thirty-first reasonably.

April the first, yes sir.

April the second in order to maintain that this would be especially so.

April the third every once in a while.

On April the fourth use your brush and comb use your comb and brush.

April the fifth rush.

April the sixth if you like it say you do.

April the seventh cook and stew as you do as you used to do as you are used to as you are used to it.

April the eighth master-pieces fairly surely surely carefully carefully entirely, entirely fairly fairly carefully carefully surely surely carefully.

April the ninth or choose it as carefully.

April the tenth happened to say.

April the eleventh as the one said.
April the eleventh as the one said and as they and as the one said.

April the twelfth fed it yesterday they fed it yesterday.

April the thirteenth when there is more or less in the meantime.

April the fourteenth ought it to be caught ought it to be.

April fifteenth as if it ought to be taught ought it to be taught, ought it to be taught as it ought to be.

April the sixteenth waited till it was finished before she budged.

April the seventeenth on April the seventeenth really really on April the seventeenth and really, on April the seventeenth usually next to it.

April the eighteenth has interested me.

April the nineteenth fourteenth the fourteenth nineteenth, April nineteenth, the fourteenth April nineteenth the fourteenth.

April twentieth makes a movement.

April the twenty-first shall it be April the twenty-first, asked to be has to be has to be asked to be asked to be April the twenty-first has asked to be April the twenty-first.

April the twenty-second not mentioned in history.

April the twenty-third and they see the point. Do they see the point.

April the twenty-third and was it.

Was it April the twenty-fourth was it.

It was April the twenty-fifth and was it on April the twenty-fifth and how was it on April the twenty-fifth.

To be to the twenty-sixth of April it is to be to the twenty-sixth of April it is to be the twenty-sixth of April as it is to be the twenty-sixth of April as it is to be. It is to be until it is the twenty-sixth of April.

The twenty-seventh of April coming nearer.

And the twenty-eighth of April which is so exciting.

The twenty-ninth of April so reasonably is the twenty-ninth of April is so reasonably as reasonably as it is.

The thirtieth of April selects selects the thirtieth of April. As it selects the thirtieth of April, as it selects. Selects the thirtieth of April. Sell it selects. Selects see ordered.
Thirty days has September April June and November.
May and might hold me tight, might and may night and day, night and day and anyway, anyway as so gay, gayly, gayly misses.

May day.

Second of May, second of May yes sir.

Third of May means that there is enough that there is enough the third of May and enough.

The fourth of May enough and enough and the fourth of May.

The fifth of May and so much to be said for it.

And the sixth of May has exactly for the sixth of May there is exactly on the sixth of May exactly as on the sixth of May anyway.

The seventh of May easily.

The eighth of May as easily.

The ninth of May may may.

The tenth of May may be. On the eleventh of May may be they will be there.

The eleventh of May as is necessary all the time.

The twelfth as it is necessary all the time.

The thirteenth of May on the thirteenth of May as expected next time on the thirteenth of May.

On the fourteenth of May expect on the fourteenth of May.

The fifteenth of May expect next time expected next time, next time.
The fifteenth of May gradually.

Sixteenth of May gradually the sixteenth of May.

The seventeenth of May is the day on that day on that day is their day.

The eighteenth of May yesterday. A disappointment.

The nineteenth of May nearly as much of an advantage as ever.

Every yours as always sincerely yours yours truly and on the twentieth of May as dated.

The twenty-first of May as stated.

The twenty-second of May as if it were as an assembly.

The twenty-third of May as much as there is to do and able to go through to as in stretches as they do.

On the twenty-fourth autograph on the twenty-fourth may they photograph on the twenty-fourth as the twenty-fourth of May.

The twenty-fifth minus the other numbers, May the twenty-fifth and minus the other numbers.

The twenty-sixth in addition.

The twenty-seventh for division.
The twenty-seventh of May, May, for subtraction, the twenty of May, May, for subtraction. The twenty-seventh of May, May, for subtraction.

The twenty-eighth of May as the result of learning.

The twenty-ninth of May in various places.

The thirtieth of May or we have it as we have it.

On the thirty-first of May remember titles on the thirty-first of May remember titles to what on the thirty-first of May remember titles on the thirty-first of May as remember titles. Little single since.

The first of June. Smile. When you see me smile. When do you see me smile. As you see me smile. Smile while mile afterwards. Smile mile while afterwards.

June the second as favorably as that as June the second as favorably as that.

And interlude between June and July and July and August. Red Indian fed Indian wed Indian said Indian. He said Indian. He said Indian red Indian fed Indian wed Indian she wed Indian. Wed Indian fed Indian said Indian red Indian, she said red Indian. Red Indian said Indian wed Indian fed Indian she said wed Indian. She said red Indian. She said fed Indian. She said fed Indian wed Indian red Indian, she said red Indian.

Shall I use that for a month or a day, to us who gave you a day.

June the third has many times three, three four not any more two three as can be one two as you, one won.

June the fourth methodically.

June the fifth two and two nicely.

On June the sixth as it happened again and was sustained too.

June the seventh very likely to be very well arranged.

June the eighth upper eat upper and ate upper and on finding and likely to be very well arranged.

June the ninth and nicely and as well arranged.

June the tenth for instance is there more is there very much more.

June the eleventh for instance.

June the twelfth if finding makes a difference.

June the thirteenth if in inattention, June the thirteenth if as well as they all know it, if in inattention, if as well as they all know it if in inattention and if as well as they all know it.

On June the fourteenth avail and too much in contribution.

The fifteenth of June and seasoned.

The sixteenth of June and habitually has habitually, it was habitually.

The seventeenth of June measured by this.

The eighteenth of June in on receipt.

The nineteenth of June was as always.

The twentieth of June changed by letter.

The twenty-first of June as an instance, instance of what instance of exactitude.

The twenty-second and on the twenty-second of June.

June the twenty-third, originally originally June the twenty-third.

June the twenty-fourth. This time the wives will sign. Today the wives will sign.

June and so forth. June the twenty-fifth, June the twenty-fifth. June and so forth.

June the twenty-sixth her name is June and very very soon.

June the twenty-seventh June and just as soon just as soon as just as soon.

June the twenty-eighth and just as soon.

June the twenty-ninth here and there a name.

June the thirtieth and here and there and the same here and there. Here and there a name.
Thirty days has September April June and November here

and there a name all the same. All the same here and there a
name all the same all the same a name here and there.

July because because July because because July because.

July the first because July the first. July the first because.

July the second jealously.

July the third in a place in the place in the place of it.

July the fourth as everybody as a sample as a sample as everybody.

July the fifth come too come to places come to places come
as comfortably.

On July the sixth the understanding which means only here
and there that only there which means that, only here and there.

July the seventh in the meantime it is pointed out.

July the eighth in which house did he live.

July the ninth ineradicably.

July the tenth makes August and September.

July the eleventh a puzzle.

July the twelfth ought to be ought to be ought to be all that
it ought to be.

July the thirteenth in which house did he live.

July the fourteenth July the fourteenth fifty, July the fourteenth thirty, July the fourteenth thirty July the fourteenth fifty. July the thirteenth fifty and thirty.

July the fifteenth the day of delivery.

July the sixteenth is historical.

July the seventeenth November September October December.

July the eighteenth on July the eighteenth it is the same thing or July the eighteenth it is the same thing.

July the nineteenth before Mary.

July the twentieth before Mary Rose.

July the twenty-first before Mary Louise.

July the twenty-second an emergency.

July twenty-third July twenty-third for this and before this and because of this.

July twenty-fourth period.

July the twenty-fifth is easily replaced.

And July the twenty-sixth still more easily.

July the twenty-seventh is not simply prepared for.

July the twenty-eighth. Fanny has a market.

July the twenty-ninth to please and please.

July the thirtieth ministrations.

July the thirty-first the first.

August and and August and and August and and August.

August first and foremost.

August the second there where there were there. Where.

August the third as may be said so.

August the fourth then I would like to like to very much.

August the fifth then to like to like to very much.

August the sixth to forget in which house did he live.

August the seventh unable to.

August the eighth all August the eighth.

August the ninth at that.

August the tenth tenth ten times August the tenth, tenth time the tenth time.

August the eleventh. To you who who to you.

August twelfth that is a nice one.

August the thirteenth and that is a nice one.

August the fourteenth forget in which house did he live.

August the fifteenth was understood to be principally for them all.

August the sixteenth on August the sixteenth usually unusually so.

August the seventeenth usually unusually prompt.

August the eighteenth unusually so.

August the nineteenth it is felt to be.

August the twentieth conviction the conviction that there is August the twentieth illustrates very well this occasionally.

August the twenty-first illustrates this occasionally.

No August the twenty-second, the second.

August the twenty-third as illustration of this occasionally.

August the twenty-fourth for the fourth time as a fourth. As a fourth. August the twenty-fourth.

August the twenty-fifth the fourth of what.

August the twenty-sixth and perfumery and stationery.

August the twenty-seventh for instance.

August twenty-eight a date. Date palm date of harm date of harm date farm. Farming.

August the twenty-ninth needless to say.

August the thirtieth thirty day August the thirtieth thirty days and August the thirtieth and the thirty days. And the thirty days, following. And the thirty and the days and following.

August the thirty-first for in a way.

September first because in a way.

September the second because in a way.

September the third house them, a house, house them arouse, house explanation.

September the fourth and as finally and as house to house and as house to house and as finally.

September the fifth formerly finally.

September the sixth formerly finally and as house to house and a house to house and as formerly finally.

September the seventh for that reason.

September the eighth in which house did he live formerly.

September the ninth and in which house did he live.

September the tenth or formerly a great deal.

September the eleventh on September the eleventh interested in birthdays.

September the twelfth as meant to be September the twelfth.

Interested in birthdays on September the thirteenth and this without principally.

September fourteenth measured measured September the fourteenth.

September fifteenth equal and as a cow.

September sixteenth anyhow.

September the seventeenth has remarkably few.

On September the eighteenth as they knew.

September the nineteenth wintergreen.

September the twentieth winter and green.

September the twenty-first no dates mentioned.

September the twenty-second thirty days has September.

September the twenty-third April June.

September the twenty-fourth and November.

September the twenty-fifth all the others.

September the twenty-sixth thirty-one.

September the twenty-seventh except the second.

September the twenty-eighth the second.

September the twenty-ninth month alone.

September the thirtieth but a year.

September a year gives it twenty-nine.

October in fine.

October first gives it twenty-nine.

October second gives it twenty-nine in fine.

October the third conscientiously.

October the fourth how many and changes.

October the fifth foremost and first.

October the sixth at first.

October the seventh one two three.

October the eighth one two three four five six seven.

October the ninth at first.

October the tenth eleven at first.

October the eleventh ten at first.

October the twelfth on which account.

October the thirteenth can it can it come, come and can it can it come, for instance come, for instance can it.

October fourteenth can it come for instance.

October fifteenth eight a day two a day two a day as eight as eight.

October sixteenth as eight, two as two, eight as eight, eight as eight a day.

October seventeenth not to hurry.

October eighteenth finally for it.

October nineteenth on October the nineteenth on October the nineteenth on and over.

October the twentieth makes it sound so.

October the twenty-first and may be yes.

October the twenty-second finally October the twenty-second.

October the twenty-third, in a minute.

October the twenty-fourth for October the twenty-fourth or for October the twenty-fourth.

October the twenty-fifth sounds like a half.

October the twenty-sixth not again.

October the twenty-seventh and not again.

October the twenty-eighth and not as as not and not again and not as, as it.

October the twenty-ninth arithmetic, follow me, arithmetically.

October the thirtieth as slowly as October the thirtieth.
October the thirtieth and in reference to it, as as and and and and and as as. As as, as and as and, as and, and as.
October the thirtieth makes three numbers.

October the thirty-first necessary and not, and not and not and necessary and not. November to repeat. Repeat November November November. Easy to repeat. Easy to repeat November, not as easy, not so easy not to repeat November and first.

November first. First and ferries. Ferries, to go across ferries.

November the second. Cross he looks.

November the third across the end across the end and where to cross the, and where is it.

November the fourth where is it.

November the fifth what is the what is it.

November the sixth when and when and as and as, as readily.

November the seventh when and when and there and there and as readily.

November the eighth and as readily.

November the ninth slightly as now.

November the tenth furnished anyhow.

November the eleventh where and where, how and how, now and now, neither.

November the twelfth. Early or, ore, this is sold.

November the thirteenth and Tuesday.

November the fourteenth happily November the fourteenth.

November the fifteenth in fifteen.

November the sixteenth or sixteen.

November the seventeenth makes a mail a day.

November the eighteenth let us.

November the nineteenth very vary very.

November the twentieth stretches.

November the twenty-first stretches further.

November the twenty-second and ministrations over again.

November the twenty-third fortunately.

November the twenty-fourth more fortunately.

November the twenty-fifth most fortunately.

November the twenty-sixth mostly.

November the twenty-seventh and now.

November the twenty-eighth four more.

November the twenty-ninth as hindered.

November the thirtieth thirty days, thirty days as. As and has.

December springing spring and sprung.

December the first strung.

December the second strong.

December the third stronger.

December the fourth surely and also.

December the fifth to change for it.

December the sixth to change for it.

On December the seventh she lost a newspaper.

December the eighth where as nearly.

December the ninth when as soon.

December the tenth when as soon.

December the eleventh where as nearly.

December on the twelfth of December where and when.

On the thirteenth of December where and when as nearly as soon.

On the fourteenth of December and to remember it as such.

On the fifteenth of December as an organization.

December sixteenth as meant.

December seventeenth and may do.

December the eighteenth if to witness.

December the nineteenth may do it too.

December the twentieth as it would would it.

December the twenty-first colored by and by.

December the twenty-second as he said.

December the twenty-third to scatter.

December twenty-fourth minstrels to mean even.

December twenty-fifth and always interested in birthdays.

December twenty-sixth and may do too.

December twenty-seventh have time.

December twenty-eighth a million.

December twenty-ninth or three.

December thirtieth corals.

December thirty-first. So much so.

A COMEDY LIKE THAT

I am going to try a comedy like that.
I am going to like a comedy like that.
Like that is like that it is like that I am going to like that. I am
going to like it like that.
Which first.
Which on what on what does it depend which first.
Which first on which does it depend which first.
Which first what first on which does it depend what first.
On what does it depend which first.
On which does it depend on what does it depend on what
does it depend what first on which does it depend what first
on what does it depend which first, on which does it depend on
which does it depend on what does it depend on what first.
On what first.
On which first.
Next evenly, next even even next evenly next evenly next
even. Even next evenly next on what evenly next on which even
next on which even next on which on what evenly next on evenly
next which depends on what first, what depends evenly next

which depends evenly next which depends on what first even
next evenly next which depends on what first.

What depends on which first.

Evenly next.

INTRODUCTION

Just the same as another.

As always interested to know as always in the way to on the
way and before by the way when there is a part, all the way as it
is used, used and added for and so much. She has no habits here.
But she will form them. She has no habits here. But she will hear
them as more. Hear in the sense of heard, hear in the sense of
right, hear in the sense of settling.

Not only over again.

Habitually corner and corner and habitually and harps and
habitually and corner and habitually and harps and corner and
habitually.

The next time as ever.

It is and not and so and to it is and so and not it is and to and
so and is and it is and it is so and it is not and it and so and is, and is.

Further than this makes it best.

Best test.

OPENING SCENE

Seen and seen and seen as to a man which if corresponded.

Answering that.

Seen and seen and seen as to and corresponded answering
that.

Seen and seen and seen and as to corresponded answering
that.

Seen and seen as to corresponded.

In the next again and has not as yet felt it to be easier.

Not remembered as a fact.

Before scenery before scenery or more. This and waiting.
Waiting on what, can be used so as if it were as if it were a as if it
were a rest and all. To them.

Actually counted and counted it all out. And counted it all
out.

If yes, yes yes, and an addition and in addition, if and in addition, if and an addition, if yes, if in addition, yes and if and an addition, larger and better.

In answer.

And and might, as well, as it is, and it is done.

Done and done so, in place of after it and between. This then in objection. Weigh, weight, and attacked, attract, attached and after it, afterwards, beginning, and satisfactory preparation.

Here as in certain for and a threat, is a threat or a threat or a half or a part or a pressure or complete or as much as in that as a case of it.

Replied and surface if the surface has been so much sooner, soon, and accounted as finished for it, it is finished as an afternoon to-day.

If mine and mine if mine if it is touched if it is mine if mine is touched. If it is touched.

Sooner have and have it in sooner. As heard away, away from the receipt. To receive when if had it even when not as or because if in in inclined and arranged to prepare. Suited to it.

The next arrangement is made as it was. As it was and second and in arrival, as late as that. The next time. By nearly all of it.

It is more as the chance of that. Found lately.

Different to be differently adhered to there. The next in and whether to have as and forgotten.

Did she say what she said she would.

All she can remember is what happened. All she can remember is that she can remember all that happened.

The next time suitable would it be well to turn around so that if the coat which if brown and the hat which is black would continue to be as satisfactory as if when a new decision was to be made it would certainly not be influenced by that arrangement. No answer as yet.

This is on this account.

Having told and having told having told and having told having told and having told evenings and more and unaccountably.

Having told it was a pleasure it was merely an apparent day. Apparently a day and day-time.

Extra and union.

Extra and union and in union.

Extra and in union and union and in union.

Extra and in union.

Not and seen nearly.

Not nearly not as near not nearly not and seen not and seen not and seen and nearly.

This is the end of that.

And very nearly as it is.

To-morrow again and in and a place. A place for everything and everything in its place.

Fortunately, fortunately it was a fortunately as it was and fortunately beside.

This is not heard and seen.

This evening see this evening see, this evening see to as much so.

And as noon.

And as noon and as there was amorning and as there was morning and more than so soon and as soon.

Nearly have to say and nearly have to say it.

Coming to a station in coming to a station does a do the trains stop.

If they do does she when they do does she do so when they do do so.

After that asking to have it clearly understood as to hearing.

Is hearing and staying equal and individual. Is it a reason or is it as a season. Can there be an ounce and ounces and may there be as often as that always all of it in preference.

She knows.

When is and when is there not all of or either all if it or all of it or either or all of it. When is there after it has been as it was assured as it is to be assured that there is no doubt. It is assuredly once and more than once and once or twice and often. Often and as often and always and more so.

She was told she had bought.

Having added having added could she have and have and add, could she add and have and have and add. Could she having could she have added could she adding could she having could she be having and adding.

Cut glass cut glass cut glass and an old and sent.

If this in the morning and if she and were she, was she and in this and in the habit of it.

Satisfied to say.

Almost all and almost all and to do and to do almost all almost all of it to do.

Though she was though if she was though if she was though would there would there be any necessity for sight and hearing. In their place there is ease.

One and two, requested to use two.

Two and one one as to have it.

Repeated.

It is easier to repeat a sentence than shorter. It is easier to repeat a sentence and longer, it is easier to repeat a sentence and longer it is easier to sing.

Left after this.

Right after this.

Left after this right after this right after this left after this.

It is all earlier.

And longer.

And after after it at all.

If the name name of wool if the woman and as much not alone that it is put there.

If at first here and there if she hears as the door door and more as a fact and never angry.

If not at all as soon as and it had for the best was she too to have heard all as well as all that.

When the same as it is when at first as well as when there is and it can when as much as it does and questioned.

How has he and not heard when he had and was left would it be and not for for them.

This is due to her sister.

Could it have have it had and the rest for its use to be seated and as much as leaning.

This and there for the noise by its use for the rest and as well when and how does she know any other.

In a way in their way in her way in a day in a day in the day time and at least.

The real and the ideal the one who finding fault does not

cause more than imitation and the other who in consequence looks again. The one who has every wish and all wishes the other who has wishes and every wish. There is no difference between two years and one year in each case they can be induced either to leave or to stay.

Part of the time.

Copy cold and copy colder copy and cold and as cold and yet fortunately it is economical and not insufficient.

In this way we say how much is there and not at all unwillingly.

A description of standard weights and measures.

Should squares which are divided in two have eight and seven which makes fifteen or can there be some other arrangement.

She came in with what. She came in with what. With what did she come in.

And then as if with cress. Cress having in itself the necessary ingredient instead of being reminded there has been more and less. And for this and as this and when if again or, can a place be made by adding places to it. Places which are added are those in which beauty is repeated. Finally and wished and succeeded. Having no doubt, no doubt having to have had an example of it.

This makes their agreement so important.

When this is heard.

Come Tuesday come Tuesday and come.

Wednesday.

Thursday.

Thursday is the day arranged.

Thursday is the day arranged seriously. For and because it is as much meant.

As a sound.

Name, his name.

Fortunately by his name.

Like that.

It will be like that.

Fortunately by her name.

Name, her name.

Fortunately by her name.

It will be like that.

Fortunately by her name.

A different occasion to-morrow, a different occasion to-morrow a different occasion, a different occasion, a different occasion, occasionally, to-morrow.

Should and no.

Having had one, one at a time, having had one one at a time having had one at a time having had one one at a time.

More than plainly.

As much more and plainly and plainly as much more.

Changing hats hats change.

Changing doors doors change.

Changing chairs chairs change.

Changing.

The next time like that.

Any more.

And any more like that.

There are not there will not there will not be any more.

There will not be any more like that just now.

As much like that.

If coming and come and to come.

When you are out how do you get in.

The thirtieth of May in the morning she had three sisters and one brother the thirtieth of may in the morning there had been another brother, who would have been older, the thirtieth of May in the morning the brother who was younger than any sister was not at all concerned with the fact that his sister being older would certainly be going farther away than any other sister. She would be satisfied.

On the thirtieth of May in the morning and there were four sisters one brother a father a grandfather and a mother. It is not at all likely that the others would be returning before the middle of July to spend the time with the others who concerned themselves with the work of the summer. The emotion would not last long.

In no sense can happiness be encouraged.

Payments.

Pointing to many places.

Obviously.

Partial payments.

Partly to her.

Let it be remembered that if and there is let it be remembered that there is to be conscientiousness.

Let it be remembered that if and there is augmentation let it be remembered that there is to be conscientiousness.

Once not.

Once and not.

Let it be remembered that at once and once.

Let it be remembered.

It is not remembered.

Let it be remembered that without its being good enough, let it as it is not good enough to let it as it is good enough to let it be remembered at once.

They took every advantage.

ONE OR TWO. I'VE FINISHED

There
Why
There
Why
There
Able
Idle.

As long as it took fasten it back to a place where after all he
would be carried away, he would be carried away as long as it
took fasten it back to a place where he would be carried away as
long as it took.

For before let it before to be before spell to be before to be
before to have to be to be for before to be tell to be to having held
to be to be for before to call to be for to be before to till until to
be till before to be for before to be until to be for before to for
to be for before will for before to be shall to be to be for to be
for to be before still to be will before to be before for to be to be
for before to be before such to be for to be much before to be
for before will be for to be for before to be well to be well before
to be before for before might while to be might before to be
might while to be might before while to be might to be while
before for might to be for before to for while to be while for before while before to for which as for before had for before had
for before to for to before.

Hire hire let it have to have to hire representative to hire to
representative to representative hire to representative to hire wire
to representative to hire representative to hire.

There never was a mistake in addition.

Ought ought my prize my ought ought prize with a denies
with a denies to be ought ought to denies with a to ought to ought
ought with a denies plainly detained practically to be next. With
a with a would it last with a with a have it passed come to be
with this and theirs there is a million of it shares and stairs and
stairs to right about. How can you change from their to be sad
to sat. Coming again yesterday.

Once to be when once to be when once to be having an advantage all the time.

Little pieces of their leaving which makes it put it there to
be theirs for the beginning of left altogether practically for the
sake of relieving it partly.

As your as to your as to your able to be told too much as to
your as to as able to receive their measure of rather whether

intermediary and left to the might it be letting having when win. When win makes it dark when win makes it dark to held to be-held behold be as particularly in respect to not letting half of it be by. Be by in this away.

To lay when in please and letting it be known to be come to this not in not in not in nightingale in which is not in land in hand there is it leaving light out out in this or this or this beside which may it for it to be in it lest and louder louder to be known which is could might this near special have near nearly reconcile oblige and indestructible and mainly in this use.

Mainly will fill remaining sad had which is to be following dukedom duke in their use say to amount with a part let it go as if with should it might my makes it a leader.

Feels which is there.

To change a boy with a cross from there to there.

Let him have him have him heard let him have him heard him third let him have him have him intend let him have him have him defend let him have him have him third let him have him have him heard let him have him have him occurred let him have him have him third.

Forty-nine Clive as well forty-nine Clive as well forty-nine sixty-nine seventy-nine eighty-nine one hundred and nine Clive as well forty-nine Clive as well which is that it presses it to be or to be stay or to be twenty a day or to be next to be or to be twenty to stay or to be which never separates two more two women.

Fairly letting it see that the change is as to be did Nelly and Lily love to be did Nelly and Lily went to see and to see which is if could it be that so little is known was known if so little was known shone stone come bestow bestown so little as was known could which that for them recognisably.

Wishing for Patriarchal Poetry.

Once threes letting two sees letting two three threes letting it be after these two these threes can be two near threes in threes twos letting two in two twos slower twos choose twos threes never came twos two twos relieve threes twos threes. Threes twos relieves twos to twos to twos to twos relieve to twos to relieve two threes to relieves two relieves threes twos two to re-lieve threes relieves threes relieve twos relieves threes two twos slowly twos relieve threes threes to twos relieve relieve two to relieve threes twos twos relieves twos threes threes relieves twos two relieve twos relieves relieve twos relieves threes relieve twos slowly twos to relieves relieve threes relieve threes twos two relieve twos threes relieves relieve relieves twos two twos threes relieves threes two twos relieve relieves relieves threes relieve relieves threes relieves as two so threes twos relieves twos relieve.

Who hears whom once once to snow they might if they trained fruit-trees they might if they leaned over there they might look like it which when it could if it as if when it left to them to their use of pansies and daisies use of them use of them of use of pansies and daisies use of pansies and daisies use of them use of them of use use of pansies and use of pansies and use of pansies and use use of them use of pansies and daisies use of use of them which is what they which is what they they do they which is what they do there out and out and leave it to the meaning of their by their with their allowance making allowed what is it.

They have it with it reconsider it with it they with it reconsider it with it they have it with it reconsider it have it they with it reconsider it they have it they with it reconsider it they with it they reconsider it have it they have it reconsider it with it have it reconsider it have it with it. She said an older sister not an older sister she said an older sister not an older sister she said an older sister have it with it reconsider it with it reconsider it have it an older sister have it with it. She said she had followed flowers she had said she had said she had followed she had said she had said she had followed she had said with it have it reconsider it have it with it she had said have followed have said have had have followed have said followed had followed had said followed flowers which she had had will it reconsider it with it have it had said followed had followed had followed flowers had said had with it had followed flowers had have had with it had said had have had with it.

Is no gain.
Is no gain.
To is no gain.
Is to to is no gain.

Is to is to to is no gain.
Is to is no is to is no gain.
Is no gain.
Is to is no gain.
Is to is to is no gain.
Is no gain.
Is to is no gain.
With it which it as it if it is to be to be to come to in which to
do in that place.
As much as if it was like as if might be coming to see me.
What comes to be the same as lilies. An ostrich egg and their
after lines.
It made that be alike and with it an indefinable reconciliation
with roads and better to be not as much as felt to be as well very
well as the looking like not only little pieces there. Comparing
with it.
Not easily very much very easily, wish to be wish to be rest
to be like not easily rest to be not like not like rest to be not like
it rest to not like rest to be not like it.
How is it to be rest to be receiving rest to be how like it rest
to be receiving to be like it. Compare something else to something
else. To be rose.
Such a pretty bird.
Not to such a pretty bird. Not to not to not to not to such
a pretty bird.
Not to such a pretty bird.
Not to such a pretty bird.
As to as such a pretty bird. As to as to as such a pretty bird.
To and such a pretty bird.
And to and such a pretty bird.
And to as to not to as to and such a pretty bird.
As to and to not to as to and such a pretty bird and to as such
a pretty bird and to not to as such a pretty bird and to as to not
to and to and such a pretty bird as to and such a pretty bird and
to and such a pretty bird not to and to as such a pretty bird as to
as such a pretty bird and to as such a pretty bird and to as to and to
not to and to as to as such a pretty bird and to as such a pretty bird
and to as to not to as to and to and such a pretty bird and to and

such a pretty bird as to and such a pretty bird not to and such a
pretty bird not to and such a pretty bird as to and such a pretty
bird and to and such a pretty bird as to and to and such a pretty
bird not to as to and such a pretty bird and to not as to and to not
to as such as pretty bird and such a pretty bird not to and such
a pretty bird as to and such a pretty bird as such a pretty bird and
to as such a pretty bird and to and such a pretty bird not to and
such a pretty bird as to and such a pretty bird not to as such a
pretty bird not to and such a pretty bird as to and such a pretty
bird not to as to and to not to as such a pretty bird and to not
to and to and such a pretty bird as to and such a pretty bird
and to as such a pretty bird as to as such a pretty bird not to
and to as to and such a pretty bird as to and to and to as to
as such a pretty bird as such a pretty bird and to as such a pretty
bird and to and such a pretty bird and to and such and to and to
and such a pretty bird and to and to and such a pretty bird and
to and such a pretty bird and to and such a pretty bird and to
and such a pretty bird and to and such a pretty bird and to as to
and to and such a pretty bird and to as to as such a pretty bird
and to and to and such a pretty bird and such a pretty bird and to
and such a pretty bird and to and to and such a pretty bird and
to and such a pretty bird.
   Was it a fish was it heard was it a bird was it a cow was stirred
was it a third was it a cow was stirred was it a third was it a bird
was heard was it a third was it a fish was heard was it a third.
Fishes a bird cows were stirred a bird fishes were heard a bird
cows were stirred a third. A third is all. Come too.
   Patriarchal means suppose patriarchal means and close patriarchal means and chose chose Monday Patriarchal means in close
some day patriarchal means and chose chose Sunday patriarchal
means and chose chose one day patriarchal means and close close
Tuesday. Tuesday is around Friday and welcomes as welcomes
not only a cow but introductory. This aways patriarchal as sweet.
   Patriarchal make it ready.
   Patriarchal in investigation and renewing of an intermediate
rectification of the initial boundary between cows and fishes.
Both are admittedly not inferior in which case they may be obtained as the result of organisation industry concentration as-

sistance and matter of fact and by this this is their chance and to appear and to reunite as to their date and their estate. They have been in no need of stretches stretches of their especial and apart and here now.

Favored by the by favored by let it by the by favored by the by. Patriarchal poetry and not meat on Monday patriarchal poetry and meat on Tuesday. Patriarchal poetry and venison on Wednesday Patriarchal poetry and fish on Friday Patriarchal poetry and birds on Sunday Patriarchal poetry and chickens on Tuesday patriarchal poetry and beef on Thursday. Patriarchal poetry and ham on Monday patriarchal poetry and pork on Thursday patriarchal poetry and beef on Tuesday patriarchal poetry and fish on Wednesday Patriarchal poetry and eggs on Thursday patriarchal poetry and carrots on Friday patriarchal poetry and extras on Saturday patriarchal poetry and venison on Sunday Patriarchal poetry and lamb on Tuesday patriarchal poetry and jellies on Friday patriarchal poetry and turkeys on Tuesday.

They made hitherto be by and by.

It can easily be returned ten when this, two might it be too just inside, not as if chosen that not as if chosen, withal if it had been known to be going to be here and this needed to be as as green. This is what has been brought here.

Once or two makes that be not at all practically their choice practically their choice.

Might a bit of it be all the would be might be if a bit of it be all they would be if it if it would be all be if it would be a bit of all of it would be, a very great difference between making money peaceably and making money peaceably a great difference between making money making money peaceably making money peaceably making money peaceably.

Reject rejoice rejuvenate rejuvenate rejoice reject rejoice rejuvenate reject rejuvenate reject rejoice. Not as if it was tried. How kindly they receive the the then there this at all.

In change.

Might it be while it is not as it is undid undone to be theirs awhile yet. Not in their mistake which is why it is not after or not further in at all to their cause. Patriarchal poetry partly. In an as much to be in exactly their measure. Patriarchal poetry partly.

Made to be precisely this which is as she is to be connectedly leave it when it is to be admittedly continued to be which is which is to be that it is which it is as she connectedly to be which is as she continued as to this to be continuously not to be connected to be which to be admittedly continued to be which is which is which it is to be. They might change it as it can be made to be which is which is the next left out of it in this and this occasionally settled to the same as the left of it to the undertaking of the regular regulation of it which is which which is which is which is what it is when it is needed to be left about to this when to this and they have been undetermined and as likely as it is which it is which it is which is it which is it not as in time and at a time when it is not to be certain certain makes it to be makes it to be makes it to be makes it to be makes it to be that there is not in that in consideration of the preparation of the change which is their chance inestimably.

Let it be as likely why that they have it as they try to manage. Follow. If any one decides that a year is a year beginning and end if any one decides that a year is a year beginning if any one decides that a year is a year if any one decides that a year simultaneously recognised. In recognition.

Once when if the land was there beside once when if the land was there beside.

Once when if the land was there beside.

Once when if the land was there beside.

If any one decided that a year was a year when once if any one decided that a year was a year if when once if once if any one when once if any one decided that a year was a year beside.

Patriarchal poetry includes when it is Wednesday and patriarchal includes when it is Wednesday and patriarchal poetry includes when it is Wednesday.

Never like to bother to be sure never like to bother to be sure never like to bother to be sure never like never like to never like to bother to be sure never like to bother never like to bother to be sure.

Three things which are when they are prepared. Three

things which are when they are prepared. Let it alone to be let it alone to be let it alone to be to be sure. Let it alone to be sure.

Three things which are when they had had this to their best arrangement meaning never having had it here as soon.

She might be let it be let it be here as soon. She might be let it be let it be let it be here as soon. She might be let it be here as soon. She might be let it be let it be she might be she might be let it be she might be let it be she might be let it be here as soon. Theirs which way marguerites. Theirs might be let it there as soon.

When is and thank and is and and and is when is when is and when thank when is and when and thank. When is and when is and thank. This when is and when thank and thank. When is and when thank and this when is and thank.

Have hear which have hear which have hear which leave and leave her have hear which have hear which leave her hear which leave her hear she leave her hear which. They might by by they might by by which might by which they might by which they by which they might which they might by which they by which they might by which. In face of it.

Let it be which is it be which is it be which is it let it let it which is it let it which let it which is it let it be which is it be which let it be which let it which is it which is it let it let it which is it let it. Near which with it which with near which with which with near which with near which with near which with it near which near which with near which near which with which with it.

Leave it with it let it go able to be shiny so with it can be is it near let it have it as it may come well be. This is why after all at a time that is which is why after all at the time this is why it is after all at the time this is why this is why this is after all after why this is after all at the time. This is why this is why this is after all this is why this is after all at the time.

Not a piece of which is why a wedding left have wedding left which is why which is why not which is why not a piece of why a a wedding having why a wedding left. Which is what is why is why is why which is what is why is why is why a wedding left.

Leaving left which is why they might be here be here be here.
Be here be here. Which is why is why is why is why is which is
why is why is why which is here. Not commence to to to be to
leave to come to see to let it be to be to be at once mind it mind
timely always change timely to kindly kindly to timely timely to
kindly timely to kindly always to change kindly to timely kindly
to timely always to change timely to kindly.

If he is not used to it he is not used to it, this is the beginning
of their singling singling makes Africa shortly if he is not used
to it he is not used to it this makes oriole shortly if he is not used
to it if he is not used to it if he is not used to it if he is not used
if he is not used to it if he is not used to it if he is not used to it he
if he is not used to it he is not used to it and this makes an after
either after it. She might be likely as to renew prune and see
prune. This is what order does.

Next to vast which is which is it.

Next to vast which is why do I be behind the chair because of
a chimney fire and higher why do I beside belie what is it when
is it which is it well all to be tell all to be well all to be never do do
the difference between effort and be in be in within be mine be
in be within be within in.

To be we to be to be we to be to be to be we to be we to be
to be to be to be to be to be to be we we to be to be to be we to be.
Once. To be we to be to be to be we to be. Once. To be to be to
be to be to be we to be. Once. To be we to be to be to be.

We to be. Once. We to be. Once. We to be be to be we to be.
Once. We to be.

Once. We to be we to be. Once. To be. Once. We to be.
Once. To be. Once. To be we to be. Once. To be. Once. To be
we to be. We to be. Once. To be. We to be. Once.

To be we to be. Once. To be. Once. To be. Once. To be.
Once. To be. Once. We to be. To be we to be. We to be. To be
we to be. We to be. Once. To be to be to be. We to be. We to be.
To be. Once. We to be.

Once. We to be.

Once. We to be. We to be. Once. To be we to be. Once. To
be. Once. To be we to be. Once. We to be. To be. We to be.
Once. Once. To be. Once. To be. Once. We to be. Once. We

to be. We to be. Once. To be. Once. We to be. We to be. We
to be. To be. Once. To be. We to be.

Their origin and their history patriarchal poetry their origin
and their history patriarchal poetry their origin and their history.

Patriarchal Poetry.

Their origin and their history.

Patriarchal Poetry their origin and their history their history
patriarchal poetry their origin patriarchal poetry their history
their origin patriarchal poetry their history patriarchal poetry
their origin patriarchal poetry their history their origin.

That is one case.

Able sweet and in a seat.

Patriarchal poetry their origin their history their origin. Patriarchal poetry their history their origin.

Two make it do three make it five four make it more five
make it arrive and sundries.

Letters and leaves tables and plainly restive and recover and
bide away, away to say regularly.

Never to mention patriarchal poetry altogether.

Two two two occasionally two two as you say two two two
not in their explanation two two must you be very well apprised
that it had had such an effect that only one out of a great many
and there were a great many believe in three relatively and moreover were you aware of the fact that interchangeable and interchangeable was it while they were if not avoided. She knew that
is to say she had really informed herself. Patriarchal poetry makes
no mistake.

Never to have followed farther there and knitting, is knitting
knitting if it is only what is described as called that they should
not come to say and how do you do every new year Saturday.
Every new year Saturday is likely to bring pleasure is likely to
give pleasure is likely to bring pleasure every new year Saturday
is likely to bring pleasure.

Day which is what is which is what is day which is what is day
which is which is what is which is what is day.

I double you, of course you do. You double me, very likely
to be. You double I double I double you double. I double you
double me I double you you double me.

When this you see remarkably.
Patriarchal poetry needs rectification and there about it.
Come to a distance and it still bears their name.
Prosperity and theirs prosperity left to it.
To be told to be harsh to be told to be harsh to be to them.
One.
To be told to be harsh to be told to be harsh to them.
None.
To be told to be harsh to be told to be harsh to them.
When.
To be told to be harsh to be told to be harsh to them.
Then.
What is the result.
The result is that they know the difference between instead
and instead and made and made and said and said.
The result is that they might be as very well two and as soon
three and to be sure, four and which is why they might not be.
Elegant replaced by delicate and tender, delicate and tender
replaced by one from there instead of five from there, there is
not there this is what has happened evidently.
Why while while why while why why identity identity why
while while why. Why while while while while identity.
Patriarchal Poetry is the same as Patriotic poetry is the same
as patriarchal poetry is the same as Patriotic poetry is the same as
patriarchal poetry is the same.
Patriarchal poetry is the same.
If in in crossing there is a if in crossing if in in crossing nearly
there is a distance if in crossing there is a distance between measurement and exact if in in crossing if in in crossing there is a
measurement between and in in exact she says I must be careful
and I will.
If in in crossing there is an opportunity not only but also and
in in looking in looking in regarding if in in looking if in in regarding if in in regarding there is an opportunty if in in looking
there is an opportunity if in in regarding there is an opportunity
to verify verify sometimes as more sometimes as more sometimes
as more.
Fish eggs commonly fish eggs. Architects commonly fortu-

nately indicatively architects indicatively architects. Elaborated at a time with it with it at a time with it at a time attentively to-day.

Does she know how to ask her brother is there any difference between turning it again again and again and again or turning it again and again. In resembling two brothers.

That makes patriarchal poetry apart.

Intermediate or patriarchal poetry.

If at once sixty-five have come one by one if at once sixty five have come one by one if at once sixty-five have come one by one. This took two and two have been added to by Jenny. Never to name Jenny. Have been added to by two. Never have named Helen Jenny never have named Agnes Helen never have named Helen Jenny. There is no difference between having been born in Brittany and having been born in Algeria.

These words containing as they do neither reproaches nor satisfaction may be finally very nearly rearranged and why, because they mean to be partly left alone. Patriarchal poetry and kindly, it would be very kind in him in him of him of him to be as much obliged as that. Patriotic poetry. It would be as plainly an advantage if not only but altogether repeatedly it should be left not only to them but for them but for them. Explain to them by for them. Explain shall it be explain will it be explain can it be explain as it is to be explain letting it be had as if he had had more than wishes. More than wishes.

Patriarchal poetry more than wishes.

Assigned to Patriarchal Poetry.

Assigned to patriarchal poetry too sue sue sue sue shall sue sell and magnificent can as coming let the same shall shall shall shall let it share is share is share shall shall shall shall shell shell shall share is share shell can shell be shell be shell moving in in in inner moving move inner in in inner in meant meant might might may collect collected recollected to refuse what it is is it.

Having started at once at once.

Put it with it with it and it and it come to ten.

Put it with it with it and it and it for it for it made to be extra.

With it put it put it prepare it prepare it add it add it or it or it would it would it and make it all at once.

Put it with it with it and it and it in it in it add it add it at it
at it with it with it put it put it to this to understand.

Put it with it with it add it add it at it at it or it or it to be
placed intend.

Put it with it with it in it in it at it at it add it add it or it or it
letting it be while it is left as it might could do their danger.

Could it with it with it put it put it place it place it stand it
stand it two doors or two doors two tables or two tables two let
two let two let two to be sure.

Put it with it with it and it and it in it in it add it add it or it
or it to it to be added to it.

There is no doubt about it.

Actually.

To be sure.

Left to the rest if to be sure that to be sent come to be had in
to be known or to be liked and to be to be to be to be to be mine.

It always can be one two three it can be always can can always
be one two three. It can always be one two three.

It is very trying to have him have it have it have him. have it
as she said the last was very very much and very much to distance
to distance them.

Every time there is a wish wish it. Every time there is a wish
wish it. Every time there is a wish wish it.

Every time there is a wish wish it.

Dedicated to all the way through. Dedicated to all the way
through.

Dedicated too all the way through. Dedicated too all the way
through.

Apples and fishes day-light and wishes apples and fishes day-
light and wishes day-light at seven.

All the way through dedicated to you.

Day-light and wishes apples and fishes, dedicated to you all
the way through day-light and fishes apples and wishes dedicated
to all the way through dedicated to you dedicated to you all the
way through day-light and fishes apples and fishes day-light and
wishes apples and fishes dedicated to you all the way through
day-light and fishes apples and wishes apples and fishes day-light

and wishes dedicated to dedicated through all the way through dedicated to.

Not at once Tuesday.

They might be finally their name name same came came came came or share sharer article entreat coming in letting this be there letting this be there.

Patriarchal poetry come too.

When with patriarchal poetry when with patriarchal poetry come too.

There must be more french in France there must be more French in France patriarchal poetry come too.

Patriarchal poetry come too there must be more french in France patriarchal come too there must be more french in France.

Patriarchal Poetry come to.

There must be more french in France.

Helen greatly relieves Alice patriarchal poetry come too there must be patriarchal poetry come too.

In a way second first in a way first second in a way in a way first second in a way.

Rearrangement is nearly rearrangement. Finally nearly rearrangement is finally nearly rearrangement nearly not now finally nearly nearly finally rearrangement nearly rearrangement and not now how nearly finally rearrangement. If two tables are near together finally nearly not now.

Finally nearly not now.

Able able nearly nearly nearly nearly able able finally nearly able nearly not now finally finally nearly able.

They make it be very well three or nearly three at a time.

Splendid confidence in the one addressed and equal distrust of the one who has done everything that is necessary. Finally nearly able not now able finally nearly not now.

Rearrangement is a rearrangement a rearrangement is widely known a rearrangement is widely known. A rearrangement is widely known. As a rearrangement is widely known.

As a rearrangement is widely known.

So can a rearrangement which is widely known be a rearrangement which is widely known which is widely known.

Let her be to be to be to be to be let her be to be to be let her to be
let her to be let her be to be when is it that they are shy.

Very well to try.

Let her be that is to be let her be that is to be let her be let
her try.

Let her be let her be let her be to be to be shy let her be to be
let her be to be let her try.

Let her try.

Let her be let her be let her be let her be to be to be let her be
let her try.

To be shy.

Let her be.

Let her try.

Let her be let her let her let her be let her be let her be let her
be shy let her be let her be let her try.

Let her try.

Let her be.

Let her be shy.

Let her be.

Let her be let her be let her let her try.

Let her try to be let her try to be let her be shy let her try to
be let her try to be let her be let her be let her try.

Let her be shy.

Let her try.

Let her try.

Let her be

Let her let her be shy.

Let her try.

Let her be.

Let her let her be shy.

Let her be let her let her be shy

Let her let her let her let her try.

Let her try.

Let her try.

Let her try.

Let her be.

Let her be let her

Let her try.

Let her be let her.
Let her be let her let her try.
Let her try.
Let her
Let her try.
Let her be shy.
Let her
Let her
Let her be.
Let her be shy.
Let her be let her try.
Let her try.
Let her try.
Let her try.
Let her let her try
Let her be shy.
Let her try
Let her let her try to be let her try.
Let her try.
Just let her try.
Let her try.
Never to be what he said.
Never to be what he said.
Never to be what he said.
Let her to be what he said.
Let her to be what he said.
Not to let her to be what he said not to let her to be what he said.

Never to be let her to be never let her to be what he said. Never let her to be what he said.

Never to let her to be what he said. Never to let her to be let her to be let her to be let her what he said.

Near near near nearly pink near nearly pink nearly near near nearly pink. Wet inside and pink outside. Pink outside and wet inside wet inside and pink outside latterly nearly near near pink near near nearly three three pink two gentle one strong three pink all medium medium as medium as medium sized as sized. One as one not mistaken but interrupted. One regularly better adapted if readily readily to-day. This is this this readily. Thursday.

This part the part the part of it.

And let to be coming to have it known.

As a difference.

By two by one by and by.

A hyacinth resembles a rose. A rose resembles a blossom a blossom resembles a calla lily a calla lily resembles a jonquil and a jonquil resembles a marguerite a marguerite resembles a rose in bloom a rose in bloom resembles a lily of the valley a lily of the valley resembles a violet and a violet resembles a bird.

What is the difference between right away and a pearl there is this difference between right away and a pearl a pearl is milk white and right away is at once. This is indeed an explanation.

Patriarchal poetry or indeed an explanation.

Try to be at night try to be to be at night try to be at night try to be at night try to be to try to be to try to be to try to be at night.

Never which when where to be sent to be sent to be sent to be never which when where never to be sent to be sent to be sent never which when where to be sent never to be sent never to be sent never which when where to be sent never to be sent never to be sent which when where never to be sent which when where never which when where never which to be sent never which when where to be sent never which when where to be sent which when where to be sent never to be sent never which when where to be sent never which when which when where to be sent never which when where never which when where which when where never to be sent which when where.

Never to be sent which when where.

As fair as fair to them.

It was not without some difficulty.

Five thousand every year.

Three thousand divided by five three thousand divided as five.

Happily very happily.

They happily very happily.

Happily very happily.

In consequence consequently.

Extra extremely additionally.

Intend or intend or intend or intend or intend additionally.

Returning retaining relatively.

This makes no difference between to be told so admittedly.

Patriarchal Poetry connectedly.

Sentence sent once patriarchal poetry sentence sent once.

Patriarchal poetry sentence sent once.

Patriarchal Poetry.

Patriarchal Poetry sentence sent once.

Patriarchal Poetry is used with a spoon.

Patriarchal poetry is used with a spoon with a spoon.

Patriarchal poetry is used with a spoon.

Patriarchal poetry used with a spoon.

Patriarchal poetry in and for the relating of now and ably.

Patriarchal poetry in preferring needless needless needlessly patriarchal poetry precluding needlessly but it can.

How often do we tell tell tell tale tell tale tell tale tell tale might be tell tale.

Supposing never never never never supposing never never in supposed widening.

Remember all of it too.

Patriarchal poetry reasonably.

Patriarchal poetry administratedly.

Patriarchal poetry with them too.

Patriarchal poetry as to mind.

Patriarchal poetry reserved.

Patriarchal poetry interdiminished.

Patriarchal poetry in regular places largely in regular places placed regularly as if it were as if it were placed regularly.

Patriarchal poetry in regular places placed regularly as if it were placed regularly regularly placed regularly as if it were.

Patriarchal poetry every little while. Not once twenty-five not once twenty-five not once slower not once twenty not once twenty-five. Patriarchal poetry every little while not every little while once every little while once every little while once every twenty once every little while once every twenty-five once every little while once every little while every once twenty-five once.

Make it a mistake.

Patriarchal she said what is it I know what it is it is I know I know so that I know what it is I know so I know so I know so I know what it is. Very slowly. I know what it is it is on the one side a to be her to be his to be their to be in an and to be I know what it is it is he who was an known not known was he was at first it was the grandfather then it was not that in that the father not of that grandfather and then she to be to be sure to be sure to be I know to be sure to be I know to be sure to be not as good as that. To be sure not to be sure to be sure correctly saying to be sure to be that. It was that. She was right. It was that.

Patriarchal Poetry.

A SONNET

To the wife of my bosom
All happiness from everything
And her husband.
May he be good and considerate
Gay and cheerful and restful.
And make her the best wife
In the world
The happiest and the most content
With reason.
To the wife of my bosom
Whose transcendent virtues
Are those to be most admired
Loved and adored and indeed
Her virtues are all inclusive
Her virtues her beauty and her beauties
Her charms her qualities her joyous nature
All of it makes of her husband
A proud and happy man.

Patriarchal poetry makes no mistake makes no mistake in estimating the value to be placed upon the best and most arranged of considerations of this in as apt to be not only to be partially and as cautiously considered as in allowance which is one at a time. At a chance at a chance encounter it can be very well as appointed as appointed not only considerately but as it as use.

Patriarchal poetry to be sure to be sure to be sure candidly

candidly and aroused patriarchal to be sure and candidly and
aroused once in a while and as a circumstance within that arranged
within that arranged to be not only not only not only not not
secretive but as one at a time not in not to include cautiously
cautiously cautiously at one in not to be finally prepared. Patriarchal poetry may be mistaken may be undivided may be usefully
to be sure settled and they would be after a while as establish in
relatively understanding a promise of not in time but at a time
wholly reconciled to feel that as well by an instance of escaped
and interrelated choice. That makes it even.

Patriarchal poetry may seem misplaced at one time.

Patriarchal poetry might be what they wanted.

Patriarchal poetry shall be as much as if it was counted from
one to one hundred.

From one to one hundred.

From one to one hundred.

From one to one hundred.

Counted from one to one hundred.

Nobody says soften as often.

From one to one hundred.

Has to say happen as often.

Laying while it was while it was while it was. While it was.

Patriarchal poetry while it was just as close as when they were
then being used not only in here but also out there which is what
was the thing that was not only requested but also desired which
when there is not as much as if they could be while it can shall
have and this was what was all when it was not used just for that
but simply can be not what is it like when they use it.

As much as that patriarchal poetry as much as that.

Patriarchal poetry as much as that.

To like patriarchal poetry as much as that.

To like patriarchal poetry as much as that is what she did.

Patriarchal poetry usually.

In finally finding this out out and out out and about to find
it out when it is neither there nor by that time by the time it is not
why they had it.

Why they had it.

What is the difference between a glass pen and a pen what is the difference between a glass pen and a pen what is the difference between a glass pen and a pen to smile at the difference between a glass pen and a pen.

To smile at the difference between a glass pen and a pen is what he did.

Patriarchal poetry makes it as usual.

Patriarchal poetry one two three.

Patriarchal poetry accountably.

Patriarchal poetry as much.

Patriarchal Poetry reasonably.

Patriarchal Poetry which is what they did.

One Patriarchal Poetry.

Two Patriarchal Poetry.

Three Patriarchal Poetry.

One two three.

One two three.

One Patriarchal Poetry.

Two Patriarchal Poetry.

Three Patriarchal Poetry.

When she might be what it was to be left to be what they had as they could.

Patriarchal Poetry as if as if it made it be a choice beside.

The Patriarchal Poetry.

At the time that they were sure surely certain certainly aroused arousing laid lessening let letting be it as if it as if it were to be to be as if it were to be letting let it nearly all it could be not be nearly should be which is there which is it there.

Once more a sign.

Signed by them.

Signed by him.

Signed it.

Signed it as it was.

Patriarchal Poetry and rushing Patriarchal Poetry and rushing.

Having had having had having had who having had who had having having had and not five not four not three not one not three not two not four not one not one done.

Patriarchal poetry recollected.

Putting three together all the time two together all the time

two together all the time two together two together two together
all the time putting five together three together all the time. Never
to think of Patriarchal Poetry at one time.

Patriarchal poetry at one time.

Allowed allowed allowed makes it be theirs once once as they
had had it have having have have having having is the same.

Patriarchal Poetry is the same.

Patriarchal Poetry.

It is very well and nicely done in Patriarchal Poetry which is
begun to be begun and this was why if when if when when did
they please themselves indeed. When he did not say leave it to that
but rather indeed as it might be that it was not expressed simultaneously was expressed to be no more as it is very well to trouble
him. He will attend to it in time. Be very well accustomed to this
in that and plan. There is not only no accounting for tastes but
very well identified extra coming out very well identified as repeated verdure and so established as more than for it.

She asked as she came down should she and at that moment
there was no answer but if leaving it alone meant all by it out of
it all by it very truly and could be used to plainly plainly expressed. She will be determined determined not by but on account
of implication implication re-entered which means entered again
and upon.

This could be illustrated and is and is and is. There makes more
than contain contained mine too. Very well to please please.

Once in a while.

Patriarchal poetry once in a while.

Patriarchal Poetry out of pink once in a while.

Patriarchal Poetry out of pink to be bird once in a while.

Patriarchal Poetry out of pink to be bird left and three once
in a while.

Patriarchal Poetry handles once in a while.

Patriarchal Poetry once in a while.

Patriarchal Poetry once in a while.

Patriarchal Poetry to be added.

Patriarchal Poetry reconciled.

Patriarchal Poetry left alone.

Patriarchal Poetry and left of it left of it Patriarchal Poetry left of it Patriarchal Poetry left of it as many twice as many patriarchal poetry left to it twice as many once as it was once it was once every once in a while patriarchal poetry every once in a while.

Patriarchal Poetry might have been in two. Patriarchal Poetry added to added to to once to be once in two Patriarchal poetry to be added to once to add to to add to patriarchal poetry to add to to be to be to add to to add to patriarchal poetry to add to.

One little two little one little two little one little at one time one little one little two little two little two little at one at a time.

One little one little two little two little one little two little as to two little as to two little as to one little as to one two little as to two two little two. Two little two little two little one little two one two one two little two. One little one little one little two little two little one little two one little two.

Need which need which as it is need which need which as it is very need which need which it is very warm here is it.

Need which need which need need in need need which need which is it need in need which need which need which is it.

Need in need need which is it.

What is the difference between a fig and an apple. One comes before the other. What is the difference between a fig and an apple one comes before the other what is the difference between a fig and an apple one comes before the other.

When they are here they are here too here too they are here too. When they are here they are here too when they are here they are here too.

As out in it there.

As not out not out in it there as out in it out in it there as out in it there as not out in it there as out in as out in it as out in it there.

Next to next next to Saturday next to next next to Saturday next to next next to Saturday.

This shows it all.

This shows it all next to next next to Saturday this shows it all.

Once or twice or once or twice once or twice or once or twice this shows it all or next to next this shows it all or once or

twice or once or twice or once or twice this shows it all or next
to next this shows it all or next to next or Saturday or next to next
this shows it all or next to next or next to next or Saturday or
next to next or once or twice this shows it all or next to next or
once or twice this shows it all or Saturday or next to next this
shows it all or once or twice this shows it all or Saturday or next
to next or once or twice this shows it all or once or twice this
shows it all or next to next this shows it all or once or twice
this shows it all or next to next or once or twice or once or twice
this shows it all or next to next this shows it all or once or twice this
shows it all or next to next or once or twice this shows it all or
next to next or next to next or next to next or once or twice or
once or twice or next to next or next to next or once or twice
this shows it all this shows it all or once or twice or next to next
this shows it all or next to next this shows it all or next to next
this shows it all or next to next this shows it all or once or twice
or once or twice this shows it all or once or twice or next to next
this shows it all this shows it all or next to next or shows it
all or once or twice this shows it all or shows it all or next to next
or once or twice or shows it all or once or twice or next to next
or next to next or once or twice or next to next or next to next
or shows it all or shows it all or next to next or once or twice or
shows it all or next to next or shows it all or next to next or shows
it all or once or twice or next to next or next to next or next to
next or next or next or next or next or shows it all or next or next
or next to next or shows it all or next to next to next to next to
next.
    Not needed near nearest.
    Settle it pink with pink.
    Pinkily.
    Find it a time at most.
    Time it at most at most.
    Every differs from Avery Avery differs from every within.
    As it is as it is as it is as it is in line as it is in line with it.
    Next to be with it next to be with it with it with with with it
next to it with it with it. Return with it.
    Even if it did not touch it would you like to give it would
you like to give it give me my even if it did not touch it would

you like to give me my. Even if you like to give it if you did not
touch it would you like to give me my.

One divided into into what what is it.

As left to left left to it here left to it here which is not queer
which is not queer where when when most when most and best
what is the difference between breakfast lunch supper and dinner
what is the difference between breakfast and lunch and supper
and dinner.

She had it here who to who to she had it here who to she had
it here who to she had it here who to she had it here who to who to
she had it here who to. Who to she had it here who to.

Not and is added added is and not added added is not and
added added is and not added added added is not and added added
not and is added added is and is added added and is not and added
added and is not and added added is and is not added added is and
not and added added is and not and added.

Let leave it out be out let leave it out be out be out let leave
it out be out let leave it out be out. Let leave it out be out let
leave it out be out. Let leave it out be out. Let leave it out. Let
leave it out. Let. Let leave it out. Let leave it out. Let leave it out.

Eighty eighty one which is why to be after one one two Seattle
blue and feathers they change which is why to blame it once or
twice singly to be sure.

A day as to say a day two to say to say a day a day to say to say
to say to say a day as to-day to say as to say to-day. To dates dates
different from here and there from here and there.

Let it be arranged for them.

What is the difference between Elizabeth and Edith. She
knows. There is no difference between Elizabeth and Edith
that she knows. What is the difference. She knows. There is no
difference as she knows. What is the difference between Elizabeth
and Edith that she knows. There is the difference between Elizabeth and Edith which she knows. There is she knows a difference between Elizabeth and Edith which she knows. Elizabeth
and Edith as she knows.

Contained in time forty makes forty-nine. Contained in time
as forty makes forty-nine contained in time contained in time

as forty makes forty-nine contained in time as forty makes forty-nine.

Forty-nine more or at the door.

Forty-nine or more or as before. Forty-nine or forty-nine or forty-nine.

I wish to sit with Elizabeth who is sitting. I wish to sit with Elizabeth who is sitting I wish to sit with Elizabeth who is sitting. I wish to sit with Elizabeth who is sitting.

Forty-nine or four attached to them more more than they were as well as they were as often as they are once or twice before.

As peculiarly mine in time.

Reform the past and not the future this is what the past can teach her reform the past and not the future which can be left to be here now here now as it is made to be made to be here now here now.

Reform the future not the past as fast as last as first as third as had as hand it as it happened to be why they did. Did two too two were sent one at once and one afterwards.

Afterwards.

How can patriarchal poetry be often praised often praised.

To get away from me.

She came in.

Wishes.

She went in

Fishes.

She sat in the room

Yes she did.

Patriarchal poetry.

She was where they had it be nearly as nicely in arrangement.

In arrangement.

To be sure.

What is the difference between ardent and ardently.

Leave it alone.

If one does not care to eat if one does not care to eat oysters one has no interest in lambs.

That is as usual.

Everything described as in a way in a way in a way gradually.
Likes to be having it come.
Likes to be.
Having it come.
Have not had that.
Around.
One two three one two three one two three one two three
four.
Find it again.
When you said when.
When you said
When you said
When you said when.
Find it again.
Find it again
When you said when.
They said they said.
They said they said they said when they said men.
Men many men many how many many many many men men
men said many here.
Many here said many many said many which frequently al-
lowed later in recollection many many said when as naturally to
be sure.
Very many as to that which which which one which which
which which one.
Patriarchal poetry relined.
It is at least last let letting letting letting letting it be
theirs.
Theirs at least letting at least letting it be theirs
Letting it be at least be letting it be theirs.
Letting it be theirs at least letting it be theirs.
When she was as was she was as was she was not yet neither
pronounced so and tempted.
Not this this is the way that they make it theirs not they.
Not they.
Patriarchal Poetry makes mistakes.
One two one two my baby is who one two one two one two

my baby or two one two. One two one one or two one one one
one one one one one one or two. Are to.

It is very nearly a pleasure to be warm.
It is very nearly a pleasure to be warm.
It is very nearly a pleasure to be warm.
A line a day book.
One which is mine.
Two in time
Let it alone
Theirs as well
Having it now
Letting it be their share.
Settled it at once.
Liking it or not
How do you do.
It.
Very well very well seriously.
Patriarchal Poetry defined.
Patriarchal Poetry should be this without which and organisa-
tion. It should be defined as once leaving once leaving it here hav-
ing been placed in that way at once letting this be with them after
all. Patriarchal Poetry makes it a master piece like this makes it
which which alone makes like it like it previously to know that
it that that might that might be all very well patriarchal poetry
might be resumed.

How do you do it.
Patriarchal Poetry might be withstood.
Patriarchal Poetry at peace.
Patriarchal Poetry a piece.
Patriarchal Poetry in peace.
Patriarchal Poetry in pieces.
Patriarchal Poetry as peace to return to Patriarchal Poetry
at peace.

Patriarchal Poetry or peace to return to Patriarchal Poetry
or pieces of Patriarchal Poetry.

Very pretty very prettily very prettily very pretty very
prettily.

To never blame them for the mischance of eradicating this and that by then.

Not at the time not at that time not in time to do it. Not a time to do it. Patriarchal Poetry or not a time to do it.

Patriarchal Poetry or made a way patriarchal Poetry tenderly.

Patriarchal Poetry or made a way patriarchal poetry or made a way patriarchal poetry as well as even seen even seen clearly even seen clearly and under and over overtake overtaken by it now. Patriarchal Poetry and replace. Patriarchal Poetry and enough. Patriarchal Poetry and at pains to allow them this and that that it would be plentifully as aroused and leaving leaving it exactly as they might with it all be be careful carefully in that and arranging arrangement adapted adapting in regulating regulate and see seat seating send sent by nearly as withstand precluded in this instance veritably in reunion reunion attached to intermediate remarked remarking plentiful and theirs at once. Patriarchal Poetry has that return.

Patriarchal Poetry might be what is left.

Indifferently.

In differently undertaking their being there there to them there to them with them with their pleasure pleasurable recondite and really really relieve relieving remain remade to be sure certainly and in and and on on account account to be nestled and nestling as understood which with regard to it if when and more leave leaving lying where it was as when when in in this this to be in finally to see so so that that should always be refused refusing refusing makes it have have it having having hinted hindered and implicated resist resist was to be exchanged as to be for for it in never having as there can be shared sharing letting it land lie lie to adjacent to see me. When it goes quickly they must choose Patriarchal Poetry originally originate as originating believe believing repudiate repudiating an impulse. It is not left to right to-day to stay. When this you see remember me should never be added to that.

Patriarchal Poetry and remind reminding clearly come came and left instantly with their entire consenting to be enclosed within what is exacting which might and might and partaking of mentioning much of it to be to be this is mine left to them in

place of how very nicely it can be planted so as to be productive
even if necessarily there is no effort left to them by their having
previously made it be nearly able to be found finding where where
it is when it is very likely to be this in the demand of remaining.
Patriarchal Poetry intimately and intimating that it is to be so
as plead. Plead can have to do with room. Room noon and
nicely.

Even what was gay.
Easier in left.
Easier in an left.
Easier an left
Easier in an left.
Horticulturally.
Easier in august.
Easier an august.
Easier an in august
Howard.
Easier how housed.
Ivory
Ivoried.
Less
Lest.
Like it can be used in joining gs.
By principally.
Led
Leaden haul
Leaden haul if it hails
Let them you see
Useful makes buttercup buttercup hyacinth too makes it be
lilied by water and you.
That is the way they ended.
It.
It was was it.
You jump in the dark, when it is very bright very bright very
bright now.
Very bright now.
Might might tell me.
Withstand.

In second second time time to be next next which is not convincing convincing inhabitable that much that much there.

As one to go.

Letting it letting it letting it alone.

Finally as to be sure.

Selecting that that to that selecting that to that to that all that.
All and and and and and and it it is very well thought out.

What is it.

Aim less.

What is it.

Aim less.

Sword less.

What is it

Sword less

What is it

Aim less

What is it.

What is it aim less what is it.

It did so.

It did so.

Said so

Said it did so.

Said it did so did so said so said it did so just as any one might.

Said it did so just as any one might said it did so said so just
as any one might.

If water is softened who softened water.

Patriarchal Poetry means in return for that.

Patriarchal poetry means in return.

Nettles nettles her.

Nettle nettle her.

Nettle nettle nettle her nettles nettles nettles her nettle nettle
nettle her nettles nettles nettles her. It nettles her to nettle her
to nettle her exchange it nettles her exchange to nettle her exchange it nettles her.

Made a mark remarkable made a remarkable interpretation
made a remarkable made a remarkable made a remarkable interpretation made a remarkable interpretation now and made a remarkable made a remarkable interpretation made a mark made

a remarkable made a remarkable interpretation made a remarkable interpretation now and here here out here out here. The more to change. Hours and hours. The more to change hours and hours the more to change hours and hours.

It was a pleasant hour however however it was a pleasant hour, it was a pleasant hour however it was a pleasant hour resemble hour however it was a pleasant however it was a pleasant hour resemble hour assemble however hour it was a pleasant hour however.

Patriarchal Poetry in assemble.

Assemble Patriarchal Poetry in assemble it would be assemble assemble Patriarchal Poetry in assemble.

It would be Patriarchal Poetry in assemble.

Assemble Patriarchal Poetry resign resign Patriarchal Poetry to believe in trees.

Early trees.

Assemble moss roses and to try.

Assemble Patriarchal Poetry moss roses resemble Patriarchal poetry assign assign to it assemble Patriarchal Poetry resemble moss roses to try.

Patriarchal Poetry resemble to try.

Moss roses assemble Patriarchal Poetry resign lost a lost to try. Resemble Patriarchal Poetry to love to.

To wish to does.

Patriarchal Poetry to why.

Patriarchal Poetry ally.

Patriarchal Poetry with to try to all ally to ally to wish to why to. Why did it seem originally look as well as very nearly pronounceably satisfy lining.

To by to by that by by a while any any stay stationary.

Stationary has been invalidated.

And not as surprised.

Patriarchal Poetry surprised supposed.

Patriarchal Poetry she did she did.

Did she Patriarchal Poetry.

Is to be periwinkle which she met which is when it is astounded and come yet as she did with this in this and this let in their to be sure it wishes it for them an instance in this as this

allows allows it to to be sure now when it is as well as it is and
has ever been outlined.

There are three things that are different pillow pleasure prepare and after while. There are two things that they prepare
maidenly see it and ask it as it if has been where they went. There
are enough to go. One thing altogether altogether as he might.
Might he.

Never to do never to do never to do to do to do never to do
never to do never to do to do to do to do never to do never never
to do to do it as if it were an anemone an anemone an anemone
to be an anemone to be to be certain to let to let it to let it alone.

What is the difference between two spoonfuls and three.
None.

Patriarchal Poetry as signed.

Patriarchal Poetry might which it is very well very well leave
it to me very well patriarchal poetry leave it to me leave it to me
leave it to leave it to me naturally to see the second and third
first naturally first naturally to see naturally to first see the second
and third first to see to see the second and third to see the second
and third naturally to see it first.

Not as well said as she said regret that regret that not as well
said as she said Patriarchal Poetry as well said as she said it Patriarchal Poetry untied. Patriarchal Poetry.

Do we.

What is the difference between Mary and May. What is the
difference between May and day. What is the difference between
day and daughter what is the difference between daughter and
there what is the difference between there and day-light what is
the difference between day-light and let what is the difference
between let and letting what is the difference between letting
and to see what is the difference between to see immediately
patriarchal poetry and rejoice.

Patriarchal Poetry made and made.

Patriarchal Poetry makes a land a lamb. There is no use at all
in reorganising in reorganising. There is no use at all in reorganising chocolate as a dainty.

Patriarchal Poetry reheard.

Patriarchal Poetry to be filled to be filled to be filled to be

filled to method method who hears method method who hears
who hears who hears method method method who hears who
hears who hears and method and method and method and who
hears and who who hears and method method is delightful and
who and who who hears method is method is method is delightful
is who hears is delightful who hears method is who hears method
is method is method is delightful is delightful who hears who
hears of of delightful who hears of method of delightful who of
whom of whom of of who hears of method method is delightful. Unified in their expanse. Unified in letting there there there
one two one two three there in a chain a chain how do you
laterally in relation to auditors and obliged obliged currently.

Patriarchal Poetry is the same.

Patriarchal Poetry thirteen.

With or with willing with willing mean.

I mean I mean.

Patriarchal Poetry connected with mean.

Queen with willing.

With willing.

Patriarchal Poetry obtained with seize.

Willing.

Patriarchal Poetry in chance to be found.

Patriarchal Poetry obliged as mint to be mint to be mint
to be obliged as mint to be.

Mint may be come to be as well as cloud and best.

Patriarchal Poetry deny why.

Patriarchal Poetry come by the way to go.

Patriarchal Poetry interdicted.

Patriarchal Poetry at best.

Best and Most.

Long and Short.

Left and Right.

There and More.

Near and Far.

Gone and Come.

Light and Fair.

Here and There.

This and Now.

Felt and How
Next and Near.
In and On.
New and Try
In and This.
Which and Felt.
Come and Leave.
By and Well.
Returned.
Patriarchal Poetry indeed.
Patriarchal Poetry which is let it be come from having a mild
and came and same and with it all.
Near.
To be shelled from almond.
Return Patriarchal Poetry at this time.
Begin with a little ruff a little ruffle.
Return with all that.
Returned with all that four and all that returned with four
with all that.
How many daisies are there in it.
How many daisies are there in it.
How many daisies are there in it.
How many daisies are there in it.
A line a day book.
How many daisies are there in it.
Patriarchal Poetry a line a day book.
Patriarchal Poetry.
A line a day book.
Patriarchal Poetry.
When there is in it.
When there is in it.
A line a day book.
When there is in it.
Patriarchal Poetry a line a day book when there is in it.
By that time lands lands there.
By that time lands there a line a day book when there is that
in it.
Patriarchal Poetry reclaimed renamed replaced and gathered

together as they went in and left it more where it is in when it
pleased when it was pleased when it can be pleased to be gone
over carefully and letting it be a chance for them to lead to lead
to lead not only by left but by leaves.

They made it be obstinately in their change and with it with
it let it let it leave it in the opportunity. Who comes to be with
a glance with a glance at it at it in palms and palms too orderly
to orderly in changes of plates and places and beguiled beguiled
with a restless impression of having come to be all of it as might
as might as might and she encouraged. Patriarchal Poetry might
be as useless. With a with a with a won and delay. With a with a
with a won and delay.

He might object to it not being there as they were left to them
all around. As we went out by the same way we came back again
after a detour.

That is one account on one account.

Having found anemones and a very few different shelves we
were for a long time just staying by the time that it could have
been as desirable. Desirable makes it be left to them.

Patriarchal Poetry includes not being received.

Patriarchal Poetry comes suddenly as around.

And now.

There is no difference between spring and summer none at all.

And wishes.

Patriarchal Poetry there is no difference between spring and
summer not at all and wishes.

There is no difference between spring and summer not at all
and wishes.

There is no difference not at all between spring and summer
not at all and wishes.

Yes as well.

And how many times.

Yes as well and how many times yes as well.

How many times yes as well ordinarily.

Having marked yes as well ordinarily having marked yes as
well.

It was to be which is theirs left in this which can have all their
thinking it as fine.

It was to be which is theirs left in this which is which is which can which can which may which may which will which will which in which in which are they know they know to care for it having come back without and it would be better if there had not been any at all to find to find to find. It is not desirable to mix what he did with adding adding to choose to choose. Very well part of her part of her very well part of her. Very well part of her. Patriarchal Poetry in pears. There is no choice of cherries.

Will he do.

Patriarchal Poetry in coins.

Not what it is.

Patriarchal Poetry net in it pleases. Patriarchal Poetry surplus if rather admittedly in repercussion instance and glance separating letting dwindling be in knife to be which is not wound wound entirely as white wool white will white change white see white settle white understand white in the way white be lighten lighten let letting bear this neatly nearly made in vain.

Patriarchal Poetry who seats seasons patriarchal poetry in gather meanders patriarchal poetry engaging this in their place their place their allow. Patriarchal Poetry. If he has no farther no farther no farther to no farther to no farther to no to no to farther to not to be right to be known to be even as a chance. Is it best to support Allan Allan will Allan Allan is it best to support Allan Allan patriarchal poetry patriarchal poetry is it best to support Allan Allan will Allan best to support Allan will patriarchal poetry Allan will patriarchal poetry Allan will patriarchal poetry is it best to support Allan patriarchal poetry Allan will is it best Allan will is it best to support Allan patriarchal poetry Allan will best to support patriarchal poetry Allan will is it best Allan will to support patriarchal poetry patriarchal poetry Allan will patriarchal poetry Allan will.

Is it best to support patriarchal poetry Allan will patriarchal poetry.

Patriarchal Poetry makes it incumbent to know on what day races will take place and where otherwise there would be much inconvenience everywhere.

Patriarchal Poetry erases what is eventually their purpose

and their inclination and their reception and their without their
being beset. Patriarchal poetry an entity.

What is the difference between their charm and to charm.

Patriarchal Poetry in negligence.

Patriarchal Poetry they do not follow that they do not follow
that this does not follow that this does not follow that theirs does
not follow that theirs does not follow that the not following
that the not following that having decided not to abandon a sister
for another. This makes patriarchal poetry in their place in their
places in their places in the place in the place of is it in the next
to it as much as aroused feeling so feeling it feeling at once to be
in the wish and what is it of theirs. Suspiciously. Patriarchal poetry for instance. Patriarchal poetry not minded not minded it.
In now. Patriarchal poetry left to renown. Renown.

It is very certainly better not to be what is it when it is in the
afternoon.

Patriarchal poetry which is it. Which is it after it is after it is
after it is after before soon when it is by the time that when they
make let it be not only because why should why should why
should it all be fine.

Patriarchal poetry they do not do it right.

Patriarchal poetry letting it be alright.

Patriarchal Poetry having it placed where it is.

Patriarchal Poetry might have it.

Might have it.

Patriarchal Poetry a choice.

Patriarchal poetry because of it.

Patriarchal Poetry replaced.

Patriarchal Poetry withstood and placated.

Patriarchal Poetry in arrangement.

Patriarchal Poetry that day.

Patriarchal Poetry might it be very likely which is it as it
can be very precisely unified as tries.

Patriarchal poetry with them lest they be stated.

Patriarchal poetry. He might be he might he he might be he
might be.

Patriarchal poetry a while a way.

Patriarchal poetry if patriarchal poetry is what you say why do you delight in never having positively made it choose.

Patriarchal poetry never linking patriarchal poetry.

Sometime not a thing.

Patriarchal Poetry sometimes not anything.

Patriarchal Poetry which which which which is it.

Patriarchal Poetry left to them.

Patriarchal poetry left together.

Patriarchal Poetry does not like to be allowed after a while to be what is more formidably forget me nots anemones china lilies plants articles chances printing pears and likely meant very likely meant to be given to him.

Patriarchal Poetry would concern itself with when it is in their happening to be left about left about now.

There is no interest in resemblances.

Patriarchal poetry one at a time.

This can be so.

To by any way.

Patriarchal poetry in requesting in request in request best patriarchal poetry leave that alone.

Patriarchal poetry noise noiselessly.

Patriarchal poetry not in fact in fact.

After patriarchal poetry.

I defy any one to turn a better heel than that while reading.

Patriarchal poetry reminded.

Patriarchal poetry reminded of it.

Patriarchal Poetry reminded of it too.

Patriarchal Poetry reminded of it too to be sure.

Patriarchal Poetry reminded of it too to be sure really. Really left.

Patriarchal Poetry and crackers in that case.

Patriarchal Poetry and left bread in that case.

Patriarchal Poetry and might in that case.

Patriarchal Poetry connected in that case with it.

Patriarchal Poetry make it do a day.

Is he fond of him.

If he is fond of him if he is fond of him is he fond of his birthday the next day. If he is fond of his birthday the next day is he

fond of the birthday trimming if he is fond of the birthday the
day is he fond of the day before the day before the day of the
day before the birthday. Every day is a birthday the day before.
Patriarchal Poetry the day before.

Patriarchal Poetry the day that it might.

Patriarchal Poetry does not make it never made it will not
have been making it be that way in their behalf.

Patriarchal Poetry insistance.

Insist.

Patriarchal Poetry insist insistance.

Patriarchal Poetry which is which is it.

Patriarchal Poetry and left it left it by left it by left it. Patriarchal Poetry what is the difference Patriarchal Poetry.

Patriarchal Poetry.

Not patriarchal poetry all at a time.

To find patriarchal poetry about.

Patriarchal Poetry is named patriarchal poetry.

If patriarchal poetry is nearly by nearly means it to be to be so.

Patriarchal Poetry and for them then.

Patriarchal Poetry did he leave his son.

Patriarchal Poetry Gabrielle did her share.

Patriarchal poetry it is curious.

Patriarchal poetry please place better.

Patriarchal poetry in come I mean I mean.

Patriarchal poetry they do their best at once more once more
once more once more to do to do would it be left to advise advise
realise realise dismay dismay delighted with her pleasure.

Patriarchal poetry left to inundate them.

Patriarchal Poetry in pieces. Pieces which have left it as
names which have left it as names to to all said all said as delight.

Patriarchal poetry the difference.

Patriarchal poetry needed with weeded with seeded with
payed it with left it without it with me. When this you see give
it to me.

Patriarchal poetry makes it be have you it here.

Patriarchal Poetry twice.

Patriarchal Poetry in time.

It should be left.

Patriarchal Poetry with him.
Patriarchal Poetry.
Patriarchal Poetry at a time.
Patriarchal Poetry not patriarchal poetry.
Patriarchal Poetry as wishes.
Patriarchal poetry might be found here.
Patriarchal poetry interested as that.
Patriarchal Poetry left.
Patriarchal Poetry left left.
Patriarchal poetry left left left right left.
Patriarchal poetry in justice.
Patriarchal poetry in sight.
Patriarchal poetry in what is what is what is what is what.
Patriarchal poetry might to-morrow.
Patriarchal Poetry might be finished to-morrow.
Dinky pinky dinky pinky dinky pinky dinky pinky once and
try. Dinky pinky dinky pinky dinky pinky lullaby. Once sleepy
one once does not once need a lullaby. Not to try.
Patriarchal Poetry not to try. Patriarchal Poetry and lullaby.
Patriarchal Poetry not to try Patriarchal poetry at once and why
patriarchal poetry at once and by by and by Patriarchal poetry
has to be which is best for them at three which is best and will be
be and why why patriarchal poetry is not to try try twice.
Patriarchal Poetry having patriarchal poetry. Having patriarchal poetry having patriarchal poetry. Having patriarchal poetry. Having patriarchal poetry and twice, patriarchal poetry.
He might have met.
Patriarchal poetry and twice patriarchal poetry.

MEN

Sometimes men are kissing. Men are sometimes kissing and sometimes drinking. Men are sometimes kissing one another and sometimes then there are three of them and one of them is talking and two of them are kissing and both of them, both of the two of them who are kissing, are having their eyes large then with there being tears in them.

Sometimes men are drinking and are loving and one of them is talking and two of them are fighting and one of the two of them is winning enough so that they are then having loving in them and are telling each other everything. All three of them are telling each other anything. All three of them are telling each other anything. One of them is listening to one other one. One of them is listening to two of them. One is not listening to them and he is having tears then tears in emotion and they are all three then drinking and telling each other everything.

One of them is then large with this thing quite large with having tears on him. This one is quite large then and has been winning in having another one knocked down by him. He is large then and kissing the other one then and is certain then that the other one is one to hear everything. He is large then and the third one then is one he would not then have near him. He was a large one then and the third one is then filling something. The one who is a large one then is one needing then that the third one is not filling anything. The third one is filling something. The large one was a large one and was leaving when no one was knowing this thing was knowing that he was leaving.

The three of them had been loving. Two of them were loving. One of them was not loving and was remembering everything and was filling something. One of them was loving and had knocked down one and was needing that the other one was not filling anything. The other one the one who had been knocked down then was loving and was then knowing that the large one was then loving. He was loving then and the large one was loving then and they were then ones having been loving. They had been kissing and the one who was a knocked down one was one who might have knocked down the large one.

Another time, much later each one of them met one of the three of them. The one who was a large one from having tears come from him when he was loving and kissing, did not meet the one who was then filling something. He met the other one and did not meet him again. He was a large one then and this was in him from not wanting to meet the one who was then filling something. He was always a large one from something. He was now a large one from not wanting a meeting with the one who was then filling something. He did not meet him. He became a very large one from once almost going to meet him. He was a very large one then. He did not go then to meet him the one who was then filling something.

One of the three of them met one of them and wanted to meet him again and to be again loving even if they did not again come to kissing and crying. He did meet that one who was just then a large one in being one not needing to be loving any one he had been knowing; who did want to be one not liking kissing, not liking any one who had been one. He was not liking that one who was then a large one in being one not liking any one who had been one. The one who was meeting him the one who was then a large one was not liking him, was not liking that large one. He had lost that thing he had lost being one liking that one being a large one from kissing and crying. He had lost that thing, the one that met the one that was now a large one, lost liking that one, lost one being a large one in loving and crying.

The one who was a large one in being one then not wanting
to meet the one who was then filling something, was then a large
one in not wanting to be knowing any one who had been. He
was then not wanting to be meeting the one who was then
filling something. He was a large one then from having this feeling
then in him. He was crying then some in being a large one.

Each one of the three of them was such a one, one they were
then. Each one of them of the three of them meant something
by being such a one. Each one of the three of them was such a
one, one drinking and talking and loving. Each one of them, each
one of the three of them had been one drinking with the other one
loving one of the three of them, loving two of the three of them,
loving all of the three of them, kissing one of them, crying some
then. Each one of the three of them were such ones. Each one of
the three of them meant something as being such a one.

The one who was filling something was such a one in being one
drinking and telling and listening and filling then something,
filling being such a one, one drinking and listening and telling,
completely filling being such a one.

He was one filling something. He was one filling being such a
one, one drinking and loving in listening and in telling. He was
one filling being such a one completely filling being such a one,
one drinking and loving in being listening and in being telling.

He was one meaning this thing in being such a one meaning
being one completely filling being such a one, one loving in listening, one loving in telling, one loving in drinking. He was entirely
filling being such a one and he was entirely meaning this thing
in being such a one meaning being one loving in being one listening, in being one telling, in being one drinking.

He was such a one, he was completely filling being such a one,
he was entirely meaning to be such a one. He was completely
filling such a one and he was then filling something, he was then
being one filling something and he was then to the one who was
a large one in being one then needing not to be meeting him, he
was to that one one filling something where he the one then a
large one needed to be having everything around him so that he
could be one leaving it behind him. He was then filling something

the one who might have been meeting the one who was then a large one in being one needing to be not meeting him, he was then filling something and being one then loving in drinking, loving in listening, loving in telling. He could then be filling something and having then the one who was a large one from needing to be not meeting him, having that one be one he was then having as one whom he might be meeting again, in being one meaning to be filling something.

He was one completely being such a one. He was one completely meaning in being such a one. He was one filling something in being one loving in drinking, loving in listening, loving in telling. He was meaning being such a one. He was meaning in being such a one. He was such a one.

The one who had been knocked down in being one coming to be loving and kissing and drinking might have knocked down the one who had knocked him down then. He might have knocked down the one who knocked him down, and then he loved him and he kissed him, and they told then that they both then knew everything. He might have knocked down the one who knocked him down and he would then not have been loving and kissing and knowing then everything. He was one sometimes knocking some one down and being then falling down something and being then one having been knowing something. He was then when he was knocked down by the one he could have knocked down he was then loving and kissing and they were then knowing everything. He was such a one and was one having been having meaning in being one being such a one. He was one having been such a one and being such a one and being one remembering coming to be such a one, and being such a one, and being drinking and kissing and loving in having meaning in being such a one and being then such a one, and being then one who might have knocked down the other one and being then one who was knocked down by one whom he was kissing then and loving then and they were then knowing everything, he was remembering that he was one who was such a one. They were then knowing everything and he was then remembering everything and the other one was later then a large one in being one not remembering anything in being one not needing remembering any one being one who had been. He was one who had knocked down the other one and the other one might have knocked down him. He had knocked down the other one and they were then kissing and loving and knowing everything.

He was a large one and he had knocked down the other one. He was a large one and he was such a one. He was such a one and he was remembering having meaning in being such a one. He was not remembering everything.

He had been such a one one loving. He had been kissing then and drinking then and having tears then coming to him. He had tears come in him when he was remembering, when he was not remembering being such a one. He was a large one in being one having tears come out from him. He was a large one in remembering, he was a large one in not remembering being such a one. He was a large one in having tears swelling in him. He was a large one in having tears dropping out of him. He was a large one in having tears remaining in him. He was one who could be a large one in having been wanting to be knocking down some one and being one crying then. He could remember something. He did remember something. He would not remember everything. He would be such a one and be a large one being full then with being such a one. He was a large one in being one knocking down some one and admiring then the one who had been knocked down by him. He was being such a one. He was meaning something in being such a one. There was meaning in his being such a one.

There was meaning in his being such a one and very many did remember that, did remember that he was such a one and that there was meaning in that thing, meaning in his being such a one.

He was such a one and he had meaning in being such a one, he had the meaning of being such a one in being such a one. He was remembering this thing remembering that he was such a one. He remembered that thing, he remembered that he had meaning in being such a one.

He was meaning again and again in being such a one and he was remembering that he had meaning again and again that he was such a one. He was remembering again and again that he was such a one and he was remembering again and again that he was having meaning. He was such a one.

He was such a one and he was remembering that thing in being a large one. He was a large one in being such a one. He was a large one in remembering his being such a one.

He was a large one in remembering that he was not meeting any one who had been. He was a large one in remembering that he might be meeting some one who was filling something. He was a large one in being crying. He was a large one. He was remembering something in being a large one. He was remembering being such a one.

He was remembering being such a one. He was remembering something. He was remembering having meaning in being such a one. He was such a one. Any one was one not forgetting again that he was such a one. He was one not forgetting again that he was such a one. He was one not knocking some one down and being then a large one in not coming to be one ever doing such a thing. He was a large one in being one coming again to be not meeting any one he had not been knocking down. He was a large one in being one coming to be meeting again one he did not come to be knocking down and to be one not meeting that one again. He was such a one. He was remembering something.

Any one of the three of them did not meet anything of any other one of the three of them. Any one of the three of them was one meeting any one. Any one of the three of them was such a one.

Any one of the three was meaning being such a one. Any one of the three was one meaning something in being such a one. Any one of the three of them was being one being such a one. Each one of the three of them was being one being of a kind of a one. Each one of the three of them was of a different kind than any other of the three of them. Each one of the three of them was such a one.

NEW

We knew.
Anne to come.
Anne to come.
Be new.
Be new too.
Anne to come
Anne to come
Be new
Be new too.
And anew.
Anne to come.
Anne anew.
Anne do come.
Anne do come too, to come and to come not to come and as to
and new, and new too.
Anne do come.
Anne knew.
Anne to come.
Anne anew.
Anne to come.
And as new.
Anne to come to come too.
Half of it.
Was she
Windows
Was she
Or mine
Was she
Or as she
For she or she or sure.
Enable her to say.
And enable her to say.

Or half way.
Sitting down.
Half sitting down.
And another way.
Their ships
And please.
As the other side.
And another side
Incoming
Favorable and be fought.
Adds to it.
In half.
Take the place of take the place of take the place of taking place.
Take the place of in places.
Take the place of taken in place of places.
Take the place of it, she takes it in the place of it. In the way of arches architecture.
Who has seen shown
You do.
Hoodoo.
If can in countenance to countenance a countenance as in as seen.
Change it.
Not nearly so much.
He had.
She had.
Had she.
He had nearly very nearly as much.
She had very nearly as much as had had.
Had she.
She had.
Loose loosen, Loose losten to losten, to lose.
Many.
If a little if as little if as little as that.
If as little as that, if it is as little as that that is if it is very nearly all of it, her dear her dear does not mention a ball at all.
Actually.

As to this.
Actually as to this.
High or do you do it.
Actually as to this high or do you do it.
Not how do you do it.
Actually as to this.
Not having been or not having been nor having been or not
having been.
Interrupted.
All of this makes it unanxiously.
Feel so.
Add to it.
As add to it.
He.
He.
As add to it.
As add to it.
As he
As he as add to it.
He.
As he
Add to it.
Not so far.
Constantly as seen.
Not as far as to mean.
I mean I mean.
Constantly.
As far.
So far.
Forbore.
He forbore.
To forbear.
Their forbears.
Plainly.
In so far.
Instance.
For instance.
In so far.

A double as in half.
Follow me slowly
Fairly has.
It fairly has.
In half.
Not at sea.
To be, not at sea concerning if at that.
Not to be at sea concerning it.
Not to resist reasonably not to persist.
Fully.
Sing Song.
As at.
Attitude.
Attitude toward it.
An attitude toward it.
An
A second apart.
Bay too.
It pays too.
To pay too.
Or to.
To draw.
In a sense.
In the sense.
Attract.
Alter attract.
The same.
Here.
Anne Anne.
And to hand.
As a while.
For a while.
And to come.
In half or dark.
In half and dark.
In half a dark.
As to it.
In a line.

As fine a line.
Bestow.
Anne Anne
And to hand
As a while
For a while
Anne
And
And to hand
As a while
For a while.
So new.
So new.
So new.
Sew
So new.
As a while.
See it.
Say it.
Say it.
Say it with sailors.
Every once in a while.
There is no use. Vienna does not really produce real sailors
nor does it very, as very nearly, as so very nearly.
All of it makes it as if it is as if it will have so many times so.
As to know.
Is to show
Are to go.
Can say so.
Letters and press.
Letter press.
Luck and cress, grass and now.
And now.
And new.
And new.
And too
And too.

BRIM BEAUVAIS (1931)

MOTTO: How could it be a little whatever he liked.

ONCE.

Always excited to say twice.

He came twice and she coughed.

Now I need reason to wonder if she went to say farewell.

It is no pleasure to be angry after in spite of what they like as often better.

She might be once and fanciful but for me she would like a melon better only did she have to not like having to need more of it for her mother.

It is very true that each one of them had a mother and now how about now will he make believe that for and forests are with cold upheld. Some have been irritated to be told about the cold.

It does make a difference if he jiggled.

As soon as to say I like it. That is to say. Finally a word. They will often talk it over. What is the difference between you did and did it. Oh think so kindly.

I like a motto.

Lotto.

Pearls by girls.

Logs by dogs.

Pens by hens.

And suits by fruits.

When should a pencil be a pen and when.

They will marry then.

Coats are principally overcoats. Hasten to overtake them.

It is no ease to have no recollection and why will they come and hasten that is hurry them.

Coats may be then. I know that there are no new ones.

It is very nice to have a lot of money when no one has been heard from.

This is why.

I know what a book is.

Time when I know. What a book is.

Please me. She sees me.

I met many of them and now I have quarrelled with them and those of them all of them of which they will come often with them. So he says.

A great struggle in tenses.

The remarkable attitude.

Boys flourish in religion that is to say if they go to play.

A great many have never heard of it.

The great glory of a simple story is this, if you tell her in a letter tell him that you will sell him. Or may they be critical critical in a crisis or example or perhaps waiting. A true story has no interruption.

So then Beauvais pin them. Oh feel with tears that they are nervous.

Should they think beckoning is welcome if they change beckoning from willing and willing to as welling. Beckoning welling. It wells up in them tearing him in a hurry she would let him. Now think clearly usually ordinarily.

It is wife who is after all very welcome in restating that they will.

But might might be right in laughing. How can Howard often soften in respect to two women.

Beauvais and Howard made it yet in intelligence of not beckoning their account on their account. Our hope is welcome. Show me just why you came.

But of course you will not. Please me.

Beauvais must be appointed. The odds are in his favor. The pleasure is theirs. The most of it is what they like. It will be an annoyance to be introduced.

They no longer need with them. Hatchets can refer to having crossed before which an ocean liner are for them. More nearly.

It does smell of fish but I thought not.

Age why age why did you like.

Beauvais may trust in trusting. They will bedew women with welcome and appointing and it would fain be a circumstance. Which they have. Oh blindness where art thou.

Just be joyful and never nervous. Call a boat a boat. Do be perplexed by uneasiness. She may smile to have it about it.

They have so largely bought all with it. In no complaint. Read happily easily. Ferociously is blemish blame Beauvais. How are ours.

Howard had hold of him. And he stepped on a board. With him. Oh should he be in shadow. It is not necessary to have life ever. In cohesion. How are Howard's words. Be necessary. Be right. Be fairly in shown. No and no they knew all who have him. All who have him.

Chapter I

A boy lit it and it was happily one. Ought she to be delighted to be near him. They must be always better in not to have them seated.

Beauvais should be toward Howard.

Beauvais all very well.

Do they know a swan when she sees one very early in the afternoon lately before one has seen one.

Beauvais should be broken their rule. He was intimidated by an offering. He came to call pearls close. By their wedding. To them.

Beauvais change Beauvais to a deafening wedding from weeding and she knew like that.

Once upon a time a ruffian was married and they thought with them.

It is marvelously adjoining to them. They will be a blemish.
More than with feathers they can relish more of them. How are
mines made by his liking. He approached she was standing by
his liking but what asking of their handling might with withdrawing, it was an incident of not exciting should then.

All this could remind but not now. How about then.

Very prettily incline.

And no moving.

It might be as well before behind with before then.

Them then.

Should accordion is in volumes of very inherent very should be
indent so come with intent for velvet invent then.

There is no use in being vacant for wicked without ours.

She very near quiet.

I know I don't know.

Was he as tired as who.

Not the same.

There is no confusion but true.

Get through.

CHAPTER II

Better beeded it comes to be again that they bless them because in them they live with better beeded as she may authorise
them.

To establish them they might to endow them with prevalence
she may bring that to doubt round and around and about Brim
how to fancy Brim. He is eight in anguish. How to fasten burly
with for him.

Brim Beauvais has vanish as an addition and they cause. However ours are made. Generous as they color. Off without it. So
sew she must be once in a while at a stretch.

Brim Beauvais can be caught. Permanently.

How can you be so pleasant around me.

Was I right to like them young.

Brim Beauvais how do you mention better. Better not. Brim
Beauvais how do you mention rather. Rather than with him.

Brim Beauvais on account.
Should Brim Beauvais of course.

CHAPTER III

Two two two can you say for two how do you how do you do.
Brim Beauvais makes a curtain be achieve.
It went away this way.
For how many pears.
She prefers him.
Perhaps it is not here any longer.
For in place of it.
As much as when they felt more for me.
She loves me.
Brim Beauvais not having come, we will take it for granted
that he is not having that pleasure. Which he could have if he
had wanted to be successful as well as hopeful. James always
had, said that he would be agreed. Always had said that he would
believe not in his name. So sadly treating it as if it was, his hope.
I hope that you will be able, to manage it.

BEAUVAIS AND HIS WIFE

A NOVEL

Beauvais is a name to contain happen and a gain in nothing.
Beauvais is why.
They will stand. What they wish. Will not. Annoy.
Beauvais and dark the sun-light is dark. They will have had
and been naming.
The sun-light is dark. Should many cry. And try. To meet
often.
However. If they wish.
Brim Beauvais conscious of which wish to be known where and
often.
Brim Beauvais and his wife Florence Brim Beauvais and his
wife Florence and bears as well as more they should he would.
Many did not come.

What has happened. Before. They married.

Brim Beauvais and will. They meet Mathilde and Aesop Am-hill. These two were married and jewelry was not the wish they had not the wish they were always. To be known. They were welcome. When they were married they were writing.

Who knows how many were married.

Martha and Bayard Bartlett were married but Martha is not a name Mathilde is a name and Lavinia and even Agnes but not Martha, is not a name. Not Martha.

Frieda and Angelo Knowles were married. Were any of them married and who has known whom.

Brim Beauvais is a friend of aunts and even ready to be grateful. To them. They will exchange partners. He will remain married to Florence.

Partly of necessity it is careless to leave well enough alone.

Just two may marry.

Angelo Knowles and Frieda. He came they came together and afterwards both grew thinner.

Martha and Bayard Bartlett as is the case with many. He came. And was intimate. He knew how many went away in a minute.

William and Genevieve Butler always know any one. They are careless together. Of leaving without them. As they frequently do. For their satisfaction. As we know. It is very likely. That they have to satisfy that and they refresh, by their knowing which way. Any one went. Who might come. With them. How are they. Further.

She might be anxious to try.

It is a time of trial for them. As they are obliging and ready to fashion a home with them. Very much as they were. For them. No one. Is useless. As all of it is in denial. Or courtesy. Or will they.

So much more as politeness.

Chapter II

Who is through. With them.

She makes many a failure and for this they plan to deceive her. He is well-known.

She makes many attempts to deceive her.

By meaning all how strange.

They carried would they.

Arthur Ranger Gurtin and felt fully owned. She knew Agnes Lillian who made many add pleasure to their delight.

It is very easy to change. By labor.

And they nestle fondly for with him. He has gone and it would not matter because they will not inquire.

Brim Beauvais does not ask if it is strange. If it is familiar. To him. Because of which. Their handkerchiefs had meant. That he found them.

In harmony of a situation. If she. Was disappointed in not surprised. In anguish. Over in because for their felt formally.

Should join and shine.

I will go away with her and be a father.

She may be left with me.

Brim Beauvais might be anxious to be a witness. Which is what he is but will he see it without wishing. For them. Forever. Over more very likely.

Do they most and liking merit best.

I do not feel that I know what she thinks.

Yes quietly.

Chapter II

A part of their feeling is in towers having houses. Which they do.

Chapter III

How can it be hoped that will be helped. As it is felt that they will like whatever it is his way. Always.

In the time. In which. There is given very much to do.

Need there be a definition.

I like a mother and a child.

I like a mother and a child said quickly.

All hope of a better yellow is there is hope for practically. For them. In winter.

They return to women and children. And will they be coming. In their way. Advantageously. It is an advantage. Independent. Of extra. Wishes.

Brim Beauvais is married to Florence Anna.

Hours crowd in hours.

All his have heard all from him that he is hers and they are pleased. Occasionally. For them ferocity is soft. Oh so softly will they make it please them too. So made a meadow do. They like to be there at that time. Favorably. In their reaching it favorably. To have lost it whether. They meant it. For them. Too.

Alright they fasten better losses. Brim Beauvais knew that they will remain for them through with it favorably adjusted to them. As well. Brim Beauvais knew it very well.

An incident. Do many please.

On account of in their way joining with and having bay leaves around them with their mine of remind them.

Brim Beauvais came to say that. Think twice. Breathe easily. All of which is. Useless. Brim Beauvais breathe as easy all of which is more useless.

Than ever.

An incident without the perfection of their dependence. They need trials to perfect them. And he breaks down. And he weakens. Because they are more careful.

She met as much yet.

He heard a protection in an analysis of dedication.

Brim Beauvais sign away.

An incident in the life of Frederick. Frederick had been perfectly leave and leaves of a tree. He had been cautiously perfectly for them. They will garnish pleasure by a season and it is as easy. Should it be fired to impatience.

For this an incident.

In the life of Eliza and Johanna or agreed for them to hear.

All four of it showed.

An incident in the life of they met with whom. They he had been pretty well mentioned by three.

I asked are we any different from the rest of them and they meant with them. He answered yes you do. I doubt it.

But what is it that they expect who are angry. Show it allowed and beside. Ours are habits. It is kindly to try to oblige will he deny others with theirs as much as they know for it to have vim. This is what he said. Rightly.

She might do through you. What she did.

How have they. Anybody has had cakes. Should they show.

The strain of that. How outrageous.

Beauvais met a master.

Chapter III

Put and push.

Lightly. They will manage. To push. Which way. They have. As an enterprise.

Beauvais felt that way. Away.

Mean. That thing is mine.

We spoke of Johanna marrying.

Would a couple. Be attracting.

Oh do be careful of souls and pairs of pearls which they know.

She may Florence be plainly. Stated not to. Go away. Oh do thank you. She knows how joining is welcomed.

By them.

Hours of welcome less.

She made a mention. Of this.

Are surprised when surprise hires velvet for flowers. That they may underway as it is for them to like to say. That they do.

Hand in hand is made thoroughly gloved by kindness.

An incident in the life of Eugenia. Eugenia is a girl who has thickened with theirs. As they planned. She bought. What. As alike. It is momentarily all which of what they made Mary Mary do have the absurd allurement of their showing their cake whether with for them. This is a bit of why all of it well welcome as a wish. There would. Be. A girl. And a carpet. He probably sat there. It is not deniable that it is a sign. Of being well.

No one can arrange that Mary should meet Beauvais.

The episode of Robins Porter

They knew they had been not at all agreeable because just as they were to start it was finished. Robins Porter had rendered all this and made it easy at first. He was willing to be able to have them think and waver with and rather just as well that they went. But which. They were at hand. To ask them. To be selfish. About it. The incident which was why Robins Porter thought everything would be to finish was this. He was anxious to please and very wary of the advantage to be taken by their hearing of a mountain. Do be sweet. And hearing of a mountain. Should they plan for their sugar just at first she would like to be angry and have to say blue and green blue two green one and then they had requested white for some and it was after all better. That they had left. The episode of Robins Porter is finished.

Brim Beauvais who wishes will he say that all of it is anxious and every day they will persuade them to have them. Call for them.

Chapter VII

How can it be that they will change two for three. All of which they will judge it is better. To stay. With them.

If you think you do like that. You know that you will have the rest of that. So that they must in all of which it is radically. A rest even. For them. Just as much as when they would like. Which they mean by resting.

And episode in analysis. Will baskets hold everything.

It is at noon that they change. From one side. To the other. After noon they change from one side. To the other.

Brim Beauvais and Agnes Douglas should they think that they have not understood. Or would they rather. Be very happy just as they were.

And would it be all of it very well and alike by means of their. Retaliation. As much so.

It would not be as strange.

And in the meantime.

For them to be sweet.

For them to know.

That they can come.

Home just as well.

As with. For them.

And so they might in the meantime know the differences.

Brim Beauvais married Florence Douglas and William Turn-
bul married Mary James. And by and by neither of them were
frightened.

Who can change what they think easily.

But which of it by which of it, is the mention of why. Will they
go. Made necessary. In their instance. They like. What they do.

Please be careful of him.

Remember how many hours each of them spent there.

Chapter Seven

Who holds them from keeping. It away farther away still.
Withholds them.

Beauvais and Richard have not been asked do they love what
they have.

Order and disorder.

Cleanliness.

Reviews.

Better.

Which they will.

They are all very well established. And yet. Might it be an
advantage. To change or should they rest as they are. Would it
matter if it turned out that it was right for them. To succeed in
giving for us with what. They could have. In leaving as well as
remaining all and more for it. It is without doubt not a question. For which they include their satisfaction. Indeed. It is quite
warm.

So that they might find. That we were. Very successful.

Chapter VI

There can be two sounds for them. And she may be very easily
asleep.

Chapter Six

He made it be as prettily as possible their way just as much as to
hide for them that he asks it to be that he wishes to feel it.

But when. Justly. Defied. Lest. They neglect their curtains.
By which in immensely. They can so swiftly read it. For them-

selves. And be very unquiet in which respect they mean in imply as for them. Radiantly more than which they were. Indeed. Very often. It is by this that they put it on high. In pearls. Pearls which do make blue a fish.

But why do you do it.

Chapter Six

Be reclaimed for themselves with their tears as their measure that they will be by themselves as much so as they ever can for them. It is highly obliged. That they do it. For further. That they mean.

Ambrose Winchester made certain that were they waiting they would wait callously with a question. How fortunate.

A chance to have a place that they make theirs with which they cloud their delight.

Brim Beauvais was fortunate. In willing. That they should enjoy. Their closing of their blessing. With this chance. Which may be the equal of it. Or indeed. Be the equal of it. Or perhaps. Be equal to it. Just as much as theirs is. More than they could in a little while ask it very well.

Brim Beauvais was married to Florence Winchester and no one is more willing than they to be virtuous. With which they have in their nervousness. No pleasure. Which. They have. For themselves. Alone. In every way. Very likely. You know they say and they oblige as well as being without any anguish.

Let us think callously of unity.

He is obliged. To banish those. Whom he finds. Disagreeable. Just as well.

As when they feel that it is now and about why they can. Be always very well.

And reasonably. Precious and cautious. Just as much.

Brim Beauvais and his wife Florence. James Sperry and his sister Janet. William Fuller and his sister Dorothy. Jacqueline Richards and her brother Henry. All these are astonishing. More than that in a minute.

Chapter VII

Why should he go with him when he stays here for him.

Brim was mentioned without mentioning them. They were usually forgetting that choice is an attention and choosing is frustrating just as others are. Who knows. Just as others are.

Oh can they decide better than beside .with their assistance besides more than they tried to have them share as they can with which they are aware of failing. There are three things that make for yes. With them. For which. They may add. And mention. For their kindness. Which is habitual. As they have forgotten. To be certain. In a minute. With their enchaining, forty in their arranging. Which they might. In substance.

For our cloud.

As soon as it has been at once with them. For them. In fortunately.

Partly without it.

It came to happen that on account of distance they looked again. At one. Which is the same as. That they have forgotten some. Of which they had been rather. Careful. Formally.

Rather careful. Continues. And more about it what they consider their fault. No one can join Brim Beauvais again. With them. As he certainly does.

Brim Beauvais was anxiety. For them. In their mistake. Which they manage. To arrange in waiting. They manage to have preferences. Just as he is told. For this and in an appointment it is a declaration that whatever he may be being with them for it which is why they have understood adding as changing. Certainly he meant. All of it a delight. It is just. What they wanted. Because it added. It to that. To oblige them to dictate. Their allowance. And so Brim Beauvais may do this with her.

Chapter Eight

She said a river is near land near water.

Chapter VIII

Put Beauvais where you please and cry will felt. Willed and will felt or Beauvais almost cry.

Just when and why will adding will Beauvais try and will cry.

It is very pleasant in the garden and they look too and see that they are looking too. At him. He is very nearly when they see him. It is only afterwards that they will cry. After him. It is only with him that. They will try. To cry. With them. Nine of them with him. It is only afterwards that they will try. To cry. With them.

Brim Beauvais and a ball where there had been. A pigeon. This is not a fancy this is a fact.

Brim Beauvais could be surprised that the taller and smaller was as active as the taller and smaller was as active. And he went with preparation to cover the situation. Which they added figuratively. And no one asked them anything. Or nearly. Not enough. To oblige them. To have meat. Ready for them. It was after this. All. That is to say. They had already eaten. Every day. Brim Beauvais.

Brim Beauvais makes every one angry.

Just yesterday they were selfish.

Beauvais has made an answer. It is a very good way. This is not an answer. It is a record.

Of what a titled lady does.

Part II

And episode in their agreement.

She said I have known three.

Three when.

That they were better than ever then.

She said it does not matter then.

That they were as much better then then when.

She said with when they resemble or resemble them when.

She said with whether they will or had rather better resemble better resemble them. And so forth. This episode was not so soon finished. As commenced.

The episode continuous and they joke.

Beauvais pleases her and misses being with her.

The episode

Who can be tall. All. Three.

Were they seen near to be. All three. As tall as she. She was careful to be left there where she did more than her share. In devotion. To the cause. Of country. She was never lost and easily filled the post which she needed and it needed. To be filled. At a very great cost. By her. She devoted herself. To the cause. Of her country.

After that what mattered.

Another one who was equally tall. Was not devoted to her country. At all. She was well. Known to be able. To say. It is mine. And it was. And she was dead in bed. Because she loved these. Who were of another country. And so that. Afterwards she was ready to gain. No one could be left to be leaving. That she would have them. If they. Went away. Did they all go away. However and rather he meant. That they were careless. Not in expression.

She was never drowned. Nor indeed in love. In answers. Oh so easily tall. There is no use in wishing that many women were even. Or three.

The episode is finished.

Chapter Eight

Brim Beauvais is not anxious to dance and as it does not happen he will not be famous as successful or thoughtful or in them alone. As they very well know. In place. Of an advantage.

They might be careless of all three. Brim Beauvais, Florence, and Hotchkins and his wife. All three are mercifully spared. So many are anxious and she will very well eat dinner. Here. Not unexpected. And alone. With and which is noticed. And so they like their interruption very nearly all of it was for the best in their liking made easily and gracious. He told them that he liked that they were. Cautious. And that they were. Fairly insistent.

Many many leave with them.

CHAPTER IX

What does he do when he thinks. Of it. With them. Which fortunately makes no difference as they mean to have it lost for them. As much as they do clearly. Which at once. It was more necessary just when they thought about it. For themselves. As they do prudently. It is of no use for them to arouse more than they leave as balance. Just as they do naturally. More than they did. Ultimately. For more than ever. Where they do particularly.

Brim Beauvais surrounded the center with what they could call flowers or only just a flower. For their chance. Made necessary in an ultimate recital of their wanting. It for them. Brim Beauvais felt very well. It is often that a welcome for him and for Florence comes simultaneously just as often. They came at once.

Who does and whom have they heard. Which is it that they add publicly. Nor prudently. In reading with and without resting. With resting. They will leave them for it or as bought. It is very welcome. All of which do. For them to add luckily.

Brim Beauvais was successful in asking it to be a chance. He was successful. In adding. It to be a chance.

He made all of it plainly.

Brim Beauvais left and right for which in there to be a chance. Needed in estimation. Nor for clarion as they look as at a daisy which has on account that she was faintly yes as ever. Do which. Strangely. Leaving fought in pieces. Owned with a joining in their reverence daily.

This is why. They have it as a leaf. As and a leaf. For farther. That she had adjoined their raining in the main where they choose. They choose admirably.

Brim Beauvais and choice.

Brim Beauvais was a man who felt that he knew older than the want of eloquent prestige and caught and further felt in choice gently. Who has heard stern tones. When they like. Florence. Think.

All are changes.

Chapter Nine

An episode introduced for variety.

One man is a man. Winning. Two men are two men winning. One man is one man winning. Two men are men winning. Two men who are two men winning are arranging for that creditably. One man one man winning is making winning learning. For their account an episode is made of very pretty laces. Very pretty presents. Very pretty choice. Very pretty choice. Which they have. In discretion. And so they marry. Glass finally is thought. To be welcome. As toast. And for a fugitive they come to go. An episode to tell them so. An episode is kindly. She is not kindly. Nor is their care. Kindly. For them they like. Partly. To have it be. A kindness. Which they do. To them. An obligation. And a relief. Indeed. Not to know. That they very well wish. For everything they have is more than they thought would leave it out. For them. More than they did. An episode is gracious. They had indeed very much rather have been. Cautious. Very much. Rather. Have. Been cautious.

An episode closes. They must have been known to have won. They must. Have been. Anxious. To have some one. Win.

Chapter X

A little yellow flower is fragrant.

Chapter Ten

It was liked that a little yellow flower was fragrant chapter ten.

Chapter X

A remarkable career in which he had been heard. And so. Brim Beauvais was best of all for it for himself. That he would. Leave it. As he had been. Very careful. One at a time. Obliquely. Which made them rise. For them. Fortunately. On their account please measure it once that they may. Share it with them. Just as it was. Remarkably. For which in their allowance. They make spoiling it. A victim. Of their obligation. That they are. Reasonably. Avoiding. To be careful to. Release it from their hold. At once.

Brim Beauvais did the commission.

He asked them to prepare whatever was all of which he would

ask them to compare. Relying. Upon their account. Of the same. That they had undertaken. And so it would be of interest to them.

Brim Beauvais had married Florence. It was not strange to add one. Just by being. In their case. Left to it. In every way a delight. Just in the hope. Of their announcing that. After the violence. Who has. Introduced violence. Into the discussion.

Brim Beauvais made it be perfection. If perfection is good. More perfection is better.

Chapter X

By the time that they are told. That a great many have been held to be very well known as when they have them with them. In the place of their wanting. That they should resign themselves to everything.

Curtains have been left to be only with them. And windows have been. Left. To be without any hindrance to living. And also. They might. Be just as well established with and without their having been very soon only known as hoping to be winning. It might need much encouraging to have them like that a beginning.

Beauvais and trimming. They will be persistent. In the realizing. That they continue. To use men. And women. And who knows who came. Who follows. Who is with them. Who says yes to them. Who after all made them go.

Just then three women saw that they could call and they must not be aware that it could be thought, that they were allowed to have it heard for them. All of this is a necessity. And they wish for everything.

Brim Beauvais had occasion to reach it. Very likely all who had been without their consent left to be reproachful could be thoughtful. It was with their help. That they were able. To have it helped to need more than they could. That was available.

Just when will they come.

Chapter Ten

It was very nearly certain that they had heard of it again.

Chapter XI

Just why will he try.

Chapter XI

Brim Beauvais may account for this some day.

Chapter Eleven

Brim Beauvais may appoint them to behave as well as they can under the circumstances. He will realize that it is very well to have them place it there for themselves. They will amuse themselves. And while. They are quiet. They will be openly and with relish leaving it alone. As they might. On account. Of their arrangements.

It will be plainly left to them to try.

Underneath.

It is by them by no means that Brim could never be annoyed. And because. In astonishment. They like. He asked for it. As they lured them. To arrange places. As if it mattered. Very much. Who makes all calls.

It is in union that there is strength. And they divided. And therefor. One of them. Was stronger. Than before. More so. Than before. And which one. Went away. And may they like. To have it intended. That it should be known. Or not.

It is a very long time for which Beauvais asked a minute. He was united and felt himself to be urgent. And he would. Be without doubt. Outwitted.

Or would they narrow it. Would they exchange it. Or only by themselves. For them. And with renown. They knew. That there were clashes. And that no one was to compare what they liked at one time. Or nearly so. For them. Frightened.

Should they mean would they think. Or hope for Susan.

Brim Beauvais married Florence. Florence had a cousin Susan. Susan was only felt to be when he Florence's brother compared one another. Susan is the same as Sarah. And they knew more than ever. That it was very pleasantly rather more than they were alike.

It is by being coveted that she thinks well of them.

An appointment, they are appointed pleasantly. It is more than orderly. Often they think well together of this arrangement. And it is allowed. Without any doubt. Carefully.

Brim Beauvais felt that the occasion warranted his interference. But was it his duty. To be polite. And express his hope. That they would arrange. Never to see them. Which is. What happened. It is ordinarily. Not a question. They will be welcome. They will come. They will be welcome. And as much as ever. Will they have it happen. That they knew. That on this account. They will join. Very fairly. In something. That is undertaken. At once. As a pleasure. And in consequence. Of their having been. A disappointment. Or an opportunity. Of disappointing them immediately. In the meantime. They were as well known. As it is at all necessary to be. Where undoubtedly among themselves. They speak of it. Which is a relish of their advantage. Over others. More than. They enjoyed. In an advantage. Necessarily theirs. This is an autobiography of one of these. And only two. Made it more an occasion. Of interrupting. On their account. Their hope.

Think singly and very often.

Brim Beauvais can easily be lost in counting.

At all events and at this time. All of them whom and because of it they had the occasion to reveal as fairly with themselves safe and safely not more than all of it as they had established. A memory.

She may be reminded instantaneously as an advantage.

Brim Beauvais knew more than as they were. Knew more. Than. As they were.

Brim Beauvais feeling a revelation in instinct. And a pleasure.

Chapter XII

A story can be told if there are conversations. There always is conversation. Whenever they meet. They tell themselves. That they do it. Or they might mutter. But not at all. He waited.

Chapter XII

And then to be then with then not with them. And to be interested and with them. They were perfectly at home with and without them. Fortunately. It was an undertaking that they had undertaken with enthusiasm. And they were remarkably adapting the obligation of wondering. Whether they were able. Was he able. To judge whether he would. Decide. About whether he was able. To have more of them. None of them. Which were necessary. As they were. He was often awful. And it is thought that there were meaning to have them come then with and without him. He was all that they could leave when. They left him. To themselves. As they were often. Just as sheltered. As on account. Of the sun. Which was why. They had decided. Everything. As very likely. Often. At that time. All who have hold. Of their exchange in exchanging it for him to beckon them. Often. To come there. With and without him. Or more constantly than they ever do. In excuse. For which they are without doubt. Remarkably. At one. With an investigation of a commonplace. Revision. Ask them for them. Rather. Which is by the use. Of elegant. Made natural. And untimely. And then. To have imagined.

There is no circumstance which necessitates the use of. As owned in an instance as have been. Recognised. As their permission.

Brim Beauvais can come too. And he will ask too. How do they manage to feel. That they will. Be very well.

To have renewed seeing him.

Chapter Eleven

It is while they are about it that they feel that they will need it as a caress. And they might without theirs for them and farther. As friendship is necessary.

Are you her friend.

Chapter XII

She thinks. That I should. Not mention. What he thinks.

For more than that. They do not care. To amuse themselves.

They give me pencils. At my request.

And at once. They fasten. Upon. My asking. Them. Would they. Be able. To admire without. Finding it out. At once. As they may.

They will illustriously. Suffered themselves. To receive. Them. In charity.

As much as they can.

Which they declare.

They are able to explain.

Whenever. They indicate. That they will not plan. It. For them. Very much more narrowly. As a comfort.

Beauvais. And Brim. And Bliss. And possibly perfection.

Brim Beauvais was married to Florence. He had married. And not at once. As they were very certain. That they would. Bequeath. A wedding.

In them. As they are. In them.

They acknowledge. And they are put. Out of countenance. Just as it is. Advantageously.

No one. Can remind. Theirs. In. Integrity.

Nor should. Nor would. If they mean. That all of it. Is. A recompense. Gratuitously. Just as shun. They shun some of them. But they meet. Some of them. As well. As an invitation. In jeopardy. Which they can. On and allow. In never. Leading. Which is why. Lamentable. Is never a bewildering result.

Brim Beauvais is the result of having nestled in a foreign kingdom.

He has been in intent lent and decorated in allowing variety to think well of when. They meant. To reassure. Him.

Brim Beauvais is always. Profoundly. Influenced by this opinion.

For them fortunately for them they fortunately for them are with them and they are with him. Fortunately. They are. With him.

He fortunately for them is there with them.

They are there with them.

At a distance they are. There. With them.

Brim Beauvais. Made it known. That he had them. As a help. In their trouble. Which came. Rapidly upon them. In consequence. Of their establishing it. As an obligation. In which. They questioned something. Individually. And on account. Of opposition. In the meantime. He went everywhere.

Brim Beauvais married Florence Beauvais. They rested very happily with the sun shining in the window. As it happened. On both sides. And they were dreadfully sorry. That it made no difference. That they were. Very likely. To be able. To have it happen. That they were. To begin it. As it were. More than they did. Not in anticipation. Or exactly. So. Shall we mind. What they do. In this way. More than they had. At once. As in the way. Of their meaning. All of it. For them. They are often allowed. To come again. Naturally. As their known. Then. All of it must. Be. An excuse.

CHAPTER XIII

Watch a watch for them. They will remember to ask ribbon for ribbon and to resemble them.

They must understand them. They will ask it for them of him. They will excuse leaving it there for them. They will add immeasurably to their hope that he will have it left there at that time for them by him. And so. They must. Make. No mistake. Because an advantage would be taken. Of any error. That they committed. In misunderstanding. Exactly. What was meant. By undertaking. To divide. All of it. Into the parts. Which would not. Be magnified. By distance. They will call them occasionally to come here. And see. What they will like. If they have it. Once in a while. Entirely to themselves.

Brim Beauvais has managed. By a chance. To be perfectly secure. Even doubtfully. In aggression. And they mean. To bother them. To the degree. Consistent with their announcing. That they are prized.

Brim Beauvais was married to Florence. Florence is not direct not directly accustomed. To deduct. From Florence. Which is in exchange. And adroitly. Who has meant to agree without. Leaving it with them.

Brim Beauvais is made happy by the dog's dreams. By the dog's dreams. Which makes him. Believe in their startling. As he will be fairly. Thought famous. As the circumstance. Permits.

Brim Beauvais has a chance. To dispose. Of it.

Chapter Fourteen

Who could chew the cud of their thought nervously.

It may be a satisfaction. To disturb. Their relation. To adopted as liberally. As chocolate.

Chickens and cows.

Who allows.

That they will win.

Without doubt.

Weddings.

Brim Beauvais never sings.

Chapter XIV

Brim Beauvais may have a chance to dispose of the rest of their stay. They will go away. Or manage. It industriously. In advance. As they catch it in their flight. It is of no importance that it is better that it is so.

Chapter XV

Brim Beauvais may always go. Away.

Chapter XVI

It is without authority that he has reasoned.

Beauvais is married to Florence.

Chapter Sixteen

Ann and Nell.

Chapter XVII

Brim Beauvais. A lament.

He will be tall. And they. Feel it to make a restitution.

He will fail. If at all.

She must. Be. An addressed. Mention. Of a. Mary. May. A. Mountain.

They will. Grant. For such. And such. Indeed. And. Nervously.
It is all. Out. Of a. Mountain.
They must be. Scared. Just now.
In spite. Of their alarm.
Just now.
Very much. Just now.
In spite. Of their alarm. Just now.
Will they mean. Just now.

It is woefully their perfection. With and with. Irreligion. In such. And sections. Of celebrated. Silence. In use. With men and main and when and diminish. All ours are mine.

Brim Beauvais cannot lament.
And they call. Hoping. He will not hear.

As they may. Scare them. In spite of no alarm. They can not be made to harm. Them. Immediately. For they are. Very much. In touch. Of. With them. Without with them. As they scare. Them. In very likely. Ways. It is just. That they will seek. To establish their repose as double. They can. Be known. Without. Any trouble. It is. Effective. To make sounds twice. Should they. Be seen. In reach. And reaching. Come to all. Who have. Gone.

It is a call. To all. Resting. Very well. I thank you.

Chapter Sixteen

Just why. May they cause. Fifteen. To rise. Speedily.
Because they answer. In. As all. It is very well known. Turbot.

Chapter XVI

With wedding Brim. Florence is with him. Brim Beauvais is married to Florence every day. With way and have and stay. Imagine that they. Will. And better. Than. If they had. It. As certain. Brim Beauvais on account of announce.

With a gracious wish they will establish their independence of killing. With a gracious wish. They will establish. Their independence. Of killing.

They may, without anguish, be very often selfish, and they had, established sanction as permission.

And then they were obstinate. And willing. To be selfish. As a wish. Without them. They bought and brought. Only. More than they taught. They were pleasurable. In changing. They were. Embellishing. In persuasion. As ignition. For their quelling. Their. Distribution.

But which. Of excess.

Made it a plea and pleasantly. They mentioned building.

They built themselves. Theirs. Among. Withdrawn. And acting. With a division. For their rarity.

Beauvais and blessed. Because of fright. And should. In course. Of division. As they might.

Chapter XVII

Brim Beauvais could because, and a cause. Of their. And grieving. It is a grief. To be saving. In no obligation. Of their use. With use. Of which. They were. Saying.

Chapter Seventeen

Gone cautiously and question. With what. He said.

They minded. Made by them. To. Belong. In connecting introduced. Connection.

Astonishing can be a covering.

Only do right.

Should they mind.

Chapter XVIII

Leave well enough alone.

Chapter Nineteen

Just cut or put into a cup fifteen made into as many as subdivision. And then they will have as provision. Their immediate welcome in delight. No name made no name made no one. Known no one.

Brim Beauvais should relieve whatever he had begun.

Which made him be better than every one. In their provision. As allowance.

Brim Beauvais should be called shortly Brim Beauvais and not welcome. No one clings to welcome in lions. Or in hearts. Or in welcome. With indifference. Or creditably. Theirs. In producing their joining. This. With them. Immediately. For theirs. Reflexion. That they will. Be welcome. As much as for instance. In redressing. Wrongs.

Have to be careful. To think suddenly. That they will perish. With their attendance. In beguiling. That they shall align. In trusting. In relief. For them. Of their hope. Of lain. Away. By this. That they. Can see. Brim Beauvais. Close. To them.

Better yet. In plenty. Of time. For preparation.

Brim Beauvais meant to keep account. Of whether. It was fragrant. To compare. Older. And younger. In all. The little while. That they were able. To apply for leave. It may be that they. Came in. Noisily.

To often wonder. Whether it would. Be best. To narrow. The research. To their opening. Not too silently. Their bought. Books. Books. Should be given. Not bought. Leave. It as a better felt. Wish. To entertain. Them. As well. As grant. It. To them. In time.

Just why should they ever be anxious.

One of the ways to be taught is this. Brim Beauvais shall miss. Being. With them.

And then. For the time. In which. They prepare. He shall be inclined. To favor it as a reason. In all of it. Incidentally. And bought. Also. No one. Will follow.

So much for that.

Chapter Nineteen

Brim Beauvais married to Florence Anna. Brim Beauvais married to Florence Anna. All made. All. Made. Of all. He thought. Just then. He will. And worship. Walk. Brim Beauvais. Which. Is why. They wish. To once declare. In spite. Of which. They came. To share. It plainly. As they like.

Brim Beauvais shall be welcome well and well. Cordially.

And well.

Cordially.

Brim Beauvais is as knees and need. Well. Well. And cordially.

In conducting Brim Beauvais to this clear and declared reason. For an established. Restfulness. In better. Than before. Left to them. Now. They may. Come to be. All of it. In their despite. To. Say so.

Brim Beauvais may need it. For them.

Chapter XX

Ten may be careful. Of money.

Chapter Twenty-one

Why should mentions be in doubt.

It is a little bit of their defeat that makes them have it come to be a seat. Which they occupy.

With them. Very little. Just as much. As they will have. They will see. To it. For them. Alone. That they have announced. Pride.

They have a great deal of pride in their home.

They have hopes. That at that time. Forty-one and twenty-nine. Make. Thirty-three. In fine. And leap-year. Makes it. Twenty-nine. Who does like. Horses. Who have bits. With which. They ask. Will they have fits. Because they think. That theirs is lost. Which is why. They have asked. The most. Of them.

Which can be purchased. Readily.

Brim Beauvais. Looks like that. To-day.

Left to be told. That an adventure. Is an adventure. To-day.

Forty-nine makes. Sixteen. Excitable. She may. Frequently. Mispronounce. It.

But why will they sing. As they may. With pleasure.

Chapter Twenty-one

With pleasure.

It is a habit to need society.

Chapter XXI

With pleasure.

Nor need they be. Without the token. Of their earnestness.

Fifty-one. With pleasure.

Chapter XXI

They will be met. With pleasure.
And if they accept. The meeting. It will give. Pleasure.

Chapter XXII

They must Brim Beauvais. And Florence. They must. Be per-
fectly acquired. As an addition. To their. Cultivation. Nor do
they. Need they. Fairly. Furnish. It around. Without their con-
clusion. And so. They extinguish. Their thought. Their hope.
Their carefulness. Their intrusion. With pleasure.
Should it be mentioned. With pleasure.
In inhabiting. More than they build. Or even in coughing.
More than they like. Nor in withdrawing. Much as they can.
In theirs. In part. In decline. And in flourishing. Theirs. As plants.
It is in decorum that they use their argument.
It is. In decorum. That they use. Their argument. With pleasure.
Should they be idle and antagonistic.

Chapter Twenty-two

It is very. Evident. Made entirely. Carefully. For them. As a
fortune. That they. Conduct it. In a revision. As an instance. Of
their regard. For many. Of their. Fellow-men.

Chapter XXIII

Just as much as a mistake.

Chapter XXIV

It is thus that. They have quarrelled.
Believe me. It is. Indeed it is. Their chance. To reinvite. Their
birthday. Very especially.
Should they decorate a ribbon.
There is a companion.
Brim Beauvais. Has improved.

Chapter Twenty-four

It has become. No disturbance. To accept. Their. Poise.

Nor will they be. Almost welcome. As they shall shame. Those with whom. They have. Been. At an advantage. Made carefully.

Chapter XXV

The history of Brim Beauvais.
He has been very careful. Not to be quarrelled with.

Chapter XXVI

Carry usefulness as an ideal. This is the story.

By accident in returning to their destination they did intend and were a little disappointed in being unable to furnish themselves in the manner they had hope. They had not intended. To return again. As it happened. When they returned. They were told. There had come. As if sent. By them. What they had dimly brought. And this was. An item. It could be a branch of their seeing. That they could. Beggar description.

It was undoubtedly. An error. And it could not be. In the present contentment. Rectified. Although. They could all use. In having to be. Merited. To be thoughtful. Without their permit. In indiscretion. She might amount to that in only briefly calling it to close. Its doors. As they may. Wonder. Should they cover. All who think well of them. With their hope. That they may do. Very well. By those. Who wish. To talk. Is it a wonder. Or might they not all. Have needed. It.

Very slowly.

And not to have. Forgotten.

She may amalgamate change and hate. And he. May amorously. Expect. Their. Representation.

It is undoubtedly unlike a cloud.

Chapter XXVI

Either she may think well of it or he.

Chapter Twenty-seven

Nor hastily. On their account. Will they furnish. Their pleasure. In intermittance. Which they may. Color. As they arise. In their deliberate thought. To be alone.

Chapter XXVIII

Just as many call. As furnish music and water.
Or either. Just as many call. For them. In their delight.
With them. In their delight.
For them. With them. As they. Exchange it. For them. With them. In their exchange. As they. Exchange. It. With them.
They exchange. It. For them.

Chapter XXIX

Did they do it. Without doubt.

Chapter XXIX

Would he be awakened if he were to be alone.
Which they meant.

Chapter Twenty-nine

It is in all a religion. To make them think with things. That they mention. They must. In their habit. Feel very well. As they may. Come. To invent. Their kind. Of arithmetic.
Brim Beauvais. Fortunately. Makes no mistake.
To be as much. As touch.

Chapter XXX

They should indulge. In leaving learning. Their change.
They should indulge. In respecting. Their allowance. Of their hoping. That they will. Underwrite. Their hope. Of their example. Of which. They will allow. In moderation. Their change.
When they are. Thoughtful. They will migrate.
They will ordinarily prepare their method with hope.
Which they will relish.

Chapter Thirty

Brim Beauvais was married. To Florence Anna. She was never appointed and they chose. With reliance. That they had bought. Thoughtfully. In return. Those have. It. Well and pray with their hope of anguish.

They will need silence to employ.

It is after all no useful hope. To have to stand with their wish. No future hope. With which. They will. Stand. With their having. A wish. Of welcome. In hope. And choice.

Chapter Thirty

She might be mentioned as. Much endowed. With pleasure. To be felt. As much allowed.

She would be gathered. As well. As she can. In reasoning. With whatever. They will. And may. That they can. Color it. With joy. In the instance. In which. They felt. Their reunion.

Brim Beauvais is made to be wonderfully. Rested. Any day. With their understanding. Such as they liked.

They may be. More. Naturally. All of it. Which. They allowed. In their reunion. It is. With all. That they. Established. In all. A lesson. To be learned. As teaching. Theirs. On account. For them. In the course. Of their allowance. Which may. Call. Their union. All which is. Made without troubling them. To be adverse. They will follow. Just and by the same. With. And whether. It is beseeching. They may. Follow. With and. Moreover. As they can. In no way blemish. Often. Fortune. Brim Beauvais. Accounts. For this. They. May. Florence and he. They may. Account. For that. In their gayety. In their reasoned plan. Of which. Amiability. And their. Anger. In a way. Never. To be. In an exchange. Of their failing. Made entirely. In such. And because. Of in vain. Brim Beauvais. Is a name. He is made. Of the same. Away. Is a name. He is made. Of that name. All the same. Brim Beauvais. When they came. Rain. Brim Beauvais is a name. They came.

Shall we join them.

FINIS

I innocently meant to go away. I mentioned digestion. I heard it spoken of and ears. I dreamed of pieces of electric lights and I meant to add that I did not care to repeat what I wished to eat. I supposed that there was more bread. I meant to help myself to oranges and butter. I meant to help myself to oranges and butter. I meant to mind the seat and to place the no I did not mean to place the plate there I meant to drink what there was which was not particularly painful. It was not particularly painful. I collected strength. I collected strength meaningly. I meaningly lengthened the time for milk. Eric. Eric he laughed. Why is there pleasure in a doctor. When do purchases necessitate books. When do questions mean sombreness. When do they go upstairs. When do they go upstairs. I saw I met, was it back of hair. When we fell and said no more when we fell and said no more, I don't want it now. Richly was the title deserved. Loud was the acclaim that greeted the rejoicing of what station do you go from. They did it. The spent hours. Sugar, tea coffee cocoa and other articles, they were generally half their value. What time is it from here. The one they went by was delayed something, we shall neither of us be in any particular hurry as we neither of us have a long journey on the other side of London. They asked if they did not ask of them. The trains are mostly travel on have not changed for years and years. Other trains are sometimes added but that does not affect the principal trains that always run. I think so. What will become of us, asked the Czar. At first sight they were much less favourable to the middle of May. There may be special things to be sent from here. They mightn't know of. It is even more certain that there will be an end of all hesitation. His men who previously had tramped down heartedly over little pieces of dust sad darkness draw on. I had not thought about darkness, I neglected little gardens. I did not neglect little pieces of garden. It is so easy not to be built with a view to an orchard now the news is correct. It was not without reason that the man is to be reminded to call. Five days earlier it was not without reason. Up there to the left. The air was thick. The air was thick. I don't believe it. I don't know if it's true. Other things too numerous to mention. He was awfully pleased with that. She could spend as much as she liked on it. I've never been. They don't keep up the gardens at all, in perfect order just kept clean. Was it named after her. I imagine so looking fatter than ever. There were curtains to match only unfortunately they were at the cleaners. These were his feelings. He acted on them. It's harder work up at that end. Never letting the war run out does making recognition easier. Suppose there was pepper, suppose noises had a special name. Suppose the packs of dogs and others moaned with hunger. Not at all.

And yet their patience will have been exhausted. But in nearly the whole of wood there is a chance to demand to undo the clumsy knot. Many of the best explanations and appeals did not satisfy the arrangements made for children and naked ladies. Not a bit.

He heard with some surprise and no dismay, he heard with some surprise and no dismay the news of firm treatment. He heard with some surprise and no dismay that you could not walk without any comfort. She is most flattering. Yes we do. It took form in the song. I'll read it to Jessie.

A haste to baby. Please may I see the water. Please may I see the water.

Against this ever rising tide of national enthusiasm, while immersed in this prodigious task, with some surprise with some surprise, with thousands of skilled stirrups with no dismay, with what is important with surprisingly great surprises, with some surprise and with no dismay, against this ever rising tide of national enthusiasm, the greatest enthusiasm no doubt, it echoed in the preliminary recitations. No I don't.

Recollect, recollect that, while immersed in this that this incident deserves special notice. I cannot be there.

The search for food and fuel became secretly cooking potatoes.

For a time early in November it was the same paper. For a time he forbore to be not something that was laboured not show not to show men, to fail to be killed and be killed. Lacking a pro-

portional melon. Everybody has one to see what I will not listen.
No why not. We find that we have obligations of honour obligations which mention more.

He scooped out of his bed what we have been saying all the
time.

He sounds just like Theo. He cannot end that sentence.

The only prudent course now was to retreat north. Cruelly and
in an obstinate fight. For a time the weather had been singularly
tried so that the sun was won won by the barometer and it did it
shone. Now then.

He clasped his now precious naturally heartless man. Two
mighty and ambitious recoveries never fully trust one another.

Oh shut up.

Keep the board and bring it to me later. Later in the day he
gave his assent. A higher will than his disposed of these events.

It's a highly trustworthy shape.

With a big and proud hear I write to tell you that Thursday
I wrote to my parents. Was she found reading in a silent corner.

No better hidden feelings. During one of their rides there
was no objection. You have no objection? But resuming his easy
bearing he gave his assent.

Purest china tea season's greetings.

A look of surprise and distrust came to the proprietors of the
watches. They were at last allowed a dog.

A short time ago he retired for reasons of ill-health. He became a way of eating each other's hay. Did he kill them all. Oh I
thought you meant that you had sat on them. I had a pin in all
Spain. Politeness and everything else.

MARK TWAIN CENTENARY

Mark Twain did a great many things and everything he did was
all he did and he did make a dead man dead. I think he was the
first man to ever do that and it was a great American thing to do.

WITH A WIFE

How can there be a difference between twice once and twice twice once. Any little way to say she loves me.

With within and mean, I mean I mean.

What is the pleasure of their saving everything. Everything saving everything. I mean I mean. In between.

What is the difference between netting and provision. With and seen. And seen I mean. And mean. I mean I mean.

What is there to be had when there is such and a deliberation. Two I mean. Two I mean. Two I mean I mean.

How can they have eight glasses and to a queen. A queen is when they do they might they will they shall they as they in between I mean I mean. Having been born a republican there is no lack of pretending pretending with seen and I mean I mean I mean. What is [the] difference between why they went at once.

With a wife.

He is with a wife.

He is with a wife.

With a wife means doing it altogether.

With a wife.

With a wife as if with a wife as if with a wife.

With a wife.

There have been many thought to be with a wife thought to be with a wife.

With a wife.

With a wife sweetly.

With a wife.

With a wife there be hold with a wife.

With a wife.
In letter with a wife.
With a wife.
In letter.
With a wife.
With a wife in fact.
With a wife.
With a wife with a wife with a wife.
With a wife.
Well with a wife.
They make.
A trace.
Well with a wife.
They make
A trace.
A trace.
They make.
Well with.
With a wife.
They make well a trace.
They make well a trace with a wife.
How can fifty-five and aside.
An aside. How far is Avignon from Oakland. How far is
Avignon from Oakland.
With a wife he went from there to there.
Felicity in spring time.
How can to disk to how can to disk to is it at first to disk to.
Felicity in spring time to and froze as well.
Felicity in spring time with a wife.
She did very well with a wife. And so did he.
A Jewish wife with her Christian lover. And so did he.
She did very well with a wife. And so did he.
A Christian wife with a Christian lover.
And so did he.
A Christian wife with a Christian lover.
And so did he.
A Jewish wife with a Jewish lover. And so did he.

A Jewish wife with a Jewish lover. And so did he.

And so did he.

And so did he.

What is the difference between three.

What is the difference between Easter and between three.

What is the difference between Easter between three. What is the difference between three. What is the difference between three.

There are three different times in Easter and four and more.

There are four different times in Easter and three and he.

There [are] three different times in Easter and four and more. Two a week three a week five a week six a week. Six a week one a week two a week four a week.

How many days are there in it. Five if they have a wife is she is a wife if they have a wife if it is a wife who is as a wife as a wife and a life and wives and besides. As a wife. With a wife. How many halves has Easter. Fifteen if four counts as one and seventeen if seven is why they like it. Fifteen and seven makes it be that they rejoice.

With a wife if they have this with a wife.

With a wife when they have this with a wife.

With a wife with with this with a wife.

Let it be a record with a wife.

Let it be a record with this this with a wife.

They might be with a wife and with lilies of the valley in season.

They might be with a wife and no asparagus could be gathered in season and so because of their being a step son a step daughter and each with a son and daughter. With a wife and with with the asparagus as much as in plenty and the season. The season and the reason. With a wife when it is well that she does not diminish half and half and half and like it to be farther farther to and play. Might she have an engagement.

With a wife. Letting it be as frequently with a wife. She could be an elaboration of having therefore to be welcome Sally. With a wife to be with a wife and to be have to be have to be with a wife and to be as income income with a wife and Harry.

Let it be uniquely in as fishes. Let it be uniquely in as hyacinths when natural. Let it be uniquely in as if on hats they imitate the blossoms that they have in as uniquely which is well after all Abelard. Which is as uniquely principally principally James and John. Principally uniquely with the understanding that if it had leaves outside it had to be carried aside outside principally better. With a wife there's to pears. Pear blossoms finish before the later apple blossoms begin and neither make any difference altogether. This is after they can be white and yet.

STUDY NATURE

I do.
Victim.
Sales
Met
Wipe
Her
Less.
Was a disappointment
We say it.
                        Study nature.
Or
Who
Towering.
Mispronounced
Spelling.
She
Was
Astonishing
To
No
One
For
Fun

                    Study from nature.
I
Am
Pleased
Thoroughly
I
Am
Thoroughly
Pleased.
By.
It.
It is very likely.
                    They said so.
Oh.
I want.
To do.
What
Is
Later
To.
Be.
Refined.
By
Turning.
Of turning around.
                    I will wait.

DATES

                    I

Fish.
Bequeath fish.
Able to state papers.
Fish.
Bequeath fish.

                    II

Worry.

Wordly
Pies and pies.
Piles.
Weapons.
Weapons and weapons.
World renown.
World renown world renown.

III

Nitches.
Nitches pencil.
Nitches pencil plate.
Nitches vulgar.
Nitches vulgar pencils.
Nitches plate.

IV

Hopping.
Hopping a thunder.
Credit.
Creditable.

V

Spaniard.
Soiled pin.
Soda soda.
Soda soda.

VI

Wednesday.
Not a particle wader.
Aider.
Add send dishes.

VII

Poison oak poison oak.
Stumble.
Poison steer.
Poison steer humble.
Prayer.

Irene.
Between.
Conundrum.
Come.

VIII

Wet yes wet yes wet yes sprinkle. Wet yes wet yes wet yes sprinkle.

IX

Thicker than some.

X

College extension.

XI

Pass over.
Pass over.
Pass.
Pass.
Pass.
Pass.
Pass pass.

XII

Not a night sight.
Pay sombrely.
Are and n and no and pail. Are and n and no and pail. Are and n and no and pail.

SUBJECT-CASES: THE BACKGROUND OF A DETECTIVE STORY

In case of this.
A story.
Subjects and places.
In place of this.
A story.
Subjects and traces.
In face of this.
A story.
Subjects and places.
In place of this and in place of this.
A story.
Subject places.
In place of this.
A story.
When the work when the work and when the work when should he work.
In place of this and in place of this and in place of this places.
Subject.
Places.
Subjects places.
In face of this how hardly in place of this, how hardly in place of this, places, how hardly in place of this, how hardly to place in face of this, subject cases, to place in case of this, to place this subject in case of this in place of this. Subject cases in place of this.
To watch. Prepare two. Prepare to watch in that way. To watch anyway. Anyway to watch.
Lighter than in there. No lighter than in there.
Subjects and cases. In case of this.
What else can you do.
What else do you see.
What else do you see.
Leave the letters at the door and more and more very nearly there do they have noises established. Let the letters be left to me

by them very often. In this way I know this tendency.

Now exactly.

If as an objection if it is an objection if it is objected that it is due to this that they have it to do, if it is an objection that they do do this if this is an objection, this is the object of this attention. He can we think. This is in building. Now now now have a cow have a cow.

Concentrate.

If in this way preparations may be undertaken. To undertake preparations. Comparative preparations. To comparative preparations.

Four heads are his specialty but it is mouths we want mouths and noses.

Sit and sit smell and smell. Go to hell go to hell.

Action and to reaction. To serve notice as well. Deserve to notice as well. Notice it as well. To deserve to notice it as well. It serves very well. It is of service to notice it as well. It is of much service to deserve to notice it. Very much. Very well. To notice it as well. To notice it as well. To deserve to notice it as well.

If the agitation is passed. Agitated, for in the sense of because of this agitation, clearly and repressed agitation, repressed as to being agitated and very needful of the adjoining pleasure. To join in pleasure. To an addition of pleasurable agitation, to such an admission admit that admitted it is admitted it is submitted, to submit agitation, agitate for admission, to agitate to admit, to submit, to the pleasurable to the pleasure of joining in that pleasure, to join in that pleasure. To agitate to be agitated, to agitate the joining in that pleasure to the adjoining pleasure, to submit to this as an admission, to admit this to submit to this, to submit this agitation so that it is admitted that there is an addition to the adjoining pleasure, to join in this pleasure, to submit this altogether with the admission of the agitation to join in this pleasure. Altogether to join in this admission. To submit this to the joining in this pleasure altogether. Altogether to join in this adjoining pleasure, to submit to this joining in this pleasure to admit this as an agitation to join to be joined in this as an adjoining pleasure, to submit this to admit to this, to admit and to join to join in this as in an adjoining pleasure. An adjoining pleasure is admitted and it is as it is submitted to

have been the beginning of the agitation and agitating this and
joining to this and this then and for this adjoining pleasure.

Accidental work, no accidental work. No accidental work in
a parlor. For accidental work. Not for accidental work not for
accidental work in a parlor. Accidentally or is it in accidentally
earning. Calmer than that. By accident. By an accidentally earned
and by anticipating by accidentally anticipating earning interest
in more and more separated parlors admitted it is to be admitted
and then to be admitted to admit that very accidentally that very
indeed very nearly and accidentally earned and to be earned very
nearly accidentally earned and to be admitted and to be nearly in
and to be admitted and to be admittedly nearly and accidentally
admitted. Do not hesitate to brush by to brush by to brush by by
accident, and to brush accidentally too.

A considerable factor it is a considerable factor in this way,
this is a considerable factor, to share in this, it is a considerable
factor to have a share in this and once again following and in once
again following and in following and in a share of this and in
following and in once again sharing, this is a considerable factor
in this, it is a considerable factor in this to share in this. And once
again more than once a considerable share in this more than once
and a considerable factor in this, it is a considerable factor to share
in this.

Plenty of this in the place of this and in place of this plenty
of this in place of this. The fairly well seen formation to fairly
well see to fairly well to have to see fairly well, to see to it fairly
well, fairly well seen information, to fairly well see and to inform
to informally see very well to it and to plentifully see and to fairly
well see and to see plentifully and in place and in this place and
to place and to place more there, plentifully, and formally and
for that and for that to be seen fairly well seen to be fairly well
and informally more and plentifully more plentifully fairly furnished with the information additionally. To add this as information and to be authorised informally.

Just a station in justice to this station, just to state and adjust
it, just to state it in justice to state it to state it in justice to it, to
adjust it, and to do justice to it and to be adjusted for it, for it and
by advising justice for it, to advise to do justice to it, due to it,
justice due to it, to adjust more than to just advisedly obstruct it,

justice do it do and do justice to it, do and do do justice to it, to
advise to adjust it to this and to that, and to do justice to this adjustment and advisedly defer to the justice of it and to defer the
justice of it. Is it just and does the justice done to it decide the just-
ness of it and does the adjustment of it determine the judgment
to be made for it. Determined to abide by the judgment of it and
to have had justice done to it and to justify the advisedly judicious
information just given with it. Indeed with it and for it indeed for
it and by it indeed by it and with it indeed with it and for it.
Justify the judgment given of it. Indeed justify just the judgment
and the judgment was given with it. Indeed this judgment of it.
Just to justify and to judge and to judge and to advisedly justify
this judgment of it. To advisedly judge just this in the judgment
of it. To advise the justification of it. To justify it.

Antedate. This is antedated. To be antedated. This is to be
antedated. Confederate, to confederate. Is it to confederate state
that it is antedated. To confederate to state that it is antedated.
Too confederate to state that it is antedated. In this state in such
a state in such a state to compensate. It is a compensation it is in
compensation to antedate it is a compensation to antedate to antedate as a compensation. Compensate for this. To compensate and
to antedate. To confederate and to antedate. To antedate and to
compensate. Compensation and confederation. To antedate as a
compensation and as a confederation to antedate, to confederate
to antedate. To antedate is to confederate. To refute it to refute
in refutation. A refutation. To dilate upon it. To dilate upon a
refutation. To presume to antedate and the presumption is that
it is to be attenuated that to antedate is an attenuation. To anticipate and to antedate or as if in a confederation. To antedate is to
confederate. In anticipation to antedate in anticipation, to confederate to antedate in anticipation. Or as a preconception or in
indication or in anticipation or for confederation or as to or as in
presumption of an intention. To antedate in anticipation, to confederate or as a confederation. To compensate. Compensation.
To antedate in compensation. To compensate and to antedate. To
confederate and to antedate and to antedate is to confederate. And
resistance, resistance is anticipate. To anticipate compensation and
confederation. To anticipate and to antedate, to antedate and to
participate.

Understood as periodical. To be understood as periodical.
Periodically fastened. Unfastened. Take it for granted that there
is an addition, take it for granted that there is addition take it for
granted there is addition. Addition antedated. Take it for granted
that the addition is antedated. Take for granted an antedated
addition. Presently presently and presently. A perfect letter-
writer.

If not what, change in cases change in case a case of it in exchange. Exacting an exchange for it. Exactly in exchanging in
case of it. In exactly exchanging because by it, exactly changing.
In changing because of it. Because of it. In changing because of
it in exchanging for it, and then what. In exchange. Now and then
and to suit and to boot. In exchange are objects colored by water.
Ejaculation and rooms. In exchanging for in exchanging. In exchanging for an exchanging and in exchanging for changing. In
exchanging for rooms. In place of in exchanging. Exchange very
nearly to change.

Last at last how many directions are there at last. By this mail
at this sale what direction was it at the last. At least. By mail and
in detail and for sale in how many directions unasked and in what
direction. In what direction do they last. It is classed. It is to be
passed as if it were to be unasked. A direction is unasked and by
mail and at last and for sale and in the past and in detail fastened
and unfastened. In reconsideration. Let it be Saturday. In reconsideration and at last and to last. Did in a direction being intended
to be at last as a last indication, did a direction intending to at last
be unasked, did it indeed the direction at last did it indeed the
indication as at last, did it indeed as an indication and as a direction did it indeed determine it as at last and as at by mail and as at
in a sale and as at as indicated in its detail, did it as direction was
it as an indication was the direction asked or was it unasked. In as
an indication in a direction as direction and in proceeding, in
proceeding and in establishing by mail what is in the sale and
when there will be divested when it will be divested of all indication as to this detail. Let there then be reasonably a history of
habitations. In this way mail sale detail indication direction and
a history of habitation at the last may be in a way as if it were
to make. To be arousing, this to be connected and antedated by
a house and houses, by houses and homes, by homes and indica-

tions given of directions given of directions given and indications given and establishment. It is established and it is meant it is established and to prevent the direction from being asked and in a direction and on this evening and antedated as to it evening.

Ineradicable to remain, to possess and to see movements when movements are approachable approachable as if it were undoubted. May be doubted. It might be without doubt. Ineradicable to remain. What is it. In as it were intentional. And to be presentable. Bows and smiles. Organisation and in time. It is not only in its interest which is in its interests. Intact, it is to be in its own delight and night, no names of praises are mentioned. To appraise means to come to a decision as to values. Traces of unity and an exact enfeeblement. To carry minutes to an extreme. May it be said of a little minute as of a little week. Exact aggrandisement and reunion. To duplicate resonances. Enjoyable governing, and mantling in that way roses and revision. Reversion makes revision stronger. And in combination, combine mistakes with mistaken. Not to be mistaken. If any one. Not to be mistaken for any one. Dividing, division, rapidity, encroaching, to transmit and to reverse. Reversibly speaking. To maintain. Did it necessitate that others wore this. To exclude pieces. A conspiracy to exclude pieces for it. Not a piece. No not pieces and inhabitants and dwelling. Not to dwell upon it and in a manner of speaking houses.

If it were to if it were to as if it were to take steps and to as if it were to come down and to step as if it were to step down and not a crown, a dog and Putnam, if in an engagement to hold the heat in place, in place of plenty of places, in a way to say repeatedly. To withdraw and to amass, to add and to vary, to interline, to obviate and to ferry, to ferry across the weight of there there need be no vagueness as to hair. If the hair is cut, what, cut, if the air is cut, and to say it with flowers, not too rapidly and outstanding. An outstanding obligation. Please and pleases. Not creditably as a circumstance and no sales needed. The futility of a policy of irritation and many majors do. Born in this way it is to be born in this way and may there be antedated purses. Not any one mentions the name of anything. It is easy to very easy to, it is very easy to and very easily too.

It was succeeded by, it was before this, it was unnecessary to mention too many and in any case two more and so to speak it was Wednesday and in a made way. When and where are obelisks washed and arches. When in that case more than in there. As intentional as that and eyes, eyes are mentioned to be singular or more than singular. In this way readiness comes readily. Markets too and after glasses, markets are too and after that as to glasses. It can be driven here and there and with some care and in that manner care is shown and not in the same as sound. To sound and to sound, to see to it. If inclination is exhausted attentively if inclination is exhausted and attentively and if inclination is tested refuse testy, if inclination is exhausted attentively, attentively remarked, and an inclination to it. Measured to measure and fit to fit. Not a ship. Shipping so to speak reshipping and so to speak reshipping in addition. In addition to this shipping and regaining and gaining and to not surprise suddenly. Not to surprise by sudden ability and so commonplace, and so so to speak common sense and so so to speak maximum and so to speak also so to speak furnish. To furnish this. To furnish this and to very nearly and very fairly, is juxtaposition the same as in case of maneuver. Maneuver is a word and a paragraph and a sentence, in a sentence, and in a paragraph a word has this connection. To be connected with antedating organs for this, canadians can carve wood for purposes of deception. This makes a street not noticeable as indeed two can be more often seen than one. One has no separation there as an allowance and no corals. Corals are again stylish. Bow to them. In this way anything can seem to be read. Not so very funny. It is not so very funny, it is not as it might be said of it not actually famous. Can antedating be so nearly and so nearly has it in the sense of nicely, has it been very near. Blue in green and white in blue green in glass and all seen through the medium of energy and precision. Action and reaction being equal and opposite when all is said exactly what is it that has been referred to. References. Begin now. As if to mount in a way from one to another. All smile.

Even and calculable, incalculable. Even and and incalculable, evenly and incalculably culpably, and inculpably, and even and uneven and calculable. Was there a background and was there a ground for deers. Incalculably around and around. Around yes and incalculable yes and inculpated yes and calculable. Calculable yes and inculpated yes and around yes and altogether found altogether yes. Inculpated yes and calculably yes calculable yes and inculpated yes. Yes a ground, yes a ground for mails yes, antedated and referred to and an instance of reaction. Action and reaction being equal a restraint is unequal. Unequal to this. In calculable and antedated and ministrations, ministered to and administered for and mentioned as a door. Best not say yes and no and do as you are told. In that as neglected, expected and directed, in that as directed expected and neglected, in that as directed in that as neglected, in constructions profoundly modified by unexpectedly balancing, balance to rest. Is it antedated if it was to be said so. Act quickly and measure them for clothes. Does it seem as if it were to be the same to be wealthy and thin. Thin it as a hem, a hem does not need wishing. In just such a way does willingness make it uppermost. Uppermost eradicates explanation and impediment. It is uppermost. In this settled distinction all can really share. And it will do.

Young among. If that is said so. Mount and amount. If that is said so. If that is so and the amount and if the amount and young among and if the amount and it is said to be so, if among the young it is said to be so if the amount is said to be so, if the amount is said to be so among the young, among a number there are if it is said so, a number among the young, and the amount and the amount might mount, it is said to be so. Among the young it is said to be so. The amount is said to be so. It is said that might mount to this amount. It is said to be so. It is said to be so and so. It amounts to that. It amounts to this that it is said to be so.

Added to it no not added to it or if indeed as in speaking additionally and abominably, as if additionally speaking and an article if it is as indicated, if an article what as it is to be chosen. If in reading, reading and writing as it may be speaking reading and writing if it as it may be it may be as it is to be sent. Sent away. It is not intended that it is to be sent in this way. And then, and if then and when, when if there is to be more and some more some do more, more and more, some do, more and more, if as follows, if as it follows, by this means and really rise, not too exactly placated as if no settled masons sit. Masonry settles in this instance and collapses too. Two and two make parlors. Parlors are as if started.

Mention parlors. Parlors are none none are in parlors, parlors are known and unknown and peculiar. Peculiarly to satisfy to satisfy a peculiarity. Can be seen can be seen in collaboration it can be seen to have been done in collaboration, collaboration and collusion, collusion and carefulness and carefulness and harmony and harmony and distance and distance and determination and determination and selections and selections and elaboration and elaboration and initiation and initiation and able to be seen it is to be seen that collaboration that there is collaboration that in collusion that there has been collusion that distance that as to distance that every indication that there is every indication that no pleasure is perceived. To perceive a perception, in a way perception is more as money is, if it is as it is does union make for strength and does it does it unify action. All to go and all to stay all to stay and all to go and all to say so, all say all are to stay and all do say so. All are to go. If there are changes, if there are to be changes if there are to be exchange of ounces, ounces have meant that and this there and here. Appear to hear, and to appear to hear. Here. Ounces and pounds and miles and miles and miles and ounces and miles and pounds and pounds and ounces and miles. In a way peculiarly. And parlors are in that way announcements.

It especially precluded violence why especially preclude violence why was violence especially to be precluded why is violence to be especially precluded. Naturally not naturally violence is naturally not especially precluded and systematically reversed, the reverse of systematically especially to preclude violence. Esther and aim and in and aid, esteem it an aid, to esteem it to be an aid and to estimate it as an aim and as an aid. Net result, an effort as in consideration. Considerably antagonised. Was it sixty and if sixty was it fifty for sixty. Sixty for fifty makes not more than three thousand. Fifteen for three thousand makes less than or more than two hundred and for four, to be surprised by and at Jane and Julia and a likely looking colored girl. To apply for it to apply for it as if an application suddenly was as related. Related to what, to what was it to be related, it was as it was to be related it was related to this and related to that and antedated as in commencing and as to antedating, as to antedating and as to in commencing to announce as managerial that which holds more and more. It holds more and more. And if it holds more and more. And if as it holds more and more, if as it is holding this much and more than this, if in this way as it is beheld, it is not in this way to be fancied, fancying nests this, nest and nest, and to see and to that search, saturday and solemnly, when is it attributable to an edge to money, to an agglomeration as if not inhabited. To have a history and not to deny extracts as extraordinarily and houses as seen to be scattered and in many cases not clearly separated, so estimated as an estimation, as indeed as if it has to be thoughtfully fed. Fairly well sawed as if it were to be fairly well noised, noised about, about and nearly for this as an integral may it be said integrally may it be claimed and in the special and in the especial solidity concerning solidity there is no repetition. To be sold. Further. Farther and farther. In this way farther and no farther and laterally as it may be. It may be. As it is fair to state as it is fairly an interstate, to understate, shouting makes for silence. When and when and when there. When there. When there is more than there is for more than there is. There is more than there is for this and for more than for this and before this is to be over-stated. In any pleasure pleasurably speaking in any antedating and in antedating making more than samples, making more than their samples securely and securing and as to security, for security.

The history and beaming, the first article antedating making more than examples. The history and this as in a measure terminating and conforming to the agitating blandishment as inaugurated. The inauguration is as it is never to be presently presented, authoritatively. In this measure in a way it was to be all rejoined. Rejoin articles and regions. They spent their past time as pastime. As pastime some gratitude differs from others. In there in the meantime how are they all to say how do you do how glad we all are to see you and we are not at all not prepared to see all of you. Mellow and mallow very mellow, and mallow as it is known to taste. A considerable instance of a foreground. In the foreground there usually are to be found grass and colors colors as if it were as if they were to be worn. Worn can be used in the sense of to be worn out and to be worn as about. Out and about and ante-dating and bowing, bowing to this as a suggestion and also to that and moreover as to discretion, indicated as discretionary and

illustration. Illustrated not angularly not angrily nor even for-
biddingly, not forbidden nor to be left over and as addressed addressed to them. In this way mistakes occur and delicacy varies
with and at variance, and at variance and to say so, to say so and
next to and nearly there. Next to and nearly there and registered
as if lingering. Linger longer Lucy.

A guide to guide and with a guide. For guidance, for their
guidance and by their guiding and with and all and to their and
you and man and riddance, to be as it is to be to be not as to convenience and purposes. The purposes are there, two and more
articles and to and for buildings, inhabited buildings differ from
uninhabited buildings in certain respects. Respect and respected
to respect, and to respect, and as expected and as it is to be expected it is to be respected and it is to be expected. It is to be expected and as it is to be respected it is to be respected as it is to
be expected. It is to be expected. It is expected. And in that and to
wait and to wait and in that and and to wait. Weight, and to wait
and in that and and to wait. And to wait. Not to be as to have it
to say not to be permanently and permanently. Not to be permanently not to say so not to say so and permanently and beyond
thirds. One third and their thirds. Their thirds. Beyond thirds
and their thirds. Permanently and beyond thirds, not permanently
and beyond thirds.

Not a guess and guessing, not to guess not to be guessing,
guess and guess and guess again, not a good guess. To guess. Fortune and as comfortably, this night is as important as any other
night and as comfortable fortunately. Fortunately as fortunately,
as fortunate it was fortunate, it was very fortunate, fortunately.
This night was as important as any other night fortunately. Fortune and a fortune, and for a fortune and fortunately. It was very
fortunate. Parlor, to be as if it were more than it might be if a
little quickly, to be quietly and quickly to be as if it might still
have to be as quickly as it might still more than and not more than
that and equally and equably, equably speaking as if unequally
preferred. Preferences, accepted as parlors as parlors are private.
Privately. Private not used as uneasiness, uneasily felt, to be more
than as if it mattered. Mattered too much, it mattered too much
and very nearly, not as if to be closeted, closeted connects again.

Closet to connect again and to closet or a closet, to further it as an estimate. To and to name to as a to countenance, and to be as if to and as a price, inquire, if a parlor really, and really, and there, to be, as well, let us as well, not to let, not to be let, not to let it be, not and narrow and to carry not to carry not to carry it away. Any day.

Monsieur Mansard and the architect of Versailles. Is Monsieur Mansard contemptible or not. The architecture of Versailles do I lie do I lie. The architecture of Versailles, to build it high to build it high. The architecture of Versailles. By and by by and by. Not to express address, egress, Negress Negress. Negress egress, address express, humbly apologise. And how to how to, and how to how to. Humbly indeed, apologies. Requesting the presidents to urge upon their governments and the governments of certain nations the immediate necessity of elaborating and restoring the expression of thanks verbally and moreover educating the administration of planning. To plan to. In this way each of them comes away. And now then. What do they seed broadcast, they seed broadcast the respect for colored glass. White and rose-color preferably. When opaque white and blue. Red white and blue all out but you. In season in the season in this season and an outburst, in season and in the season and in this season. Chances many chances, and some chances some chances are taken and other chances are not taken. Antedate and a plate, and to placate and to antedate. Other chances which are not taken are those of which being reminded it can be recognised it would not have been judicious to attempt the undertaking. A great many people reason justly. And not very trenchantly. To advise and to advise, it is advisable to entangle to disentangle, to disentangle one arbitrary decision after another. Another and another. The coral remains the same. Just now it is an attraction. To attract and to attract. To attract to the attraction without indication without any indication of the nature of the attraction. Be beset. To be so beset. To be so beset and so beset. Finally.

Not poppies for poppies to poppies as poppies, turns to poppies, pansies turn into poppies, as poppies, to poppies for poppies in poppies into poppies, and so as to turn and so as to return, it was returned and the following was closed inclosed, closed in, and as to a lot of it, it was so to say the group to be seen and heard, and as to reading and as to illiterate if it sprang away, if it sprang and sprang in that sense sprang, a few months suffice and twice, it was to be definitely dissolved and so to obtain an interest as interest and in their interest. It is intended to interest to be of interest and to introduce the approach to that as a parlor. When they arrive and they examine they observe the depth the length and the breadth and the pleasures of purchase, then in order not to compare, they come and declare what can be declared ostentatiously, what can be declared to be in order. Everything in order, in that order in order that there is no value. There is no value in our having been right. Alright. To ground a ground and on the ground, to be as if it were to be found here and there. To be defended, if it means, no, no, and if it means yes and no, and if it means no not at all and if it means in order to excuse. Excuses made, and to be as if to be made. Excuses made, to have to have excuses made. To excuse the recognition of and the interest in and the description of and the delight in and the request for and the determination to and the denial of and the attribution to and the defence of and the interruption for and the disappearance of and the declaration with, and the combination with and the distribution of and the negligence for and the abstention from. Why abstention and smell, very well why smell and smelling and very willing and very much sought for. Can a declaration that a door as a door, and as in question, as in a question, this as in question, to question this. To miss and to miss. Amiss and amiss. Not too much to-day. Any day. For a day. To call for a day. To call for a day. Joiner, a joiner was once a carpenter. A carpenter was once a carpenter and to carpet is to cover. To cover as a cover. A cover is not embroidery. And so women appear and disappear readily. Favor, and as to flavor, to know very well that they ate very well.

Plentifully it may plentifully pay. They can absolutely say, as to display, to display and absolutely say, plentifully pay, it may pay, as to display, as to plentifully pay, as to absolutely say, to say to pay to display, for pay, to say, as display, to plentifully display, to absolutely say, to adequately pay. As to a parlor, alright as to a parlor, for a parlor, for the parlor, to adequately attend to the preparation and transportation and singing, transport as it were, from port to port from door to door from the door, away from the door. In so much as it is plainer, in so very much as it is so very much plainer, as if in a history as historically known, to be known and a tone, to be thrown and as it shone, to loan as to a loan, as to lean, as to lend, as to lend as to advise as to advise as to be seen as it is to be seen and to be as if in relation to a parlor. How can it be said to have been so. And so. And so. To see, as if to say it severely. Severity if described is as an index to a silver set. Silver set of course. Of course and restlessness and easily, very easily as a settlement. A settlement means an exchange. An exchange of this for this, and exchange for this of this. Of and for because and why, when and shall and it and all, all and more and asked and ended and defended. In a way to be defended. Necessarily closed. Admirably adhered to, indefatigably circumstanced. And a reference to it as antedated. To be restated. Restate, in this way north and south and east and west are directions. In this way north and south and east and west each one is in that direction. Directly it was furnished it was furnished for them. A name is always astonishing.

Articles, are to, close to, articles as protests may, to be pronounced to be protesting or merely said to be providentially, providentially common rose or odors. Proving it as it may come to be no bother, no bother if at all. In this way before and also afterwards, afterwards as if in this not being in any way different contemplation authorises authority others as in their authenticity, remind to remind, reminding and reminding it considered as protesting and as in no way catalogued, catalogued uniquely, universally tinged, tinged with this and that and more nearly reluctant. Unions and safety and firstly and intermittently and if there is a monopoly, monopoly and not cowardice, in wishes in organised wishes, to wish to wish and formerly, formerly it was very well understood, formally to be personally and not in any way responsible. Can it be said to be in this way not proven but established that not even indications make it plentiful in the sense of having been adapted to change and conditions, adapted to change and conditions, in this way it is very well known that establishments are not at all are not all found at all found and in this way, days and ways, understand it to be said, they know colors to be another subject and more exactly.

Attach to it to attach to it, as attached, and when it is attached, and lessening, to lessen, as it lessened, lessened and to be avoided, as to avoid, avoiding evidently and not to be planned and carried there. To carry as an extra, extraordinarily and just as soon, just as soon too. If it is to be absently and urgently replenished and not undertaken not to be undertaken it is not to be undertaken, not to collect parlors in parlors. Parlors and in a pet in anger and not angry and plentifully papered. It is no longer necessary to use paper. Antedated and so forth. In repeating and four followed when they were sitting there. Where. No one knows as certainly as formerly. Informally has been mentioned and so has pursuit, pursuit and in pursuit and in pursuance, in this way in pursuance of their intention. Can it be ascertained how incompletely and repeatedly and heatedly a parlor contains the elements of enjoyment. To enjoy and relish to relish and refashion to refashion and entertain, to entertain and to vindicate, to vindicate and to indicate and to indicate. As indicated. It was as indicated. To be indicated. So many thousands have thousands. So many thousands have so many thousands. And as thousands. And as thousands are to be considered indeed to be as considered as many thousands are to be as many thousands and as considered and as many thousands. As many thousands have as many thousands. Many thousands have many thousands as many thousands. To be considered to have. Have to be considered to have and to have and to have to be considered and to have to as as to have indeed to have. Have. Have to have and to be considered to have. This is the best yet and matters in hand and the matter in hand and to the matter in hand is to be added intensity and reiteration. Reiteration is said to have been said for them. Parlors and parlors and for their parlors and in their parlors and to the parlor, to the parlor into the parlor for the parlor and in fact for it and in fact more than a fact. A fact is a fact. It is a fact, and facing and replacing, in replacing, to replace, to replace here and there, and so much. In so much and so quoted and as quoted and so forth and for the most of it, for almost all of it and so and in that way not investigated. As to investigating reasonably preparing, preparing to do so. Do so and do so and to do so and as it were to be as if it were to have contributed and furthermore not more than as to stating. To state. Behind them to state, behind them and not to wait, behind them and more frequently and as it was very frequently they were merely as to have it attributed. Attributed to all of it and so satisfactorily as stated. No one heard them, and no one is to understand distinctness. More of them and in a way more and more. More and more and more was said to be and all of it and instead, finally to do so and finally do so.

In that little while for a while and for a while to while away, for a little while and for a while for that while and to while away and for that and for a while and for that while and to cause it to and because of it, for a little while and for that while and for that while. A while. In a little while, for that little while or for that little and a while for that little while and for that little while. To cause it, for example to cause and to close and to be close and to be closely and for a while and too closely to as one may have said for a while and indeed for that while, formerly a while, formerly for a while and as one may have it said to have it said in a way said to have had it to have in that way had it as if once in a while as if once in every little while, once and once in a while, as if once every once in a while and as to have it and as to as to have and as to have had it once in a while once in once in a while and as if too closely to be close to be close to it once in a while every once in a while, and as one while and as for one while and for one while for a while.

Every now and then and when, when every now and then and where, where have they heard it. Who told them to who told them and who told them to and when and where every now and then. To startle as if to start and when to separate, to separate and to sort and to assort, no one knows how clearly it shows how very clearly it shows and where it shows and to expose it and to reconsider it and afterwards to expose it weigh it and the weight of it for the weight of it and by its weight by the weight of it, what is its weight. When is it important and why do advantages accrue. To accrue and advantages to accrue need to have it reestablished. To reestablish is separately useful and to be used what is to be used and why do they mean to say yes and yes.

Yes and yes, guess, press, address an address as address, address can be useful more than a meaning or many folds, fold and folding to follow, if the praise of it if in praise if it is in praise of it, to praise it, and praise in that way very presently and to present it as a present or as present. It is present, and better pleased than before. Before and more, more than that before, more of it than before, more than that of it and they say it changes, as change, as to change for them to change and to exchange, exchange parlors for parlors. To exchange and to be in a parlor and to change from being in that parlor to being in another parlor, in this sense to change a parlor and to exchange to feel funnily, very funnily to feel that there is more advantage than there was than there would have been than they would have had.

Instead of dwelling upon it, instead of selling instead of planning not to introduce more than they meant to have considered, it is very well to be considered in that way. To be considerably in their way, to have it considered and to be ready to consider it and commenting and as for consideration can it have the same ceremonial certainty for this and for that and considerably felt as if it were in consideration for all of this. And this as if to please and this and please, moderately to venture, at a venture and in moderation and in moderation and to settle quickly into a place that has this particular satisfactory quality. Quality and equality, equality and irritation, irritation and installation to install everything. Everything and if as wishes if they wish, to wish and to present wishes presently. And to furnish it as well and not leave it there, then too and nearly as if it had been an offer. It was offered to them. If inappreciably there is a difference as to delivery, and notably not at that time it was not as an interruption but not in any way to please themselves. So thirdly it can be as it was to be if it had had to be antedated and in this as it is and was not to be shown. Not at all shown to them and not found there not to be shown to them and not further to be shown then to them.

Indicated vindicated, it was and it was as it was, it was as it was, and indicated to be indicated, to be vindicated, to be vindicated to be indicated as usual, usually, usually as to choose, usually to choose, to choose and organised when and why and organised,

if in outline, to outline to more as if it were an inclination, incline
to it, able to be and to rebound to their credit. To and from and
from there and to them, and moreover suitable suited to this as
situated and not partly, not partly and situated and partly and
partly this. Partly this and very and when can when did it where
did it and for the time and in time and may it be traced. It was
traced literally traced, traced as to invitation not an invitation.
Not and not and not in choice, not a choice, not chosen not to
just chose, chose and to have as chosen, not to have as not and as
it was chosen, and those, to be counted one to count and account,
one and two and to count and as to a count, as to a count, cups
and saucers and put it away. Close, close to it, close and not to
close, fully state what, fully state what is what. To fully state and
to fully compare, compare and compare, in this way all of it is
passed in a review, as in a review, as in a pretence to oranges.
Pretended to, they pretended to. Silly and not silly not to nor
evenly not to, not to show, not to be shown to be accurately defined. What is a definition, it is a definition, definitely and more
sheltered than ever. If it is exactly stated that to be drawn blinds
can be drawn, doors can be made, windows can be entitled bay
windows and all parts of a parlor are copied by them and not at
all. May they have it settled, may it be is it able to be and in
question, is it in question. To question, a question, come again
soon. More of a question. Come again soon, to be questioned, and
come again soon, with them and by themselves, come again very
soon and come again and as to very nearly very nearly to be
coming out and going in there, very nearly to be going in and
very nearly going in there. Not as it would have been added,
added to.

Protected and partly protected after six months of protection
after being with an object, helped, protected, helped and protected, protracted help for themselves and either or for this, in
the exchange of helping themselves, protecting themselves and
adhering to, adhering as if as it were protected by and very near
by, very nearly by means of not nearly as newly as before, sent
to them without mentioning the permission, permitting it, as a
permit and if it can be helped, can it be helped. Partly and partly
this, settled for them it was settled for them partly for this they

parted it and in question it was in question. By nearly all of it
having had and in not vacating as if it were valued, valuable as
it can be. To be as valuable as it can be. Sizes, as to their seeing to
it, seeing to it as if it were traced to them, traced to them as if it
were inclined to be doubted. May be they do but do they have
doubts about it. May be they do. In doubt, when there is a doubt,
can they be in doubt, and rectify, rectify antedating, antedating
yesterday. In a day more than that in that and to defer to that.
Deferred and referred and to refer, as to reference to it, as to a
reference to it, referring and delighted to refer, to refer more than
to refer to it more than it was to be expected that they would need
it to refer to. Obliged to stand still. Standing more than that and
standing more than that. To change for it in exchange for it. Not
violently as exactly for that situation. Situated where.

They as well very very well, and as well, largely readily and
if they might as well tell. Collectedly, as to collectedly, very
nearly to be as to selections, and in order to be for their sake.
Connectedly tracing, a trace can be so much for their interest in
their interest. Afterwards and known, known to be afterwards
and settled known to be further and it does matter in that way
as if returning in returning that. Much of it fairly and nearly,
fairly well, and afterwards as if in connection with and fairly
well managed and as to an understanding, no not depreciated,
appreciated and fairly well and connectedly speaking, connectedly speaking and they thank you. To and to them and so
much for the use of a parlor. In return, in in them, in the return
and none of this is not for much of it and when much of it, and
when can it be correct. To correct, and four four are more than
if they call out the same as they have said that they did. Come
faster than that. Have to have it come to have to have it come so
many times, time and time again.

As stated or as stated. Finders keepers, and kept as found,
found that it was kept and to be kept, found as to be kept. Finding or to be finding it, and to be finding it and to be keeping it,
or to be keeping it and to be keeping it. If they mind, do they
mind, do they mind and if they mind, if they mind, if they mind
and they do find, if they find if they mind, find and mind or mind
or find. Find or mind. Find or find or find. So indeed so indeed a

parlor settles that. So indeed and so indeed and so indeed and a parlor settles that and so indeed a parlor and so indeed a parlor settles that. A parlor. Indeed, and as to a parlor. Indeed as to the parlor. A parlor settled that.

Makes music. He was in love with his wife. He makes music. He was in love with his wife. A long gay book. Oh see. Thieves see see to see. See to see, season this season for only this season, in season, for a reason, for this reason, he was in love with his wife and see to see, for this reason, in season, and in season, see to see and to see, unrelated, tell it to them, related, tell it to them to be related to tell it to them, to relate it that is if to tell it to them, to tell it, relate it, tell it to them. Practically well, very well, practically, and practically, so that is thereby when it is obligingly feeling for it. To feel for it and so by themselves and so to say by themselves, so in a capacity, capes and capes, come for this, see to see, and come for this, come and come, and come for this, come for this and to come for this, so near that it may be said as if it were so nearly as stamps, not stamping but just and especially so nearly retained. To retain means permission to find it more than convenient. Conveniently is that word and absurd. To be added and in addition. A long gay book. To stay. A long gay book. A day. In a day. To-day. To stay. After six months and after six months. To introduce them in a parlor. A long gay book, I took. You took, the long gay book. Along. Thank you very much.

Usually one, unusually two, unusual too, usually too, use one, and if too, use one, and if one, used to use one, and if two, not any use to use two, and if two, there were two, and they used to use two. They used to they used to use two, they had no use for those two, they had not used the two, they did not use two, they did not they never used to. They can see them as they fall, they can see them as if at all as if they were at all there. They can use them as they do they can use them as they used to, they can use them as they do, they do not use them at all, they have no use for them at all, they were there as if they were used to it too. They never used to they always used to they were used to they were never of any use to they did not care to and the circumstances, can it be useful in that way, in the way. Two thirds too, two and two thirds to two and two thirds and to depreciate the

difficulties and incidentally prosper. Prosperity clauses, incidentally and not at all and difficulties and definitely and praise-
worthy and have they happened to incidentally, it happens that
definitely it is antedated. Too in a memorandum, to and two
again. Again, men and mention, again women and two, too and
two, to a seat, and the other way too and in that other way to
and to that farther there, come again here. So that as in so that in,
in and by that, buy that, buy that, come to be and as to a parlor.
This makes it in the way on the way by the way.

Indicated and also ransacked and so much as to all of it as
precarious, as to unlimited and in no need of parcels. Parcels in
place of sights, in sight, to be flattered, and to be flattered so that
there is more and their name, so they name the direction for the
parlor. It is undeniable that in this direction it is as reliable that
coming to meet all of them coming and if in a parlor there is
more than recently was flattering. To be flattering too. All tie
they all tie, and a variety, in their variety as to a very seldom and
related, as to relating, relating this to a difference from all of the
same all the same and not relating and not so nervous, not so
nervous nearly, nearly this as they say. Later they came they
came later. Economical and there, here and there and a slip, a
slip of the central baggage as baggage and what did they manage,
they managed it as well as ever. Hardly ever. Readily, going
back to that. Under the circumstances. In the large building they
already had they had already they had it ready, as to the large
building it was already it was as ready it was to be ready they
were to be ready, readily, to change to that, readily, in change
for that, readily and to exchange to change more than that and
to be attached to readily attached to be readily attached to be
more than that as if in attaching, that to the space ready for it.
And so forth. And so for it. So for it and so to see so. Up and down
steadily as if when a knighthood is in flower. I effect an exchange,
in effect. Was and expose, was expose, and to show, and to show
and settle as if so carefully attending, in tendency, able shall it
spend and too more. Consenting. A parlor for consent. And detri-
ment. If not having advanced and as across it, to plan an opposition
to this and more so as standing. It was as standing in the relation of
here and of here. Hear. Shall they speak of it. To it and more than

was accounted for to be considerable. Considerably too. And so if there can have been all of it to announce and stating and so much more as if a parlor has in it what. What was it. Commenced allowing as if to manage as it was. It was. So near. So much can the rest not actually. Actually as to that. Thank you and come again. And in speaking.

CHAPTER II.

Exploration.
The party prepares to depart and starts to leave having first put everything in order as a preface. They and their companions install themselves and look over everything. This once one, and at once over and in addition all the material of which they can be careful is carefully placed in the safest place. Alternately they are carefully looked over and arranged and not replaced. It is preferable even if there is not much space not to put anything where it can not be easily found. With this in view everything is accomplished and no one is mistaken. Mistaken for something unexpectedly, unexpectedly to mistake, to misstate to make a mistake. In the meanwhile they note that everything is in order and they verify their collections immediately. Immediately entertain. And so forth. To entertain and so forth and ultimately finish, finish which is in a way taken for granted. In the beginning not, not to and to and to go and at hand everything was at hand. In plenty of time. And as preparation. And valuable. And for divisions and at most, all most, almost, congratulate, prepare and all about it. Practicably, every one practically, as practicable and as practicable. And so forth. Whether, and whether to go. Or whether to go. Or whether to go. And as to it. Indeed stretches as to it and so have they had hold of the half of all of it. In the meantime what is the floor for. For that. And all three. All three, all of them and all of them allowing allowing for it. To show. All there for three for three all there. All there for three, for three and four all there for three and for three and four and all there, for three and for four. Therefor they were there.
Settle to a second and as secondly, settle to a second and three, four, and not as undertaken finally. They met and to try indeed

and to untie and to have energetically all of it as in the circumstances they do need to. They do not need to. Indeed not to have it as nearly as it can be left, left to them altogether left to them. Windows are nearly round. If in plenty of time, have it as in leading them there. And almost all and why, not so very much too much and so and there and so. As parting any way. In there as at all and they have met and come as long as they are there. Not provided, and as for the rest, not arranged and as for the rest, not at all to rest, not more than the rest and they have not only agreed but they have been thoroughly and formerly and farther behind. In no case was there any right to provide and provided they needed the road a road connecting in connection. So easily can in between, so easily can there be that and all of it conspicuously directed. In that direction. They met with orderly and dutiful appearance and delivery. And all that can be further attended to is further attended to. A plan and all of it so arranged that in spite of inconveniences no disturbances can occur. Could they go away. Having come have they any interest in what is happening all of it makes an end to an itinerary and all of it shows that nevertheless they recommence. In a way they do. Stretches and so and stretches and so. So and so very readily. To begin as has been practically particularly tolerably acquired. And so forth. Now not as an exhibition but more so than cemented. And after all two years are plentifully arranged as to bridges. If three bridges are said to be so, and is it fairly clear. Weather and they say so. So much reminds them and antedating and once more and parlors and twice more and more and come more and more often and come more often and to come more often. Or to come more often. In all of that and when a part of that and by having that parted parted in two, two and partly four for this they said they were practically shining. When all of it makes it able to be traced, trace it anyway, anyway there is a trace of it and they will originally follow as followed. No one must disagree not enough if all of them agree. They agree. Alright. They agree. Agreeable.

In sight and by sight, and insight in sight and by sight. They knew them by sight. They kept them in sight. To keep it as quiet as it is it has been necessary to sit down to get up and to walk around. By sight, they can tell it at sight. Unsuitable in every

way they say. To suit them in this way. Next to it nothing is
nearly offered. In offering as an offering. Offering for them. They
have to balance it as they can. So next to that and so next to that.
It is so and next to that. And next to it. In a way to resume and the
preparation is, measurements for them measurements by them. In
a measure, they can as a measure, they will as they measure, they
have to measure, and as they can be advantageously so soon, ready
as soon, they can be ready very soon. By any perplexity, fully and
as for instance it may be, and may be that. Quarrels may be conducted they conduct them to their seat. Beginning again when.
And beginning again. To be beginning, fancy, as to a change in
any instance. In this instance. Not repeatedly. Conducting not
repeatedly. Beginning again and when. For instance. In this case.
As intended and in this case and more intentional. Not more so
intentionally. No circumstances warrant the use of all of it and
so many say so and very nearly all of it is mentioned systematically
and in no way has there been there and there and there were there
then there and there. They and their intention. Not more than
helping. So many have it as they may say attested.

They will attend to that. Intend to and nervously too and adjoining. When it is joined so that there is no reason for felt and
it is infelicitous, there is an absolute standard. In their fashion. A
background and leisurely approached by them in the meantime.
Not mentioned as care, to care, by their care, in their care, as care,
come carefully and see farther and never interfere. To interfere
and to prepare and to endow and to share it with them. As in
speaking. Hearsay. By hearsay. As in speaking and by hearsay. In
speaking and by hearsay. Carefully to see farther and to accept-
ably organise. Organise a victory.

Planned as to use. In next to nothing and of course. Shall they
reduce it day by day. Shall they, do they will they pay. As to in
general. They do not care about generals or anything. In general.
They do not care about the general or anything. Or in general. As
a general. Or in general. Generally. They do not care about a
general or anything. They do not care about a general or about
anything. They do not care about generals or about anything. Not
in general. The reason for this and this is a reason and their reason
and for that reason. Reasonably. Reasonably speaking to address as

their address. Their address is this. For all of them and not particularly, for all of them and particularly, particularly for all of them. It is particularly for all of them. This is particularly for all of them. They and before, before or, and before or before. Do they do do they do, they do do, how do they do, how do they do it, do they do it as they do it and is it done. It is done. As it is done. A parlor. In the meantime. From it, away from it, not away from it, in it, and in it, and in it. And so they were there and they can very nearly estimate have as an estimate, decide to estimate, remember an estimation, in their estimation, to seem, having had in no and at no time and as a share and as their share there. So nearly have they had an understanding and a division and for this and their account on their account and as an indulgence to indulge themselves very nearly here. Here and there and to all and they have to be met as they come and they are to come, come here. Seeing to it makes of it, seeing to it as it is seen to and to be seen, never decide, they decide and tried they tried and have it as if they had it. They had it and for it when was there when did they intend, when have they any avoidance of a feeling of inquietude. Correct and correct, as correct. It is as correct as it is. Corrected and corrected. To be corrected as it is corrected. It is to be either corrected or entirely corrected. Have you finished with it. Or have they had it finished for them. As it is finished it is to be nearly finally and as in preparation. A preparation for in preparation for, their preparation, they have prepared it and they may do they prepare and may they repair this. If there is any attention, attending and in offering. They offer what they have offered and it has been offered to them.

In plenty of time, there is plenty of time and as there is plenty of time and as they are in plenty of time, there are plenty of occasions and indeed yes. They have seen no reason to hurry. In a hurry, they have not meant to be in a hurry. Hurry. As to this and as to the difference, there is a difference, there is this difference there is no difference, indifference and in no way not in their way, any way not as a way. To weigh, they know, to weigh they know, underweigh they know, to proceed, they know, underweight they know, to concede they know, to have it and they know and they know that they have to have it.

Leaving it at night, as it is right, leaving it as it is right, very right, they are right, they may and they may, as it has been their habit they may and they might have as they may have. May and may, might and they might. If they might. Measurements of them as is necessary when an expedition has returned. Have they returned. If they will be neither here nor there. Here nor there. Will be. If they and if they and they and so much it is as they and they and not at all as they. Remember their claim to it and that they are very willing to be as if it were and so them. Very well and very well. The sixth in the series.

Imagine comfort imagine the comfort of it, imagine and the comfort of it, imagine it and the comfort of it, imagine it for the comfort of it, to imagine it and to imagine the comfort of it and to imagine the comfort in it, imaginable the comfort as comfort and imaginable as in the comfort the comfort there is in it. Unimaginable that there is comfort in it and the comfort of it and in their and at once and so at once and in their and at their suggesttion and in their and for them and in their reception of it. To extend, to extend, to blend, to extend to extend, and to send to send and to send, as if to send as if to extend, as if to extend. Prepare, kindly prepare the parlor. The parlor is prepared. Kindly antedate it, it is antedated, kindly attend to it, it is attended to, they are so kind, they know that kind, they are that kind, they are so kind. Will they be so kind, will they be as kind, are they more than kind.

Incidents as they might close up and go away. Incidents and wonderful wood and incidents and wonderfully and incidents and incidentally and for instance. As an instance they their insistence, they may, formerly, as formerly, they may have, fundamentally, as they may have had, intermediate, and in the meantime, as they may have had to do. As they may have had to to do. As they may formerly have had it to do, and as they may have it to do immediately as they may have an immediate necessity to determine not to do it. As they may have come to some decision and as in deciding they may have closed up at once and gone away for the holiday. Not indeed carpeting, as carpeting it is laid on the floor. Actually carpets, as actually carpets, no one needs this. They have carpets actually laid on the floor. In this way around and around.

At once if at once, if they are there at once, it will happen at once, it will be happening at once, all at once, it will all be happening at once and at once, at once, can they at once, can they and at once, at once, as at once. All at once and can they be there at once. Can they all be there and at once. Have it at once and at once. They have it at once, they have had to have it at once. And at once. They and with their and with them they and for them with them with their, whether, whether they were there were they there and whether they were there at once. Whether they were there at once. As they, were they, as they were, were they there, whether they were whether they were there, whether they were there whether they were there once, whether they were once there, whether they were there at once, when they were there, they were there at once, as they were there they were there once, they were there at once, as they were there, and as they were there at once, more than once, as they were there once, as they were there more than once, and at once they were there, after two years two days, as soon as they were there, they were there as soon as they were to be there. As they were there they were there soon, they were there as soon as they were to be there, at once, as soon, at once and as soon, as soon and as soon as they were to be there.

LAST PART

If they do not move if they are sensitive if they are sensitive if they do not move, going, as going, if they are sensitive and as it can have been illustrated, if they do not move, going and as it can be illustrated, as it can be illustrated. If they are sensitive.

As it can be illustrated if they do not move as it can be illustrated. Come together, as they can be illustrated and as they come together and as they can be illustrated. The illustration of it as an illustration of it, and illustrate, to illustrate, as illustrated. As illustrated, for this illustration and as more illustration of it. For the illustration, as an illustration, for illustration, as it is illustrated. As it is illustrated it is fairly well illustrated and as an illustration it is considered a good illustration. Action and in action, they are satisfied as they have to have it as they are to have it. No more than

that any way. In any way. As there is more than that in a way. In
a way as in case of it, more in case of it than before and the finishing touches. The finish may make it shine, a bottle of wine to make
it shine and two little niggers to squeeze her. Finishing touches as
to the best way of establishing it as at present. Presentable and
presented. For the permanent use of joining. As many as that.

Fairly hilly, they should not have and as it was fairly hilly,
they should have and fairly hilly. As fairly hilly as fairly hilly and
as they should have. Meanwhile in the meanwhile and not at that
time and particularly, as they particularly as they very particularly and as it is fairly hilly, in the meantime their establishment
to establish entertain and rest. The rest as for the rest in the meantime as the establishing and as established in the meantime and no
reason, for no reason and because of the reasonable request, request them to, to request it of them and as requested. It was as
requested. A request, they request, as to that request, when they
need to go there and not at all as it is not only not requested but
not even investigated. Do they establish and as an evidence as the
evidence as to the evidence and for it as evidence and evidently
more than ever and evidently more than ever as it is evident. It
is more evident than ever. Not than ever. In the meanwhile in the
meantime as in the meantime there is established definitely established and not requested and not evidently not very evidently and
as evidence and in evidence and for evidence as to the establishment as to their being established and as being as an established
thing, it is to be so much in evidence. Believe them. Evidently they
do. As it is to be kept up and as it is to be kept up and as it is to be
kept up. To keep it up so that to keep it up, it was their request it
was there by request it was to be kept up at their request. To keep
it up and as it necessarily means this, it necessarily has meant that
as it was being established and in earnest and as an evidence and in
evidence. More in evidence it was more in evidence.

Not very hilly yes and will they discharge their obligations to
themselves and to their other friends. Their obligations are there
and they see to it. If in obliging themselves to do so to discharge
their obligations there are no complications and no further pleasures, farther and farther and then in no wise and then as to the
way of spending themselves, they spend themselves repeatedly.

It is like this. If they have said yes, if they have said yes and no, if they have said they have said so, if they have at all said, that this is said to be originally the same they would not have said that they said that this was originally the same. The afternoon passed pleasantly and on the return a great many saw them. It was not at all hilly and it not being at all hilly it made them more certain that they were easily between hills. As hills are even, evenly, as hills are evenly, and more evenly even more evenly as more hills are even more than evenly, as more hilly as hills are more evenly hilly, it is very hilly. It is even more hilly, it is easily seen that it is even more than hilly. Nevertheless and nevertheless than there are more copies of it, more than to copy it. Tissue paper, tissue paper fairly certain to be inherited. Tissue paper is not as useful as oiled paper and oiled paper is often left about. Left and about. Tissue paper and oiled paper and left and about. It is often left and it is often left about. They meant to use the center as well as the left, the left center, they meant to be left in the center as well as to be left. They meant to be left in the center and they meant to be left and to be left in the center and they were left in the center. To stand up to sit down and to walk around.

So Nice, a town.

Treat and retreat seat and reseat receipt and seat and able able to be seated, suitable, suitable as a seat.

A seat, to be seated on a seat. Reseat, to be reseated, to be seated, to be on a seat. A seat, to be seated. Reseat. To be reseated, to be seated. A seat. To sit on a seat. To be sitting on a seat. Sitting sit, seated, seat. The seat, this seat, and sitting and seated. Reseated, as seated, a seat.

As scenes.

As seen.

Or as seen.

Or as meant.

Or as to mean.

Fairly finish it as seen.

Subject-cases makes a dressing, subject-cases or as pressing, subject-cases or as seen, subject-cases have to mean, as sent. They sent it in that way. Distress. No distress. Yes, very nearly yes, intended as intended, reliable as to being so reliable, in question, as there is no proceeding, in fact or very nearly. Designed for this. In the meantime as meanwhile, in fact, so they can have it. Have as you can, antedating, exactly, more than so, and as if it were not unsuitable. No more as when there can be no more so there can be, more so that there may be more so that there may be. As more. No hurry.

And more as soon.

Or in as wanted.

Can it be or ordered ahead.

Not fairly sorry not so much nearly as that.

For nearly as that.

That is the end of it.

EMP LACE

Emp lace.
Miserable.

Next n time

Seat.

What is a say mow grass.

Night a steam pen.
Night a steam pen penny.
Night a steam pen penny pennier.
Night a steam pen pennier penny.

This is puss.
Polar share.
Pole pair.
Polar.

Knee nick.
Nickle.
Knee nickle Knee nick.
Knee nickle Knee nickle.

Picture and steam boat extra sail boat.
Not a no not a long suit pale mail.

Why is a sole a dumpling.
A sole is a dumpling because there is swimming.

Little lights of kindness news in all the branch where all is
the weeding when the perfect set of tracing is poodle. Poodle
when.

Pole in ore. Pole in ore up till. Pole in ore up till soon lay.
Soon lay spook. Spook tie. Spook tie told top.

Oh my way sit.
Oh my way sit how glass.
Oh my way sit any an now.
Oh my way sit any earn now.
Oh my way sit any now.
Oh my way sit any an now.

Net and some silk.
Suppose it was in glass. Suppose an investigation and a relay
a relay of large size. Suppose it is a burst, suppose it is egg glass.
Not in sent.

Not a sill in bellows.
Noise is claim climb.

Are perches in cream.
Not or nest or.

Little thunder brick ates.
Let or mine shine.

There is no use in a pilaster there is no use in a peel laster, there
is no use in a pilaster.

Color it cup, color it cup why is why is hair is.

Climbing in tights climbing in tights climbing bits of button. Tiny nuts tiny nuts make week, tiny nuts make week straw. Legs look like less. Leg look like less.

Tiny week tiny week hum moan day, tiny week hung moon, day, tiny week hung moon day secure.

Neck lace in laces, laces and keeps back, necklaces and keeps back.

Not a peal not a peal sounder, not a peal sounder eggs use. Eggs use twos, eggs use twos two specks. Eggs use two specks. Two specks sounder. Two specks sound in admit safe. Two specks are or in is it, are or is in it in, is it in or is it, is it in or, or is it in.

Next a place next a place hawk next a place hawk cough.

Angel of weeding cake, angel of weeding cake, angel of weeding cake ate, on a step by a stem, all a pack sew a glass necessary necessary by wear eight.

Tender piece of a section of is to there. Most so.

Lack of roaring mutton. Sold pigs sold pigs wretch wretch eating wretch.

Knock about gate knock about gate must it must it must it.

In the agreeable, in the agree silk great or in the action not a shape or paid a sacrament to be a real coal leaf or pass. A curtain, next sugar rest, rent sugar rent not a smell not a smell salt.

It was funny it was peculiarly reacted by a necessary white knit way boat, way boat when call the looks for it. What in lace, what in lace to, bowl of nor or so let or.

Nest let nest let be. Accent and be have accent and be have no no sigh wake no sigh wake peace or.

It does get funnier it does get funnier, it is does funnier, it does is funnier, it does is dunnier. I have no inclination to be scolded.

Come to pearl ton leave stretch, most or climb step, climb step tight.

Pail of clover. She was a spectacle to win to win a dressing table. She was a spectacle to win a dressing table. The nice nine, the nice nine pours.

Earn east in gay, earn east in gayly, earn in east in gayly good, earn in gayly.

When should the ill boat show excellent pail, when should it cause a fly beam.

Nest to extraordinary and curtain and little special, real trimming, not a shade, not a horizontal piece of coat, not nearly finish.

Please sudden please sudden dough, please sudden dough nuts, please so rendered so rendered so rendered.

Later exchange no pet is stolen oh the lovely cool satisfactory on when on when.

Plunder in collars plenty in collars plenty in plenty in collars. It does change nuts. It does reduce burns. It is sell out in.

Earnest. Earnest is a chamber.
Earnest. Earnest.

Representative essence. Essence.

Following feet, following feet for, following feet furnish.

A longer curious a longer cup and stand.

Pledges pledges nearly.

Please fasten white please fasten white, please fasten white white please fasten white.

White eye-glasses, white eye glasses and a ribbon a real ribbon a glow a glow a gone gather a little seed spell and a natural gas. Piles of strange piles of strange in a special reason. If it is warm it is an hour glass, if it is cold it is a saddler glass if it is rain if it is rain, if it is rain it is a celebrated glass, if it is rain if it is rain if it is rain it is a safe in last old solid, last old solid grain last old solid grain of trained lips.

Clouds of willing seen in the bird day.

Able to exact bicycles.

A personal survey of frost.

In general.

Perhaps he has perhaps he has.

A wood below a wood below jerk, a wood below a wood below aid or excellent.

It was a transitive a transitive leave height.

Allowing allowing allowing allowing.

Put a pull put a pull all leather.

This time not so well on limb.

On none part let par on eat touch par.
Going to stop singing stop it stop it stop it stop singing.
Perfect pleasant place wire lily.
Put see put see put see put see.
Leave a glass mass leave a glass mass curling is a pressed sense.
Words cousin by words and cousin by, words and cousin and by words and cousin and by words and cousin by.
Left grapes or shade of real colds or pieces steak or little way shoulder steps.
It comes to the present interdicted and really poised really poison really pointed necessity to be collided agreeable and a commoner a comprehensive rendered so present and nearly persuadable nearly power.
It is a credit to be it is a credit to be.
Nearer a glance to thee.
A little reasonable parcel a little reasonable parcel.
Shatter a pan cold more a ground lease with mite and less line and check go lights with peaked peaked pats widow grown not a spell soup not a spell soap actually actually in in.
Morning gate. Pepper calls. No use.
Read oceans right burn rubber hose nerves color in a ten agreeable and a lest woes.
Knocks eggs know better. Knocks eggs nor better. Knocks eggs nor eggs nor eggs nor better.
Lay colonel lay colonel.
Paper chews.
Hinting and boldness, hinting and boldness, way waiting, way waiting.

Mention leader.

Little stands make meadows and beneath all and beneath more and beneath pants.

Have it at hand, have it at hand have a pear to smear why it.

Able stamp planter able stamp curtain, able stamp bowl dear slow.

Pearls, pearls pages, extra summer one, minor chin laugh, pearls pearls pages, extra some more one, leave minor changes, let powder let powder let powder.

Extraordinary purses, extraordinary purses.

A pleas rather fine a pleas rather fine.

It was a pew it was a pew it was a pew in places.

Widen pour lets.

Papers of cranberries.

Laps in covers.

Age in beefsteaks age in pear shapes age in round and puzzle.

Witness a pair of glasses. Extra win eager extra win eager.

Piles piles of splinters piles piles of splinters.

English or please english or please or please or please or please or please.

Weighed in skirt weighed in weighed in skirt.

Anguish anguish anguish.

Puzzle a tower.

Real button.

Real butter or nuts.

Real button nuts.

A measure of muss, a measure of a muss meant.

Little eyes of peal ax resting by the clothes makes a pillow show a grain and makes a left hand restless back wards.

After noon. Extra toweling.

Persons.

Persons nearly bower.

Plain tags to a dozen. Yellow sponges to a piece.

If it was necessary if it was ameliorating, if it was ameliorating.

Loud center wheel loud center wheel.

Paper satchels.

Little sequestered lot shown countenances.

Angles agreed.

When stares.
When stares.
When stares.
Flute flute how are you.
Way of web stairs way of web stairs.
Why or lean.
Door hum door hum sew.
This is a change.
Wheel or wheats.
Lettuce excuse.
Heap heap heap.
Or a plain.
Personal bestow personal bestow buck eat wheat. Personal bestow buckwheat eat personal bestow buck eat wheat.
An irregular an irregular and irregular an irregular.
Please lean wheat.
Away in pay real suspect away in pay real suspect can, in away away in pay real suspect can argue ties, away in pay suspect ties away in argue suspect ties ties.
Mounting slate.
Extra fort.
Whine cold straps, whine cold straps angle trace.
Not in corner pigeon, not a regular rice not a chin reading not worry goal.
These are oiler or glee.
Wade in cake.
Come in.
One one.
Come Come Come Come.
Two queen.
Come into so.
Of two or two.
It was necessary it was necessary to purchase twine it was necessary string it was necessary so on it was necessary reasonable sweet, it was no pole it it was an example.
Let it agree.
Lovely eye lamb.
Red in red in parlor notes red in red in parlor notes.

Red in eye lamb, red in red in parlor notes.

Red in eye lamb red in parlor notes red in eye lamb red in parlor notes precious precious precious precious.

Red in parlor notes precious precious precious.

Red in parlor notes red in parlor notes red in precious precious.

Lovely eye lamb red in red in precious

Lovely eye lamb red in parlor notes.

Precious Precious Precious.

Smiles and miles.

Colored board.

A collection a collection poor at a collection poor at pencils, a collection poor at pencils patients, a collection poor at pencils patients.

Please over debt please over thumb.

Lender tender.

It was putting.

Scissors or cheese scissors or chase scissors or james.

Lamp lighting.

Pen a sable.

Peacocks. coil balloons.

Tea knows.

Lick in plains.

Cannery. Cannery catastrophy.

Length.

Weed spare those.

Able able to take sugar.

Less in bright.

Not a louis in filip.

Hug or. Hug or hug or.

Lump in a wheel lump in a whole lump in cousin sand.

Narrow bend.

Twisted twisted lake.

Vestibule paul.

Near jenny.

A whole season a rode a rode a rode.

A whole season a road.

Pleasant stem.

Next to shake.

We say.
Examples and earn say burn.
Acres again acres again.
Spot or less.
Need berries hot.
Wave who mean.
Leave be leave be.
It was a positive corner.
A white extra syllable.
Neither pressure.
Can you see sit.
Cinder judge land hear.
Susan spoke what.
Susan spoke sweetly.
Read birds.
Susan spoke what.
Weighed.
Leg light.
Ancient washing tone.
Red tea let.
The power of his violin line. He transformed it into hair.
Loads loads and loads loads.
Paper cut in water water chair.
Neat niece or egg.
West in stoves.
Natural lace furniture.
Old cheap gray. Mustard.
Why should pepper mutter.
All all all all.
Ready sign tax ready sign tax.
Naturally cunning. Weather scope.
Ee's last.
Ready little a.
Color two pieces.
Wait a garment.
Not a flake hater.
Needs pearls tiles.
Oh pay oh pray open.

Oh pray oh pay open.
Not a regular bay day.
Weeding butter.
A left over into a left into or a left or into a left into over.
Nuts in nights nuts or nights.
A clamor.
Pay special stains.
Coil or puss.
Whiter ship.
Eight o'clock.
Rubbish.
Eight o'clock pussish.
Eight o'clock radish.
Eight o'clock and a lump.
Eight o'clock more.
Sew soon.
Eight o'clock equal.
Pun in baby.
A clock feather.
Eighty day.
Cunning.
Feeble foliage.
Rain air neck.
Pay stairs.
Pair recapitulations and tender tender tender titles tender
tender tender titles.
Able to seize able to seize separate separate separate.
What is a dictionary, a dictionary is thanks.
Nerves curves nerves curve less nerves curves curves curve
less nerves nerves less nerves nerves less nerves nerves less.
Waiters double cherry waiters double cherry.
In the course of conversation. In the course of conversation.
Needs a pin.
Needs as a pin.
Come out.
Come come out.
Out.

Mercifully mercifully mercy fully mercifully.
Which is a lit.
Lighter.
Wedding chest.
Wedding chest pansies.
Hat is across.
Across far.

Next to next to near soled tip, next to next to near to next to near to near to next to. Next to next to next to near to next to near to.

Cow come out cow come out cow come out come out cow cow come out come out cow cow come out cow come out cow come out come out cow cow come out come out cow cow come out cow come out cow come out cow come out cow cow come out cow come out.

Honey is wet.

Paint on paint in paint in paint in paint in paint in paint in.

Left order neither.

Yes I have been to come. Cow come out cow come out cow come out come out cow cow come out come out cow.

Become become. Polish.

Dress well dress well dress well.

Funny little bore or link

Next next.   .

It was a way to say say say say.

Inch and inch met or met scale or stamp, stone or paper drawer, rent or rent needs address excel wood and wood and only stick out either, by a place but not more sudden when and all July.

MORE GRAMMAR FOR A SENTENCE

PART ONE

The Almonds

Buy me with this.

Will you be well will you be well.

A lily smells as green as when it is annoying that it is right about it.

If for long she had been with or without them. That means that her name had not been changed but not known about. She had been with the and without it making a matter with at all. Why then. She is the mother. Her father. Her brother died a young man so did her husband. He was a young man and the house was bigger. Without it to do. She was very well very well to do very well to do with them. After they are a while. Like that in a sound.

There is no other family with at all.

To go on with going on with it.

It makes it safely with them and who.

Wordly worthy worthy worth were they were or were they with be.

Worth bitter.

It is better or are they better.

It is better or are they bitter.

She had held spend when she was sent.

In and uninvited by the mention of that.

Think of their weeding. They were cutting without it at last.

Not only not it but not it.

Try it out. How do you do. Do they love you. Or curiously. When it is different to be agreeable or agreeably older. There it is not to be mistaken.

They made it a danger to have avoided a door which they meant to have had and a hinge in undividedly an attention.

Remark that a recalled pleasing having for them makes it immediately known which is theirs. They have to be without doubt well known. He likes to have him be hired for that in that

with their care named Bradley which made whenever they do
more than that deliberately making a mine of use of their acknowledge meant for them a reason assistance made curious and
by and nearly which is that. Make without call. It is very beautiful
to have the winning language.

This a paragraph in substance.

Of course it looks like it in that shape and they always remind
it of it. This may be spoken of why. When they are alike they
resume a plant which has that for them that they did which was
theirs because of ordinary less than white. Ivy leaves resemble
harbors. He harbored added it as in order having had it in detail.
This makes a paragraph attached.

What is in amounting. Who is in power with having find.
Now or then there never is a need of having nine or mine in a
name, a noun with thinking of currants makes it different alright
but without their say so they will even will with an account so
that there is namely that if they turn they will please do with
hesitate. Finally they refuse. All this is how they cannot use
the name currants after they were women. This whole paragraph
is explanatory.

It is very true that it is of use to after to you. With you they
will withdraw with which they have to do with you. After all
why will they meet with which.

It is very likely that they tell that they liked when they liked
it which was which they have as much as an instance of which
it is as well. Known as paragraph.

He fortunately was as playing with him. They need know
that he thought with them. With by which it is remain and remained about in by with in having they made it have them with
and to do. This is a paragraph that plans of thinking it with as
Etienne.

It is at adding in remaking tens. Every little way of calling
May away from them. With whom were they careful. They will
have been thought well of without. Every little nicely by a paving
with when by this in and announced. She let fall something which
made a little racket. There is why they need now and know their
paragraph. A paragraph is not natural. Who knows how. A noun
is nature personified. Alike. A sentence which is in one word is
talkative. They like their moon. Red at night sailor's delight a

vegetable garden which is when there is a cage wherein they add with add withheld with string. A paragraph is not natural. Peas are natural so are string beans all sausages are natural, butter is natural but not cream paragraphs are not natural, quinces are natural even when they are late and with them they are natural without cherries they are natural. A period is natural a capital with a capital with and with a capital. It is beautiful. A word which makes basket a name. If it is a name will he be confused with whatever with it they make to name. There is no doubt that a mine is natural that always is natural that appointment is natural that nearly is natural that will they have their board is natural. It is natural to remain once again. It is natural. A paragraph is not natural but needful. There are more needful with what they do. Think of everything that is natural. Now. It is very beautiful to have a birthday. In which they invite prefer. With them. A paragraph is not nature. Not unalike.

If I leave with them now if I leave it with them now if I leave it with them. Now. A paragraph is not a division it does not separate. Because if they must go they will not have gone. Not now. Be with a wife. Wifely. Enthusiasm. Natural. They will think about who says. She liked their coffee but she does not like it now.

A paragraph without words. Why are mainly made in comparison.

With having lost. He was not discontented with having lost. By that means he was received without having mine and then it was nearly by the way of fastening. With in union for they made it do. Without them as they could for which they were in an opposite reason of a placement. For their attachment. Which made it be by the time that they could diminish. Upper. and more.

The difference between natural paragraph and moving paragraph.

A little at a time.

It is as good as exercise.

A paragraph of why they will apply theirs to this. Infinally acute hire that they can. Appeal that it is very times to be.

A natural paragraph is not waiting.

They will it is not natural to speak of them. It is not natural to speak. It is not natural to have them. They have them come with them. It is natural not to have them come with them. Reduce remaining without them. It is very natural to have returned with them. What has a paragraph to do with it. They are not having it to do it as they wish. Providing they are coming with which they made it anyway. There is no use in a paragraph which is outstanding. A paragraph has not naturally as an encumbrance without which they are with wither a blessing good which is as good. What can a paragraph do eventually. Do without but he minds it. A paragraph is naturally that they are disappointed. a paragraph is made in between continuing which is that they will have it bloom. How can you tell the difference between eat it all and a pea. Which they mean. It is not that they are without equivalent.

To think well of any paragraph they must have affection.

There is no such thing as a natural sentence but there is such a thing as a natural paragraph and it must be found.

It makes no difference whether he gets tired first or whether I do if we continue to go on it is not necessary that we have both went and rested without there after made it be a different in the way. This is not a mistake in wasting which when without theirs as they do needed all alike which if it is a part of inclusive that they make in agreement and after all it was hers I used.

There is no such thing as a natural sentence and why because a sentence is not naturally. A sentence. With them they will detest without whether they will belie it. A paragraph in when there is a little valley in noon or as it is in the way of a little of it as soon as there has been is a moon. That makes it not naturally be a paragraph. When he is afraid he is after afraid and if it is then that it is that it has been might it be in with which it is in return. Rarely afraid. After afraid. A paragraph is naturally after. Afraid. After afraid. To look after. It is after.

There is a difference between after and after afraid. A paragraph is not a sentence after it is a paragraph after.

Supposing three things a will they be having met and at a time with while and after without not at a time with which to trouble with advising why they weeded without grass. Because they prefer separating salad. This and they come alternately again. It cannot be naturally a paragraph because they are there and they have left one shovel so they will be willing which is why two hundred salads are as small and will be larger. A paragraph is an hour.

After every day they think.

About their wheat. Which is coated with bread. And they like grapes. Because a dog looks at it as a ball. Why if they are currants and made it with it.

If a dog looks like it does with them.

It is very nearly a paragraph to cry.

She knew who whose when they lent. It is a basket which they covered with a and with in it. It is very actually fine.

A paragraph made a mention. And Nora or no or a dove which is widen.

Partly relief.

Nobody knows what I am trying to do but I do and I know when I succeed.

Plainly attaching the string to keep they string beans within. This is nothing.

They know very well how they stand and are thinning but did they. Very likely they always did. It is not a representation of unified attaching to them. Now then she always knew she would be everything. He always knew he was becoming. They are accepted as being in very mainly if intruding. They will accept as well. Well enough alone. They know how they are standing with without moving. I do not think that they never didn't. Well and. Just as very well. In hive and in him. Every and one.

Forget how beautifully Marin has his hours. With his hours. She with out him with her son with out him. He may sail. Not with his same as with a name. If he has not asked him she will come and call of him with of her son. He has since been with women and named them attaching inclining for it to be other than their name. A fox which is that it was right basket was a name. There is no need of a paragraph without amounts. This time a paragraph was not natural because he said. If they had three men then they lose it with his good-bye and an offering. There is no use in an unnatural parting. Pears and apart. And will they leave with pillows. With them. This paragraph is not natural. To-morrow is not natural. Without with them. Is not natural.

May full of weights a darkness all in declare.

What is thought about whether with will they go.

Resist having a natural sentence. There are a great many ants in apricots but they can be blown off without very much of an effort.

A natural sentence can not remind one of startling.

It is of very little use to like to walk.

With them.

It is of very little use to like to walk as well as be with them.

A paragraph is why they went where they did.

A sentence made it be all when they were through indeed how are they after all may it be for their sake and ridges. With may if it makes more than at most will be for in for instance. Now a sentence can come and be no disappointment. She criticizes. But which week.

A sentence is natural. He did not come. This is a joke. A sentence is natural. He did. Which is variable and they will offer him liver with and without oil. A sentence. Made against. His will. Will he do it. He will. A sentence made with his meaning.

There is no difference between a paragraph and at once.

If it is better than ever. If it is finished. This is no paragraph. They will remember like that. This is inviting his confidence which is not withdrawn mainly but with it.

A paragraph does need a two by three. Without doubt. Which it does. By the time. They will deliver. With adding. More than they can. In need of a reliance without a difference in their name they have it a name. With them.

A paragraph is mentioned as silly. As silky. As a silky saving that he had.

That is a good paragraph. Thank you. He came. It was so good. Which is that he came. May be he did.

There is no effort in without a paid relief.

What is a trait which they have. They made more.

Forward and back.

Sashay forward and back.

Think quietly of how to do with out a way of which they were well out of it.

Folded wrong.

The salads have been wet.

The salads have been made wet by water. This is as useful as a doll.

Now this is the sort of thing that she would write. I know what a paragraph is after all.

What is he willing to do. For you. As well as for him and they will be asked to come if they answer. They will wave it as many could have made change in a firm hoping for it now. Why are nasturtiums natural which they have as which they are. Awhile at a time. It is our they hope. But they will see. To it.

Did he drink out of his water because of well well. Who can be cured cared while they may. Who while they may. Now do you see how wrong that is.

Leave sizes to paragraphs.

Paragraphs are one two three one two one two one two three paragraphs are sizes.

That is without what paragraphs there are. Paragraphs are sizes.

They began with using me for them. Will they be well and wish.

Paragraphs are named.

They name a paragraph without with this.

Why is a sentence natural if it is not in disuse. A sentence is not natural. Why is a paragraph not natural. A paragraph is not it is not not natural a paragraph is not it is a paragraph and it is not as that that is as a paragraph to tell. Do tell why is a paragraph just as much as ever natural.

A paragraph is natural. They will mend by the time it is mended by the time. A paragraph is natural by the mended that it is by that time. This is not in used. A paragraph if they were occupied which they were there and care. It was foolish to care. Have to take care. Which they have to care.

A paragraph is natural that is it is that it is is very well to know is very well known. Thank you for forgiving with them to with him.

A paragraph is natural with forgotten. That is with may and said.

Think of a paragraph. Reminded and remember. Remembered.

A paragraph is natural. They will be a paragraph will be a paragraph will be as natural. As should never be used for likely.

A paragraph. Which is natural.

They will know that each sat as they lay there. A paragraph is not with drew.

William and who. This is a mistake.

A paragraph is natural.

What can be expected of paragraphs and sentences by the time I am done. With or without. What do we do. We do without. Why is she stout. Because we do do without.

It is perfectly easy to make a paragraph. Without a sentence. Because they like it better. So.

If they do not tell them what they have. That is a natural sentence because it is without this which they finish.

If they do not tell them what they have they will be able to have it as often. This is not a natural sentence. Any more.

Need they be always one of without that. They do have. To like it.

They made it be naturally. Without a place. With theirs.

Think of a natural sentence in religion.

As we went along.

She made it appoint them. They will like which they had being alike.

One of which.

You can have a natural sentence if you look alike.

Reliable they made a bee.

A bee hive is made for once and with is kisses.

Will they cry with their with their with thin with. A sentence made from anxious.

I am thinking a great deal about which sentences are, left over, asked, and leaned, made for it in easy. They made it walked around.

With which do you think me.

That is a natural sentence without Baltimore.

What is the difference between and with made easy, that they came, made why in their amidst with in them, they are tallied, in remainder after soon. That changes it to all of their time. It is very easy to miss a sentence.

But not a paragraph.

It is very wrong to miss a sentence.

If they move they will move with welled and they did not like it for them as fish.

That makes it change readily from Baltimore to Belley. In with when. When announced as added then.

They can refuse paragraphs.

It is.

Baltimore west. Belley east. Boston.

They made it different to have tears.

Let their be paragraphs why or not.

They are no paragraphs. Belley. They are paragraphs. Baltimore.

It is by this wish which is.

What joins which is and which it is. Boston.

There are no paragraphs.

Paragraphs they will bequeath weddings.

Thinking thanking.

A solace.

Natural sentences do exist in arithmetic.

If we both say he threw that tree away.

It does not make any difference how old they all are.

These would be natural sentences if they were at all to call harder than for her.

She does use that which will there oblige it with either at very heard for advent in refer to a sentence.

She does not make it a paragraph.

No nor at all likely.

There is a difference.

There can be natural sentences if they are halting which whichever that is with renown that without that waving that if they or through. This is a sentence.

A sentence is halting with but as a cow gives and is gives it is sent has calves.

The Almonds have women.

A sentence leaves cows out about left where with all it takes.

This sentence is around.

I think naturally not with have their things they like with their shone as add or fancy.

This sentence more and more grows wider without carrots.

A sentence can be natural with wheeling.

With can be natural.

Some say forty. And some say one.

Now make all this into a paragraph without me.

Bend ended wagon. This is no sentence nor a pastime.

A paragraph is natural but not to be amused.

Bend ended wagon here nearby they will paper with comforting in rejoice.

A sentence is without their dear. Dear me with.

A sentence means too much a paragraph doesn't, therefore a paragraph is nature nature we we are averse.

Assent. Recent. Assert. And question. Do stop. When you do. It was a rotation. In regard to their fixing habitual arrange meant.

A sentence needs help. And she cries.

A sentence is why they were folded. Please have it folded.

Who helps whom with help. Withheld help yourself.

That is or or hour.

A sentence will come.

Chiefly. Will come.

That is a natural sentence. A sentence will come. Chiefly. Will come.

It must be wonderful to hear about these things and then see them.

The difference between not reading and not inviting may do.

It was opposite wholly in directing.

What is a paragraph when they predict rain.

There used ordinary sentences to make it apply.

Really not to care really not to care makes it a hole with a well. A well is not used any more. That is an ordinary sentence and is it satisfactory.

Count again. Fifteen.

This is in a tradition. They will be as careful.

To make it do.

This is a paragraph.

What is it. A paragraph. Grenoble. On the way to Grenoble you pass a hill without a town where you might stop which I see it is used by it in a main while in the way. A usual sentence is placed anywhere. What is a sentence. Without a trouble. They will be just as well aware. Without it. This is a paragraph without delight. They are after it. After awhile. An ordinary paragraph. Which they have.

How is a paragraph. Taken by themselves. Or right away. What is a sentence. With them a paragraph.

Think carefully about a paragraph. Nobody knows whose is it.

All of which makes how is it. Now think about that. How does it have a help without them they will in relight right away.

A sentence is not in naturally made in part. It is easier.

What is it.

I see what is the trouble with a sentence they will not be two a day. That is the trouble with a sentence. Now try to make a sentence with this experience. Not to care. But with whom by the time they have finished. A sentence by the time. No thank you not to thank you. A sentence by the time who has been named with them. It is nice that they do now.

It is easy to know that a sentence is not a paragraph.

With will with them do. Will they do.

What will they do with them they will want them. They will do what they want to do.

Is this a paragraph or are these sentences. Who will know that about them.

Sentences are not natural paragraphs are natural and I am desperately trying to find out why.

Neither for as turkey which in ended May. She tried to get a sieve in many towns.

It is easy to sound alike and to diminish with their welcome that they state.

What is a paragraph, no place in which to settle. Because they have been moved.

A paragraph is different that is it affects me. That is it it is why they are relished. As for a sentence in what way do they stop. They stop without. And why. With is noon. It is with them it does not make a difference they will wait.

All this leads to me. I can be careful of what I do. That is a sentence. If it is repeated and for days there can be hopes that Florence will marry which she will. A sentence is a plan. It is never plain. Think of a sentence by its birthday. What is a sentence. With or without an ado. A paragraph is why they will at with their other brother. And they are hurried. They like the best of all when they made it a part of which they can do. If they feel well. What is a sentence. No. Nobody.

All of it. Content to be obstinate.

What is a sentence. He may mean that he is very nearly his cousin and that he has been made fortunately for him with a tendency to remain thin. That would be a sentence if one did not use anything to have him tell them.

There is this named him. This is a sentence with his name.

Feeling the same.

A sentence is a hope of a paragraph. What is a paragraph that is easy. How can you know better if you say so. A sentence is never an answer. Neither is it. Who answers him. He remains with them. They have to have him because they took him. And they with this are what they are saying.

What is a paragraph. Right off. Write often. What is a paragraph. He drinks as if in wishing. He drinks of if in washing. And so and so they will be out of mind out of hand. This makes no difficulty. Have they thought of that.

A paragraph is naturally without a finish.

A paragraph is alright.

With or without a chicken fish or vegetables she came to pay for a harness. This is what they were taught.

A paragraph always lets it fall or lets it be well and happy or feels it to be so which they never were themselves as worried.

What time is it.

A paragraph has to do with the growth of a dog. They talk about it. She says. No. A paragraph is never finished therefore a paragraph is not natural. A paragraph is with the well acquainted. It languishes in mediocrity. It makes it doubtful if lips are thick and the eyes blue and the blonde which they have it might be

cupped and alike which whenever a reliable made to order as
plainly. There is nothing troubled with how about them. They
are ordered to make it more for them. A paragraph ceases to be
naturally with them with cream. With them they are enthused by
holding it off. A paragraph is natural if they walk. It is natural if
it has not come. In order. Which was given. And no blame.
A paragraph reads why do they like where they know why they
have gotten all of it back not all of it because a part of it has been
missing. This is a paragraph naturally.

There is a difference between natural and emotional.

Who can sing. Sing around and about. If one thinks of a paragraph without thinking one does not think of a paragraph or anything. A sentence is why they like places. He replaces it. She replaces it. She replaces the amount. They place and replace and re-
correct their impressions. They do not change. They do not
with how do you do. How do you do. How are you. A paragraph
never is restless. That is easy. What is a paragraph.

I like to look at it.

What is a paragraph.

She likes it better than Granada.

She likes it.

I like to look at it.

A resolution is a paragraph.

What is a paragraph. I thought a paragraph was naturally a
paragraph was naturally a paragraph and now I did please my
retaining a paragraph.

What is a paragraph.

She will be with women. She not. She is places where they
can hear it which they wherever it is replied. Will she open the
gate. She will in spite of an appetite which she has. This is a paragraph and it sounds strange. They may be made to have a calf
that they feel which that it is for them to sell. They make all of
it well will it do. A paragraph need not be a finish. They will be
and think with what they said. A paragraph has changed hands.
A paragraph made a noun. A noun is the name of anything. How
in a paragraph. I like a name use and lose. They will use the name.
Some will use the name. A noun is a name. Basket is a name. Will
they come for him is a name. What is it is not a name. Why do

they like me is why they have it as a name. They change from some.

It is a change for some who come. This is a sentence that is unreliable. A paragraph is of sentences that are reliable. A sentence is very well when it is as if they had sat and waited. Do you see how they sew. This is a sentence of which it is for which in part of the time they will see me. This sentence of which I speak. Made in pairs. Maidens prayers. Made in pairs. With which they are placed. With may which is mainly. This is a mistake. As spelled. It is very beautiful and original.

Now any word made an impression. They will in three make Mrs. Roux. We always speak of her. Mrs. Roux. This is without an opposite with her.

Withdrew, they withdrawn have withdrawn, they withdraw.

It is unbelievable how many sentences have a mistake. Unbelievable. How many have. Very few have. They will do well not to have a mistake. They will do well not to have a mistake in competition. They will be very careful too. Which they are. Whatever they do. Now this is an example of just as well. A sentence is very often more than added. A paragraph is in that case not just a paragraph not at all now without this. What is a paragraph. Who is with to blame. Change meant to mean. A paragraph has been motioned away. And now sentence is natural if they redivide it.

Redivide. Who will be winning by their half.

It is alright that a sentence and express what is it they will see to it. I know what a sentence is or is not and a paragraph is not a sentence even if it is all one because they shrink from it. Not from it. This is a paragraph for them.

A paragraph is if it is natural that they will change it too. This is a paragraph which is natural. It is a sentence which if it were a paragraph would be natural. If you introduce as natural you do not make it too.

A paragraph is natural because it falls away. A paragraph need not fall away to be natural.

A sentence can not be natural because it is not rounded that is round is natural but rounded is not natural. A sentence is not natural. They will go on. A sentence is not not natural. If a sen-

tence is not natural what should it be. If a paragraph should not
be because to help it is to go away, she said he would be busy.
This is neither a sentence nor a paragraph the country says no.
This is neither a paragraph nor without it. A paragraph is natural
because they feel like it. A sentence is not natural without that
with that. And now think about damage. It is no trouble to wear
green, thank you Len. This is a sentence which they know. If
they know. Thank you if they know. This is a sentence. Thank
you if they know. What is the difference between rounded.

In other words a paragraph is not naturally a natural thing
but it is.

I have suddenly gotten not to care. This is an old sentence. To
say so.

She knew she was right by the way that he said so. This is
simply that.

There is no distance to come. With them come is came. She
came.

No sentence when they were careful. A sentence when they
were careful.

It is why they were aware that they were carried away by
her. That is a nice sentence but not a natural sentence because
they were divided in a sense. They were divided by leaving them
about when they were ready. A natural sentence has nothing to
do with how do you do. A natural sentence is vainly made by
butter. It is in vain.

A natural sentence. A yellow peach may be ripened. There
is a kind of a pear that has a rosy center which if felt is not in itself.
What is it that made her know with a measure, she said there
had been enough.

What is a natural sentence. A natural sentence they need not
write. A natural sentence. After all. Who is here. After all who
hears him. If they can.

None of that has anything to do with how a sentence is held.
A sentence thinks loudly. Why must must is by me. Nearly beside made by then. A sentence cannot be natural. It must be
returnable. To be returned. As well. What is a sentence and why
cannot it be natural. Because it is a sentence. A sentence is not
unnatural. A paragraph is not made of sentences. A paragraph

with a precious sweet with eat. A paragraph is not pressed for
time. Ever. A sentence if it returns or if it is added or if it is ended
or simply in each way they make it do. They always can. Make
a sentence do. You see why a sentence is not a part of it. A sentence should be ours. Now listen if he makes believe loving and
eats in playing he eats in resumption, this is the same as anything
and this is not a margin they make either stopping or not it is a
paragraph with how and treasure. A sentence should be within a
lope, that is why they had with him. Now think of these things.
With them. A same with in all either shawl. Nothing to do with
it. What is a sentence. There is no use in telling a whim. Nor in he
sews. It is alike. Everything they show is piled alike. There should
be a sentence in some arithmetic. But with fair they had it as may
fairly hand it our like. No nor should it be my fish. A fish can be
taught as a lake. What is a sentence it used to be that they liked
it. Without a notice. That they liked it with that they had to be
mine. What is a sentence. Often I will make a paragraph.

It gives all the effect of a mountain but it is on a plain.

Make it have it. It is a part and a part is not where there and
have more. A part is not that it is belonging to the same plans.

A sentence if you thin then you thin sauces and sauces have
need of Leon and Rosa. Every time you end will you have a refrain. Refrain can only mean that they wind and leave. He has
disguised his action by his delight. He is delighted with it. Now
these sentences do not make a paragraph. Nor do they make an
end without it. Without doubt. That is a sentence but two words
cannot make a preface. Is a preface a sentence. Very well. Send
it. A sentence is a present which they make. In that way a sentence comes without a paragraph. Do you see. To say, do you
see, is finally without employment.

Think of a sentence in two places it is not natural but engaging and very frightened. That is a sentence with waiting for
them. It is very disagreeable to be waiting for them. This is a
cadence. A cadence does not resemble a sentence it looks like it.
A cadence does not resemble a sentence it is partly without a
paragraph. Without is vainly made true. Mainly, mainly is the
idea. That a paragraph is returned. It is not. It is mire which is
not where they used. A paragraph is our, signed William. What

is a paragraph, a paragraph is not a partition. A sentence never can be set apart.

A paragraph is this she discovers that the lake which is far away is not absolved in a partition. That is to say the land in between does not belong to them. It is very kindly of them to be back.

This is not completely a paragraph because of hoping that they will hear it alike. If it were a paragraph listen they would be told. How are they. Now a sentence is made by happen to distance.

They will be called anyway. This is neither a paragraph nor a sentence.

After a while.

I feel very differently about it.

Is conversation sentences. Is it paragraphs. Is it seeing them. There is an advantage.

When is it taken the advantage.

By them. Made by them. They will be willing. A conversation changes to paragraphs. With hope. Will, they be pleased. If they go. What is a conversation. They have learned all of it.

A sentence it is so easy to lose what a sentence is. Not so easy with a paragraph it is not so easy to lose what is a paragraph. What is a paragraph. Who loses a hold on him. That is a paragraph. That is not a sentence. Why is it.

What is it.

What is a paragraph.

I can come to know.

I have been known to know and to say so. A paragraph is not varying with the summer or anything.

This is a paragraph because it says so. Do you see. It says so. If you do see and it says so. Yes we do see and it says so. A paragraph says so. A sentence if it could would it say so. Would a sentence say so. If it said so would it have it as if it had it as said so, no. A sentence has not said so. A paragraph has said so. Think of a sentence. Has it said so. Yes it has said so. Two to a sentence. Yes it has said so. A sentence has not had it. It has not had it to say so. A sentence has not said to say so. A paragraph says so. A paragraph has not to have to have it say so. Easily say so. Too easily say so. A paragraph not too easily to say so. What is a sentence. A paragraph is not a sentence exactly not many more. There have not been sentence whether they say. A sentence always returns if they are happy. A sentence always returns if they were happy. A sentence is a sentence. This may be but it is not with arrive. Arrival. A Rival Sentence. Will Dan come and meet me. If he is meeting there. Think of a sentence. They will part. A sentence can not exist if it does not come back no not if it does not come back. A paragraph finishes.

This is it.

PRACTICE OF ORATORY

Practice of Orations.
Four and their share and where they are.
Practice of Orations.
A.
B.
C.
D.
A. b c and d.
Practice of orations.
A.

ORATORY.

I withdraw you draw and he draws, I withdraw neither I nor you neither do I neither do I. It is not as if I spoke, it is not.

Now no more character.

No more character at all.

No more as character.

Let us remember.

Let us say that grant to-day granted any way, let us say grant to-day, he was in cream. In cream and in cream I do not eat cream I do not heat cream I do not heat cream I do not for I do not and yet when you come to think it is not the country for it. Let us forget to say let us begin as if we were addressing, addresses are easily obtained. It is as if in some determination he had dwindled and even so selfishly, can you smile as if it were three long sales. What did we do. If he did do it she was not needed from time to time. And she wore, and she was and now remember what they will say. Let me ask are you ready yet.

ORATIONS.

When I very nearly hear it and I hear it and you hear it when you very nearly hear it, to see is said when you hear, to touch is said when you crowd to fall is said when you call. Call again this can be said when hail, that is a hail-storm is mixed with rain. We know very well then that it will not in that case do as much harm.

I do not care if there is no way of expecting all four and knowing them apart. Do you know what do you know. You know you know. Well then.

In the practice of orations and the relief of fears, in the practice of orations and the relief of fears, in the practice of orations and in the relief of fears, he we and they, they and we and he, he and they and we and in the practice of orations and in the relief of fears may we accept that which when sent is not only not acceptable but in a way need not be regarded as a surprise. It is astonishing that nearly in the meantime no one is surprised that that which is sent has been sent and with the choice of sending as if it were to

be received. So unequally have astonishment and unalterable re-
covering astonished the process. I have a weakness for exits, and
you, and you and you and you, also you and also you and you also,
and also and also you, and as for change of places and as a request
come again, as a request. To come again and as a request. I feel
this to be oratory.

Let me practice oratory and the practice of orations.

Leaving more to come has it a pointed settlement has it been
appointed as a settlement is settlement there something that has
been appointed. Have they appointed this as a settlement indeed
more so than imagined. You and I indeed you and I you and I may
carry pictures to Cahor and in this way a lot we say no one has
given or taken away, no one has given and no one has given and
give and take, to give and to take.

SPEECH.

A speech to him and for him and speech with him. We not
speak and are we to speak. Have you spoken. Do smile to yourself.
Do, do. Do and do and if you do, if you do and do, and do, do do.

This is meant to be studies in orations.

EXAMPLES OF ORATORY.

Example A.

An address is a simple way of what to say when they come
and go away.

And why has there be[en] no declaration of an undertaking
and why have they mentioned blue glass and pale yellow glass. In
the case of both and also red glass in a summer house the landscape
has a different appearance. Why do you smile.

Example B.

An example of how to explain what there is indicated by such
examples joined to other examples.

And why have you almost felt the strain why indeed have you
and when you are very inclined very nearly inclined to parade
packages and certain colored blue colored and very well colored

signs, why then indeed it is astounding, they were astonished to learn that there were frequently mounted police at a crossing. In a way it was an announcement. No one felt to blame. No one felt that there would be blame. Not any one certainly would come to be at all blamed and moreover there was representation and addresses. Listen to the addresses.

The first address. If you look to the left and do not see that there is a description below and above and indeed if you hope to be admirably sustained remind me and in so doing remind yourself of the illustration. The illustration that has been brought to your notice is the following.

They are amazed, no no exchange, they amaze, it is an amazement, and a pretention, no pretention is necessary ruins are ruins and reestablishment, are establishments that have been reestablishment. In this way they are authentic. And allowances. Allowances are made to all and for all and by all and in this way union and celebrations succeed each other in quick succession.

Dream for me.

In dreaming of Mrs. Andrews as you did surprised me.

Example C.

Many many instances of distribution reconstruction and restoration.

If you do do you believe that we have entered after we have mounted the stairway. Indeed not if many are waiting in turn. And what then. Why then we watch something entirely different and do not stay to see it accomplished. And is there no question. Of this there is no question. We do not avoid pressure nor insistence nor even dismay. I do obey. Of course you do.

Example d.

Example d is necessary to show that the emergency if there is an emergency is satisfactorily met.

Meet and met and very well and very well, this may be misread.

To be very kindly reminded by this of Spain, not really of Spain, not really of Spain, not very minutely of sand and strawberries not very minutely of rain and rivers. Have you met with some distraction. Very nearly intentionally and now for an address.

He addresses this to every one.

And mounting, upon this evidence we can decide as we have decided and more beside. And very much more, and very indeed very much more.

I know how linen braided in a certain way enhances the beauty of one whose beauty is conceded. We do not spare pleasure and praise. I am here in praise of you. For this purpose and for this purpose alone I have added this observation. Do not fail to observe the reason of the pleasure we have, you have and we have in corals and colors. Can you find pleasure in such a way. Indeed we can and we do. Do you.

Examples of real oratory.

Allow it, to allow for it, plentifully too the rain will do.

Not not not no.

I am making it easy.

Not not not.

I am making it easy.

Not not not certainly uncertainly.

Not not not nervously.

Not nervously at all.

Not at all.

Not not at all.

HOTEL FRANÇOIS Ier (1931)

IT WAS A VERY LITTLE WHILE AND THEY HAD GONE IN
front of it. It was that they had liked it would it bear. It was a
very much adjoined a follower. Flower of an adding where a
follower.

Have I come in. Will in suggestion.

They may like hours in catching.

It is always a pleasure to remember.

Have a habit.

Any name will very well wear better.

All who live round about there.

Have a manner.

The hotel François Ier.

Just winter so.

It is indubitably often that she is as denied to soften help to
when it is in all in midst of which in vehemence to taken given
in a bestowal show than left help in double.

Having noticed often that it is newly noticed which makes older
often.

The world has become smaller and more beautiful.

The world is grown smaller and more beautiful. That is it.

Yes that is it.

If he liked to live elsewhere that was natural.

If he was accompanied.

Place praise places.

But you do.

Partly for you.

Will he he wild in having a room soon. He was not very welcome. Safety in their choice.

Amy whether they thought much of merry. I do marry del Val.

I know how many do walk too.

It was a while that they did wait for them to have an apple.

An apple.

She may do this for the Hotel Lion d'Or.

II

Buy me yesterday for they may adhere to coffee.

It is without doubt no pleasure to walk about.

III

The romance of the Hotel François premier is this that it was seen on a Saturday.

IV

In snatches

A little a boy was three, two of them were three others.

She may be right I told her. I thought it well to tell her. They told them. They were avoiding nothing. And so.

Do they and are they will they for them to be remarkable.

Now think.

V

Repose while she does.

VI

An aided advantage in touch with delight.

VII

Just as they will have by nearly whether.

What is the difference between a thing seen and what do you mean.

Regularly in narrative.

Who is interested in Howard's mother or in Kitty's mother or in James as George. Dear James as George.

A target.
Those of course of us who have forgotten war have been mean.
I mean I mean was not spoken of the sun.
Do think of the sun.

VIII

A chance to have no noise in or because.

IX

They change being interested there to being interested there.

Hotel François Ier

To and two to be true.
They will be with me
To have you
To be true to this
And to have them
To be true
They will have them to be true

X

Just as they were ten.

XI

Who made them then.
Which made him.
Do they come then
Welcome
Join and just and join and just join them with and then.
It is very often that they are dissolved in tears.

XII

Should it show where they are mine.
And his care.
It was that they might place them all of them.
Just why they do so.
To call Howard seated.
I never leave Howard.

Hotel White Bird

She may be like that
Do
For me to choose.

II

Our just as assume
Leave riches with her
Are dovetail an origin
With wood.

III

But she
Can go clearly
To pieces
By adding act one
By add may meant scene one.
Left done right and left done.
She will never think in pointing in property inviting.

IV

Just shown as their agent.

V

Just shown.
As their
Agent.

VI

Mutter.

VII

They will read better

VIII

With other

IX

They have known a platter better.
Thank you
                              My dear
    My dear

How are you
This is for you.
Dear
How are you
This is
For you
How are you
My dear
How
My dear
How are you.

II

Love which
Love which
To love which
Which to love which
My dear how are you.

III

Just why they went.
They went
They were to have gone
And they did go
And they went.
What did they do.
How are you
My dear
How do you do
How are you.

IV

Oh choose the better
Oh choose you
Oh choose for you

V

She made it better.

VI

By the choice of more
That is why

My dear
You are
Better
How are you
How do you do
You are better
Two.

VII

She meant well.

VIII

Much better

IX

Very much better
Well.

X

She had eight
As the date
Full date
We date
We have to relate
The cause
Of bringing
It for her
It was light
As weight.
But she enjoyed it.
For it was
Not more than
Not too late

XI

Not at all

XII

She is very well I thank you.

For them

Just joined James.

In no way a disappointment.

They must have met with them which was in the capacity to lead and leave.

Our house contains. That is made back with idem. Idem the same just please come and claim our house as a lot which we have in a home. This is what made a pioneer.

Leave a nature to rain.

It makes no difference if they use it.

A narrative oh how often have I thought that a narrative.

How often will a narrative do.

Complain about fifty narratives perfectly.

He is waiting not for his food but for his appointment. Dear dear.

Plenty of bread and butter.

He is waiting not for his food.

Resignation does not mean narrative.

He is to come welcome, as well as having left welcome is not a narrative but foolishly.

I was completely persuaded by Mrs. Tolstoy but she told me.

She was completely persuaded by William but she told me.

How should either have been headed very often.

That is astonishing a narrative and I would so much rather be poetical.

For me.

I love poetical history for me.

I love poetical and still for me.

I love poetical will poetical for me by me.

The best of wishes

He wishes he came away he wishes.

Just why he wishes.

Joined by

He wishes.

A narrative of relieve

He wishes.

Think William
Poetical

So few this further.
I will reward
An error
Of regard.

Hotel François Ier

Was there
A surprise
In nearly not to face
Imagine
That the name
Was the same.

I

How far are you not to leave them.

I

With a colored message to know colors were. To know there
his coloring there.

I

She made no mistake. To take not only with it. When she came
to mend they say.

I

Garments were a separate desire pleasure. She made hours a
desired separated measure. With them they actually considered
why it is a treasure. Must it become be how even much with
pleasure.

I

She used pleasure exactly.

II

They are neither here or there.

II

Or there it mostly widened for in invite there. Them there who how did it. Do this for them.

II

Should it be shown. No how who ever coupled a dog out of a pleasure or round. Around. See me a round. It is polite. Let us congratulate ice rice.

II

They made no mistake to be indifferent. How which come faithfully or. Will it be easy. Not for me.

II

Adjust, add edge to adjoin wine. Wine is a drink. Water. Watered wine. We weigh wine.

III

They must expect one of you.

III

She may expect two of you.

III

What does she expect
You to do.

IV

Come with me and sit with me

V

I am afraid if she waits longer it will do her an injury.

Forests

She liked forests in a pity.

I

With forest too.

II

Will forests do.

III

What is it a pity will forests pretty.

IV

Forests are there

V

Saturday

VI

She must be without it

a

Old when

b

A forest deer

c

Makes it pay me

d

To call her.

With them

When they came in some one was waiting
When they arrived they said something
Some one was waiting when they came in.

Just Church

We stay gathered
With them intentionally
Have they met them
With Church
Just as if in incompetence
It must have leaving weather
As much with confidence
In Church.

Regularity

Be wider with lather
Rather a darkening

Of with gather
That they will
Suffice
Just why
They have this
As mother be occasion
To have rejoiced then ring
A bell soon.
She must be just which they do.
Outright.

Behave

Why cups of butter.
They will
In the morning
Happen
To be fatter.

Articles

Drop him for me.
Does wish.

Tidy

They make her mending large
To have a doll
Do be careless
In hope
Of pointing
Their dispatch
Of hurry
Hurry and come in.
It is of no use.
Hours of trying
That is what breaks
In cups with more rather
Than
They wish.
Do I know whether she has come in or out.

How ours

Very fairly selfish
Some sealed fake ponds
Very much as they hear like
May down in implied
                  Shells
Ears if they accustom to born
With counted help her
I do not think better help is ugly
By which
In win.
Just why a repelled for her
They might in nature
Come for
They caress
A dove tailed
In succeeding.
Nobody knows me.
Our too.

She is my bride

They make safety in seventy plus fourteen. As known as never hearing figures.

What will she see when she hears me.

It is after.
All mine.

Powers in because of up with their resource.

Careful

There is no use in eiderdown
But yes
Leaves which have been that they can win
With yes.

To guess
Would she choose what he would use.
He asked tell her to judge when
And because it is fine.

Allan

Allan Ullman knew me
He was prepared next of kin
To sink and swim
With magnifying carving
Should make
It is well to have held a pillow
Or other corals

At fourteen

It is extraordinary
That she made fourteen
And will make fourteen
And does fourteen sixteen
Gradually
It is extraordinary.

How are they hoping

It is old to think of welcome heavy women
She was fourteen.
They liked to have owls look unlike a pigeon they do look
like. That is a pigeon can be mistaken. For an owl.

How many things happen

A great many things happen

Every time

Every time they mix they make it different women
Who has sung men.
Do be careful of sung.
Checkers among.
Half of them sung.

Every time they changed they forgot all they bought.
However they bought.
It is very not useful but exceptional.

A part

Allan Ullman who knew me.
Separately from three his brother mother and father. He knew
me. He said when he knew me he separately regretted one two
three not he.

Our page

How could it be a little whatever he liked.

Morning glories

He made as stable morning glories
For the next to handle
Their regret.
Morning glories were eighteen to the dozen
Forty made fifteen.
Everybody who has been for them.
In add her add coming.
Too many thousands
Have a link with a king.

Francis Rose

Shut up
And stay shut
Where they drink all the better
For families of yet get her
With them in ravishes
Between them with dishes
And they came then with her
In precious labor with love
He may yet get wealth in getting tender
Which they make stronger
With us
Thank you.

How many cakes make jell for jelly
And how many loves make bless
A little flower of rather think better embellishment.
Just why join mass
A mass is a towing to a lock.
At towed they devise
How to a challenge.
Challenge has nothing to do with him.
How are heads held Howard.
She cooked and seized.
Cooked and seized
She cooked and seized.
Forbearance
Cooked and seized.
Bridle is paths.
Just as about a path
Just as a path
Just as a path.
It makes no difference whether four
Ate one.
Sum to sum.
Our adding is more hours.
Ate one
Just as well ate one
Just as well eight one
Just as well eight
One just as well
Eight one.
How much are they like me
Like.
After walked.
Before walked
He made her talk
To have her
Walk
After walked
And leave a walk

Leave walk
Or leave her leave walked.
It is an error
Oh.
Join me
With observation
She may be
Our hour glass
Which we sought
And have not bought
For our hour be
Be an hour for me.
Such is sought
And here bought
For our be
Her be
Err be
Come Francis Rose
Or be
Forty leave fifteen
Thrilled be
Or sought by
It for him
Or for
Her
For him to be
When they may
They may
Shall shelter
They make
Shelter
As they may be
For and to be
Nobody knows how old showers are.
Or how should hours should be.
In inlay should be
That with mean

With be
With held will then
In to be.
What is a square.

She should be

What could it prove
If it made no difference
To them

Dear dog

Dear dog
What do and does it leave
Dear dog.
He likes to see
Dear dog
But did he know it was he.
Leave dear dog where he is
Otherwise it is.
Not satisfied.

With him

Just why they ate
In state
With him.

Why does it come like that

He so happily is present.
When it comes like that.
From him
She so pleasantly is present
When it has come from him.
She so happily is present.
When it comes from him
So happily from him
When it comes so happily out of him.

He says obey

I obey which is to say
They come to-day.
And she closes the door
With delay.
But will
To happen to happen yes.
She sits with him for him
We know the difference

Than

I little thought of how it went
When they were told
It had been better with them
Than
Just yet.

Better heeded

Should rejoice be to arrange
Will they tell they until they are strange
Let them be for me to estrange
That they will until they change
For them will they until they have caught it to arrange
They will estrange
Because they can be blamed for the arrangement of their change
to change and arrange to be strange and well intended to come
to derange them then for them in abundance to them in a vice,
who held them
In a vice
Twice
To them to arrange
For them it is strange
That to them for them
They arrange
In them for a vessel which is meant a book
A book look twice

He held him twice
To make him twice
Shake dice
To be thought tranquil
In their wear
Aware
Come catch with capable
To be to like
A tree
For them capable
Underwent in anger
One
Two
Three
They must be sensibly made with them for them
Three
Ultimately
She might hinder
All of them
Ultimately cornered
All of them as meant
In clouds
Who ate them
Three
Ultimately
Made in generosity
For them to have it
In undertaking
Restively
She might be wonderful
Ultimately
They might in undertaking
Shall he have pleasure
Ultimately
In their recognising
Why they were often
Just as much as three

Which they may would
It may weight wood
For them ultimately
Better than could.
It might be careful
Who has made them
Who might have made them
Ultimately careful
With them.
For them.

GO IN GREEN

Go in green. Go in, case. Go in green.
Go in green. go in. in, go in green.
Go in green.
Go in green.

PRUDENCE CAUTION AND FORESIGHT

A STORY OF AVIGNON

It is just what they would do eventually.

Leon was married. He had a wife. He had four children. He had four girls.

He has come

Who has come.

That does not attract the attention of anyone.

Who has come

He has come

He has not come.

Leon was married, he had a wife, he had four children he had four girls. They were all young. Leon had been told, he told that it was better to be nervous than to be neglectful. He was not nervous and when he received a reward he was rewarded.

In varying religion he did not mean to write for them. Nor did he. Nor did he die fighting. Nor did he differ from the men who sang. They did not sing to be told that they were singing. They did not sing in order that they would prefer tears. How can you cry and not die.

Prepare to be a little astray. Do not prepare to describe to-day. He described how he saw all he saw and he had not seen bridges and water and climbs. He never climbed there because his friend had not been there before he had not been there before or after he had been there. He told us what was more important than this to him.

When he had not been left alone and could you be really prepared in a mine or in a ditch or in a room when he had really never been left alone he rarely felt that he had forgotten to mention the matter. And regularly when there was danger he could recollect that he could see before him his four children who were four girls. He never thought then of calling the littlest one a one languaged butterfly, nor did he speak to us of heredity. He felt that his wife had had sisters and brothers. And where were they please.

If you please.

Leon was necessarily dead not necessarily dead.

Leon had not been perfectly immune. Nor had he chosen to see to be.

He had indeed followed advantageously. And in following he had not felt very nervous nor very timid nor very aggressive nor very dangerous. He had indeed felt that he was to be spared. And was he. He was.

He collected readily he recollected readily and more easily than not he was angry. And when he was angry what did he say. He said he had not neglected his own affairs. But he had. And then the contradiction was made and he contented himself with work for himself and others. In coming to addition he again added that he was no immune. That he did not know this and that he had not neglected to add in addition.

We see opposite to us another older and we hear opposite to us a calendar. Leon did not mean to be more assiduous.

Can you have their adventures with a mother. With their mother. Their mother later arranged a little writing table for herself.

Leon did not prepare pleasantly. Oh yes he did.

Leon very nearly entered in here and he very nearly entered in here again.

From this there was no appeal. And in reality catch as catch can is not a plan.

There is a bridge at Avignon can you believe that it is a suspension bridge when you see it or when you walk on it.

I arrive.

I arrive here and I leave here after I have arrived here.

Expenses color me in a way.

PRUDENCE.

Leon neglected no fanaticism. He did not neglect any fanaticism. Nor did he fear to consider that he had escaped the rest. He was not nearly so easily restored not nearly and he undertook nothing else. He was not extraordinarily circumspect. He was not more cautious than he was prudent and in a manner of speaking he had slept well.

CAUTION.

When I was connected and caution was said to be more meaningful than patience I remembered that I had meant what I said.

Leon was not more cautious than he was patient. Prudence and caution do not mean being prudent and being cautious. In Avignon every other day is every other day. In this way they separate night from day. This did not concern Leon who was not readily adaptable. How can you please to see. You do not deny any occasion to preach repetition to me.

Leon was useful and necessarily satisfied. How can he visit this on himself. And where does he prepare to stay. Leon was not more cautious more patient nor more prudent than in war and in peace.

FORESIGHT.

To foresee changing places. If you foresee changing places do you change Avignon for Marseilles and Marseilles for Avignon. If you foresee do you foresee what there is to foresee. Do you foresee that you will be pleased and not seen when you no longer care to see to it.

Leon died.

And this made it easy to foresee that he would have been better pleased if he had been very well.

It was easily felt to have been left to remember there was plenty of foresight.

Prudence caution and foresight, and she foresees and he foresees and there are a great many hills in Marseilles and none in Avignon. There are hills around Avignon. Avignon is a walled city and the river is close to it. Marseilles is built on hills and the river runs into the Mediterranean and Marseilles is on the Mediterranean and the Mediterranean is close to it.

Prudence caution and foresight.

Leon had a wife he had four children all of them girls.

Foresight.

Leon was nearly as well attended to as if he had been married and had had the attention of his wife and he did not have necessarily to have pleasure in repeating this to them.

I foresee that he will see to this and to them. Now it is all changed. If you change you change that and if you change that you change this and if they change this they are not more than changed.

He did not die to cry. No indeed nor did they hurry. You hurry where they hurry, and they hurry where he hurries. He does not hurry here and there. He did not hurry.

And yet in his movements in his movements he was very hurried in his movements and in his ways he was hurried in his ways and in his way there was nothing in his way. In his way he was very useful and proud and decisive.

Ring again.

Pleasurable.

How pleasurable.

I foresee an added alarm.

What did Leon see.

He saw just the same and he did renounce his attention to pursue himself adequately. Do be gloomy to-day and do say that Leon went away. He did not go away in that manner of speaking.

Hear him express himself readily, hear him recount and recount and yet he and yet he had seen the same when at the same time violence was all the same. Is violence all the same and is his attention the same and is his intention the same and is his attention the same and does he answer the same answer and does he answer and does he deserve and does he serve and does he ob-

serve and does he quiet them and is he quiet then and did he
answer and did they ring and did they ring and did he answer
and did he address and did he have address and did he come to
say what did he come to stay and did he stay there where did he
say. Do say were you interested in what he did say. He said well
he was conversing then he said he understood very well and
naturally he was not neglectful.

Foresight means going to Rome. A frenchman does not roam.
No indeed. Leon was a frenchman. And his wife. Did I say his
wife. And why was she faithful and why were there four
children. The four children were little girls. In the meantime
cheerfulness can be me met and so can energy and economy and
foresight and administrative ability and too great abstention.
And in the meanwhile were we sorry. We were very sorry when
we heard of it. And the way to place a name there his name
there her name there, she placed her name there his name there
not their name there.

Not the name there. Naturally not the name there.
She stayed there.

I

Thank you very much, how often I have thanked you, how often I have cause to thank you. How often I do thank you.

Thank you very much.

And what would you have me do.

I would have you sing songs to your little Jew.

Not in the form of games not in the way of repetitions. Repetitions are in your first manner and now we are in the South and the South is not in the North. In the North we resist even when we are kissed and in the South we are kissed on the mouth. No sonatina can make me frown.

I love my love with a g because she is so faithful. I love her with a p because she is my pearl.

Can you subsist on butter, oil and edibles and rosebuds and weddings. Can you have weddings in many countries. How do each how does each mountain have a hill a steep hill, and I, I am always good.

Coo-coo, Mona. Plan away.

Have you seen a mixed dream. I dreamed of dances and guesses and cooing. How did you guess that.

Eighty pages of love and blandishment and small hand writing. And now a poem a conversation an address and a dialogue and a rebuttal.

Birds are fat and roses are yellow.

Tea is a color and tileul a drink.

Politics is a subject and obedience is necessary.

Blandishments are long and the buds are budded.

Who budded the buds.

I do love Tubbs hotel very well with Eucalyptus and palms and Godiva and a mistress.

A little hand writing is precious.

And now a conversation.

Let me neglect you. Do not let me neglect you. I do not let you neglect me. I am reproachful.

I have been reading. What. The book about Russia. And you

have loaned it to me. No I was personal. In the french sense. In the french sense. Do not be elusive and remember the last sign of the Moor. We walked far for that. I forgot that it was a conversation. That it is a conversation.

And now an address.

Address me to number thirteen rue San Severin and St. Anthony, address Saint Anthony too. And building blocks. Address building blocks and the can for the oil, address the can for the oil. Address it to all.

A dialogue.

I love you, I know it, how do you know it, I know it by my feeling.

And a rebuttal.

We do not use coal, we burn wood, we find it more economical and pleasanter. Before the war we used to wish that we could afford to burn wood instead of coal, now that we are no richer and wood is dearer we find it more economical to burn wood. Can you reason with me. I do not wish to.

And now as to cooing.

Coo away.

I miss the Mistral.

And the wood.

The wood misses the mistral.

And misses. Misses does not miss the mistral. Eighty pages are not eighty leaves, there are forty leaves, forty leaves make eighty pages.

And thunder.

The thunder comes from the door.

What can roses do, they can grow red without being seen.

How faithful is Caroline.

I can tell you a story about the North west.

Northwest from here is a hill and above the or rather near the top is a village. They grow orange blossoms, olives and winter grapes. The olive crop has been a failure for two years, the orange trees have been frozen, and the vines which are now just budding have been affected by the fog. In spite of all this the village is extremely prosperous. This is owing to the constant visits of artists and tourists. Thank you very much.

Pussy said that I was to wake her in an hour and a half if it didn't rain. It is still raining what should I do. Should I wake her or should I let her sleep longer.

Coo, coo.

The coo coo bird is sitting on the coo coo tree, budding the roses for me.

Why is pussy like the great American Army. Because she buds so many buddies.

And now I want to explain again the difference between the South of France and Brittany. In Brittany they have early potatoes. In the South they have early vegetables. In Brittany there is a great deal of fish caught. In the South they catch a great deal of fish. There are trout in the streams in some streams of Brittany and in some streams in the South. They grow camellias in some places in Brittany. They also grow camellias in the South.

I am very pleased to be in the South.

I address my caress, my caresses to the one who blesses who blesses me.

I usually say it for each separately.

I am going to say it for all of them altogether.

White yellow and pink roses, single ones.

Pink roses. Single ones.

White red and yellow roses.

An elephant.

Pink roses, single ones.

White roses.

Lilacs white roses and red roses and tea roses.

I need not mention the others.

How can gaiters cover old shoes.

How can rubber heels come off.

How can oil be thick and thin.

How can olives flower.

And why don't figs.

If Napoleon had a son, we could see Corsica in the morning. We have not seen Corsica yet. Everybody has mentioned it.

Why can butter be yellow or white.

She is so political.

And Mrs. Johnson is so afraid.

Coo, coo, I mention it. Coo coo I hear it. Coo coo let us be moderate. We are personal. We have a personal husband.

How can you read a book how can you read a book and look. I have no book.

I look.

Coo coo don't listen to me.

Do you know how to say buggy wagon riding. Do you know how to go slow. Go slowly. I go very slowly. Coo-coo I love but you.

This is old fashioned stuff. Now we say, Coo coo, I am all to you.

Cover up roses scratches, with what with black oil, and what else frog's noises.

I can understand copying gallo romaine pottery but I do not care to spend much money buying original ones. You can buy them for almost nothing.

Egg shells. Who sells egg shells and oranges and green peas. Who does. Answer me.

Eight out of eighty is how much. It isn't out of eighty, it's out of forty. Eight out of eighty is how much.

I said hastily that I was very rich.

I can think of everything to say.

Call to me with frogs and birds and moons and stars. Call me with noises. Mechanical noises.

I do not disturb you unnecessarily. Oh yes, you do.

I aspire to acquire every virtue and the allied armies. They will ride and we will see them. At a distance perhaps. And she sneezed. I am quite sure that it did not portend a chill. No indeed brilliant sunshine.

Gladys Deacon is so brilliant and so is Chicago. I do not mention either of them here.

Coo coo a message to you.

And she did not make cheese very well.

We see no necessity for reductions.

I please myself and I please Mrs. Johnson. I pay her. Who payed her. You payed her. Why certainly you payed her.

Let me tell you about yesterday. Yesterday I was Lindoed and you you were so gracious. And to-day. To-day I was still lindoed and you were even more gracious. You are extraordinarily gracious and I am very contentedly grateful. In this way we are adjusted. Pinions are adjusted. They are not like a bird. They do not fly.

I spy a fly.

It was a bee.

You are my honey honey suckle.

I am your bee.

You are my honey honey suckle.

I am your bee.

We saw a blacksmith making springs and we waited in the dust and were content not content to wait but content with the springs. We hope we have cause to be content with the three springs.

Two weeks are less than three weeks. We will see everything.

Olives for wood, butter for cheese, milk for honey, and wind for sunny sunny weather and clouds. How can you distress me. You can't. You can please me. And an apprentice. You can please me as an apprentice. Apprentisage.

A nice library a very nice library, she mentions it as a very nice library.

Coo coo come dirty me, coo coo. I am for thee.

Do we like corn bread.

Here is an interesting story. In visiting churches we find many little colored images pretty renaissance altars and late colored glass chandeliers and flowers and we said what we liked best were the colored glass and after that the little colored images on the ceiling and after that the flowers. We sent our servant to see these treasures. She walked 5 miles and enjoyed them very much. So had we.

We have a multitude of roses and mountains of lilac. We pick everything as it shows. We are a model to every one. We are wonderfully productive.

This is another interesting story. We found ourselves suddenly without eggs for supper. We were quite near an Italians and we bought some very good sausages. We also bought some anchovies and cakes and then we came home at a very rapid pace.

We came home so rapidly that we were able to go down hill slowly. We always prefer going down hill slowly. When we had finished supper we were very certain that we were not hurried. We always linger in a chair. To-morrow in a fashion of speaking is the Holy Sabbath.

How can you think of everything when roses smell the most and tea pots lean on elephants and a spring is lost. How can you mention orange wear when orange blossoms last how can you laugh at me all day when all day has been passed, splendidly with an Englishman a negro and a Pole who might have had a Russian name.

How can you easily please me you can do so very well and how can you laugh as asparagrass when peas will do as well, and gloves. How we appreciate doves. Gloves and palms, please take care. Take care of what. Take care of electricity. Electricity takes care of itself.

A reform for two is not to stew.

A red poppy is for decoration and a daisy is a humble expression of a husband's love. Together they make a bouquet. Joined to nasturtiums and pansies they show unexpected tenderness.

If the South is cold and the North is colder, if the wind is strong and the palms are stronger, if there are no palms in the North only lilacs what emotion do canticles express. Canticles are religious.

Can we still be a necessity.

Counting horses, a large horse is named butterfly.

Relieve me relieve me from the Turk. He was not a Turk he was partly Negro. His father came from New Orleans in Louisiana.

Can you prefer one who is not Italian can you prefer cooking that is not Italian. Can you prefer rice that is Italian. Can you be selected to look through the window. And what do I see. I see you.

Can a cow keep sweet. Yes if it has a blessing. Can a cow keep its retreat. No not if it has a blessing. Can a cow have feet. Yes if it has a blessing. Can a cow be perfect. Yes if it has a blessing.

I bless the cow. It is formed, it is pressed, it is large it is crowded. It is out. Cow come out. Cow come out and shout.

Have Caesars a duty. Yes their duty is to a cow. Will they do their duty by the cow. Yes now and with pleasure. Mock oranges do not mock me.

We have the true orange the orange blossom. And do perfumes smell. Yes in the grass.

How can I welcome you. I do.

Now there is a case in point.

I arouse, you arouse we arouse and Godiva arouses me. This should not be. We should tranquilly think of the remedy. I arouse the sympathy of Grasse. Why is grass white. Because it is covered with white hail. How pleasantly we back out.

And now mountains, and now mountains, do not cloud, over. Let us wash our hair and stare stare at mountain ranges. How sweet are suns and suns. And the season. The sea or the season, and the roads. Roads are often neglected.

How can you feel so reasonably.

And what were the pages.

And why were there men who had hurry as their reason. Not now. They were not in a hurry now. How precious you are.

A poppy, need I say a red poppy. A poppy by its color is a symbol of the decoration a grateful country gives you in recognition of your devotion to duty and the daisies are a humble expression of a husband's love. Now take it.

Can we count a nightingale. Can we escort one another. Can we feed on artichokes and olives and may we sell anchovies. No we may buy eggs. And now often do you say, I argue often about words and houses. How are houses entered. By the determination to be well and happy. How kindly you smile. How sweetly you smile on me. How tenderly you reward me and how beautifully you utter your words. We have no use for botanically painted plates.

How can I thank you enough for holding me on the ladder for allowing me to pick roses, for enjoying my fireside and for recollecting stars. How can I thank you enough for all your kindness to me. How can I thank you enough.

If I could I would make this arrangement.

Here donkey and he brays, so does not my mistress.

Here donkey. Just a minute. Monte Carlo. Just a minute.
Here donkey. We crave sweets.

Not because we like honey or landscapes but just because
we have ancient habitations. We are placed under a torn sky,
and the Romans were lenient and paused on the road. How nicely
we go up hill.

When I was wishous, when I had wishes. When I wished I
wished to be remembered to you.

How can you silently think of me. Rest easily on the terrace
look out on the blue sea and think of me.

How can rows of roses spare matches. How can matches
strike. How can images be blue, temples are blue and how are
brooches red. Fish come in summer. They need rain and warm
weather.

I can lean over a parapet, you can lean over a parapet, we
can lean over a parapet, she can lean over a parapet, they can all
stand as if they were waiting for their king. There are no kings
there are nothing but princesses. Princes and princesses.

And where have I seen you before.

In a way a honey moon is not treated to hail. It is not treated
to rain, it is not treated to mischief, it is not treated to threats. It
is treated to pleasure and prophecy. I prophesy good weather.

How do I care for hair. I care for hair by cutting it.

That is an excellent method.

And how long does an inventory take.

It takes all day. Not every day. No not every other day. I
leave mine behind me. You are so wise.

Do you despise decorations.

Do you admire gypsies.

Do you really wear a chinese hat.

We do.

Can we eat to-day, to-day is the month of May. Can we eat
to-day largely.

And how nicely we sing of the thirteenth of April. The
thirteenth of April is the day which is the month of May. On
that day we hesitate to sing. Why because we are so happily
flourishing.

We make a list, a sauce dish, a saucer, a tile, a gilded cushion, a handkerchief, a glass, two plates and an oratory. And what do we do in the oratory. We tell about our blessings. We bless the day every day. We say gayly the troubadour plays his guitar to his star.

How can we whistle in our bath. By means of oxygen. Oxygen in water makes oxygenated water. Thank you for all you are doing for me. And don't mind the rain. It is not going to rain long.

The song of Alice B.

Little Alice B. is the wife for me. Little Alice B so tenderly is born so long so she can be born along by a husband strong who has not his hair shorn. And what size is wise. The right size is nice. How can you credit me with wishes. I wish you a very happy birthday.

One two one two I come to you. To-day there is nothing but the humble expression of a husband's love. Take it.

I caught sight of a splendid Misses. She had handkerchiefs and kisses. She had eyes and yellow shoes she had everything to choose and she chose me. In passing through France she wore a Chinese hat and so did I. In looking at the sun she read a map. And so did I. In eating fish and pork she just grew fat. And so did I. In loving a blue sea she had a pain. And so did I. In loving me she of necessity thought first. And so did I. How prettily we swim. Not in water. Not on land. But in love. How often do we need trees and hills. Not often. And how often do we need mountains. Not very often. And how often do we need birds. Not often. And how often do we need wishes. Not often. And how often do we need glasses not often. We drink wine and we make, well we have not made it yet. How often do we need a kiss. Very often and we add when tenderness overwhelms us we speedily eat veal. And what else, ham and a little pork and raw artichokes and ripe olives and chester cheese and cakes and caramels and all the melon. We still have a great deal of it left. I wonder where it is. Conserved melon. Let me offer it to you.

How can you sleep so sweetly, how can you be so very well. Very well.

How can you measure measures I measure measures very well.

To be a roman and Julius Caesar and a bridge and a column and a pillar and pure how singularly refreshing.

We know of a great many things we are not to do. We are not to laugh or be sarcastic or harsh or loud or sudden or neglectful or preoccupied or attacked or rebukeful.

He is so generous with the towels. He leaves her two fresh clean ones.

How can you worship extras. I find it exceedingly simple to do so. I have but to see.

I see the sea and it is a river not a murmuring river nor a roaring river nor a great river nor a callous river. I see Saint Anthony in the river. Saint Anthony the fruit of the olive, the crown of the orange the strength of the cork. Saint Anthony, pray for us.

I feel nearly everything.

How often the wind how often the wind resists iron. How often it manages to show. We have tall walls and so have palaces.

I can be seen to be a queen. I can be seen declaring that wine how can wine be so cheap. It will be cheaper. And is there a providence in Provence. There is no comfort in a home, because they are not as reasonable in their hopes as they are in their fears. Wine makes no water. Water makes wine. The wine, the vine needs water and we we wish to eat our lunch in the department of Vaucluse. And we will we will arrange the department to be willing. Napoleon, why did they declare their purpose. Napoleon listened to music in Avignon, he felt the strength of the violin and the composition. We were not inimical to women nor to men, nor even to educated strangers. We liked best of all the soldiers and the salt. How many leaves have pitchers. And what is the difference between white and yellow. And how many lions are golden. All dogs seen at a distance, run.

Willy nilly with a roasted kid, how can you be so delicious and give it to the cat. I gave to the cat because we were uncomfortable. We are not naturally uncomfortable, we are a little nervous. I took a piece of pork and I stuck it on a fork and I gave it to a curly headed jew jew jew. I want my little jew to be round like a pork, a young round pork with a cork for his tail.

A young round pork. I want my little jew to be round like a young round pork. I do.

A special name for careless is caress. A special name for answers is tenderness a special name for Master is Mrs. C. A special name for an enormous hotel is very well I will not answer back.

When the swallows fly so high you mustn't cry because when the swallows fly so high the sun will shine out by and by.

I never answer back.

Back there.

How can the mother of a priest see through your glasses.

The times, the times is a rose, the rose is a nose, in time the nose arose. To arise means to clean, to wash out. Thank you so much.

What have little museums in them. They have dutch British English and austrian things in them and when we see them we say they are copies of French and when we see them and we see them when we see of them we read of them. We know we will like them. And we are not mistaken.

We did not stay where St. Stephen was to pray we did not stay we did not play we saw the guns and what did they say, they said that it was not necessary to be protected, it was only necessary to be firm and numerous, it was only necessary to be stoned it was only necessary. A great many people hesitate about St. Stephen. We didn't.

When we came away we came away to stay we came away steadily. And where are we. We are in the land of sky larks not in the land of nightingales. We do not mention robins swallows, quails and peacocks. We do not mix them. We murmur to each other, nightingales, we please each other with fruit trees we allow each other melons and we throw each other shoes. And pork. What do we think about pork and asparagus. What do we think about everything. It is necessary for us to know what we think. We think very well of butter and church cheese. We think very well of cracked church bells.

How many is four times two. Eight. And seven plus one. Eight. And six and two. Eight. And how much is seven. Seven is five and two and four and three. We are free. We are free to have false smiles. I smile falsely and I do not hesitate to give pleasure I speak sharply and I hear the sound of falling water. I linger and I kiss a rose. How often do I kiss a rose. Everytime. I approach the wonder. I wonder why I have so many wishes. I wish to please and to be repeated. This is in my first manner. Thank you so much for your first manner. That is most kind of you.

Misses meet Mister.

Is that what you were doing.

I quit early. So does every one who works eight hours a day.

Georgie Sand is in my hand and what are omelettes made of, of oranges and lemonade and how did you see the new moon. It was not the new moon it was the first quarter.

Don't make fun of me.

How sweet to tickle little sweet and how prettily little pigs eat, and how interesting to collect treasures and how admirable to celebrate pleasures. Napoleon was a great pleasure.

A sonatina followed by another. The public is not invited to laugh. Who brought the turkeys to France. A Jesuit father brought the turkeys to France and ate them and then they grew and then we ate them and then we grew. Let me see the cups. How often do we say let me learn to stay. I stay all day and all night too.

How can I be relished by lunches. How can I be stolen for tea. I cannot. How can I be earnest in churches how can I be wise in a chateau. We say so.

False smiles are wiles to make one's styles realise the difference between a tone and a tone. I atone with smiles and miles.

How many forests believe in Carpentier and will he win on a foul. How many times have I asked this and how often has a fowl replied. Oh the dear dear fowl oh the sweet false smile oh the tender tender while, we while the time away so pleasantly and she, she is my nature's daily food and she is wooed and chewed. Respect me.

I see the moon and the moon sees me god bless the moon and god bless me which is she.

II

A sonatina followed by another. This ought to be the other. And it is.

A sonatina song is just this long. A sonatina long is just this song.

Come along and sit to me sit with me sit by me, come along and sit with me all the next day too. Come along and sit with me sit by me sit for me, come along and sit by me sit by me and see.

Seneca said that he loved to be wed. And he said that was what he said.

Carefully meddle with me.

If you think, if you think much, if you reflect if you reflect me, I reflect that I have not been serviceable. But you are very serviceable.

Do not be plaintive and sing, meddle with me, meddle with me, medal, who has the medal.

Sing reasonably.

How happy we are on the fourth of July.

There is more short hair than long hair here. Hear me. I will be clerical. And researches. Researches rhyme with churches!

Rachel says Rachel says she is my aunt. I do not deny her. Nor do I blaspheme the saints. I am always to see Saint Anthony thought of.

Please be very still. And repeat, let us lead it by ourselves. And we did. Godiva did. And happily.

What can Beauvais say, Beauvais can say come away. And we did. We will go to Brussels. Brussels rhymes with muscles.

I look very pretty in sculpture.

Make a new way to say, how do you do. I can write to there. And how will you do it. By measuring from there to there. France is french.

A sonatina caressed. I like that best.

I have a fancy for reconciliation. How can you reconcile beets and strawberries. By knowing they both are red.

How easily we release images. And why do we worry the blacks. Black and blue all out but you.

I reason, we reason we reason for a reason. How prettily I shimmer. We have assisted ourselves. And sunshine. We brought rain, in our train, Godiva Godiva Godiva.

Let us and let us and let us say. We go away and absolutely we reason in this way. Why are pages open and why are we not disappointed. Why do we moisten our hands. Because it is hot. I breathe freely.

Birds and pages and Brussels. Lobster will be cheaper. Lobsters will be cheaper after a bit. And how often do we intend to go a mile.

Summaries are precious to me. Left over every where is precious to me.

Continue to purse your lips and remember that fruit is not abundant this year.

And how much patience is there in singing.

All the mouths are near and all the mouths are here and all the mouths have that.

I am still satisfied.

Wedding jelly.

Have that colored white.

The reason is not far to seek.

The honey honey honey suckle. I am the bee.

Words and sizes. There are surprises. Can you quote speeches. Can you quote speeches. Words and sizes there are surprises. And little screens. How literally we screen her. We have barricades and weaponless sisters and all sorts of repeated curtains. Curtains let us take advantage of repetitions. She tells a story so brightly. And a hero has patience. He leans this way.

How can so many sonatinas be followed by another. Everybody smiles.

How can you press me to you.

All the rest of the bale is filled with down. We find it very compressible.

Can you thank me for so much.

A great many numbers indicate the number of places to which we can go. A great many numbers have this to say. Go this way. A great many numbers have special sizes and under them there is a large F. Be so pleased to see for tea.

We are going to remember this very soon. And recall her. And recall her call her.

Now no motion is so fast as hurling.

She is immovable.

Have a chance repeatedly for the use of this have a chance repeatedly collect me.

I have been useful to her.

ANNEX TO NO. 2

SONATINA FOLLOWED BY ANOTHER

NOT YET SAT BUT WALKING

I can but think I can but think, and what do you stare at. Cultivation.

In the forest by the sea in feathers, two white feathers have decorated Normandy. They have been placed there by the girl who came by sea from Barbery. Casablanca is now entirely a french city.

We are spending our honeymoon in Normandy. We are following in the footsteps of our brother who found that the inhabitants singularly flattered his wife. He has been married a long time and has a son twenty five years old.

How old are brave women. We find that a disrupter we find that a disrupter is singularly useful in an emergency but entirely impractical when used too continuously. We have returned to our normal footing. We love the hand. The hand that forbids collisions. The french avoid a crisis and the Americans arise to it.

Do not think that we are safe.

We are safe in a safe deposit that is in a hotel found for us by our brother.

And now gently guide us up hill.

Uphill and down dale.

How is it that the English do not mind remembering that they once possessed Normandy. How is that they do not mind noticing that all their civilisation resembles the civilisation of Normandy. How is it that they do not mind me. I love to mind to remind to remind them and they remind me of everything.

Why is there a certitude in recreation. Why is there feeling in antithesis.

Leaves cabbage grass, apples trees gold cream oaks and ears, now many people need me.

I need her, she needs me, she needs me, I need that she is splendidly robust. Please me by thinking at ease.

Good-night now.

Sincerely yours,

Augustus Wren.

Flaubert have a care. Have a care Flaubert. Flaubert don't be hurt don't be hurt Flaubert.

When we were traveling we saw cunning, we saw cunning in women, we saw cunning in men, we saw cunning in children, when we were traveling we hesitated before wishing and then in the evening we saw a star and we start wishing. I wish I was a fish with a great big tail, a polly wolly doodle a lobster or a whale. This was not what I wished. I never tell my wish.

Earnestly we notice that a pharmacy has a green light that a railroad has a red light and a green light, that an automobile has a white light, that a ship has a green light and also a white light. We also notice that distances are not deceptive.

Please recall to me everything that you have thought of.

And now for squares. It is astonishing that it has never been observed that squares are frequently expressive of ignorance on the part of the inhabitants. They inevitably consider those who come to them as strangers, they certainly feel lonely in their inter-course with another. Some are too young to marry and others never will be of service. Some appear at windows and again others say we have joined a circus. In France it is not easy to join a circus. Barges have a boat to lead them. How do you do. I forgive you everything and there is nothing to forgive. Some prefer going up hill quickly and down hill slowly and some really prefer going up hill practically all the time. I myself am to be remembered among the number of these. I understand what she says. Peas and beans and barley grows. You nor I nor nobody knows. And yet flowers are very pretty.

The fruit that falls from the tree and is picked up from the ground is often sound.

I am always glad when I please you.

Around the world around the world there is a square. How can I forget the square. It is very large and the town is small.

We have been very pleased to hear him say that he likes to be where they play all day in the Casino.

The apple marks a day, the day when in the evening we heard of the ocean. Water does not resemble water at all. I am not worried about breadth.

Let me tell you about museums. When glass was made and there was no shade, and buildings were necessary for symmetry, then objects which of which many are beautiful were collected together. They were placed so that they might be seen. They give pleasure. As for me I prefer purchase. I even prefer that the seller breaks his treasure. The buyer of course does not. Thank you so much. We are sincerely remembered wherever we have been. She said that she regretted but the staff had already been sent away and the inventory had been begun.

Sixes and sevens oh heavens oh heavens.

A fig an apple and some grapes makes a cow. How. The Caesars know how. Now. The Caesars know how and they know how now. The Caesars know how. How can you be able to obey a whim. Whine and shine is not the same as whim and vim. How can you be stout. By eschewing reminiscences. And how can you be on time. How can you be left to serve me. An Italian has not gone yet. We are very pleased to see that a woman wears the medal of Eighteen seventy of Alsace and Lorraine. We wear the medal of the Reconnaissance Française. Thank you so very much. We sign ourselves respectfully yours, Mrs. Herbert Howard. We like Breton names such as Patty Requets. I do not smell nicely. Seasons are upon us. And the snow threatens. And the sea is soft. Please me.

Back, we do not go back, but by a back we go across, we Godiva and Saint Christopher.

Back and over, how well I remember that song. Back and over and is he a good father. Back and over over there, we and Godiva and Saint Christopher and the pair, the pair and the pair. Father and son, and one another. Over there. When there is no bridge there is a river. I might have said this in another way.

This is a list of my experiences. I cannot describe beauty. I cannot describe a square, I cannot describe strangeness. I cannot describe rivers, I cannot describe lands. I can describe milk, and women and resemblances and elaboration and cider. I can also describe weather and counters and water. I can also describe bursts of melody.

I was reasonably gratified that we did not lose that.

How often have I said, what do you wish.

The question is is the broom a broom and I cannot mention this. I cannot mention the half of a honeymoon which was finished too soon but there are always plenty of them shining in the sunshine. I am your honey honeysuckle you are my bee, I am your honey honey suckle you are my bee I am your honey honey suckle you are my bee.

Treasure measure pleasure, whether it is a pleasure, whether it is a pleasure. Treasure measure, whether we consider the placing of the treasure, whether we consider that the treasure is whether we consider that the treasure is a pleasure. Measure, whether we consider that the treasure is a measure of a treasure, whether we treasure, whether we measure whether it is a pleasure. I remember with so much pleasure the crossing of the river. I remember with so much pleasure all the pleasure and all of the pleasure we had crossing the river. I remember the pleasure we had in looking at all the treasure that was made of steel and had to do with instruments that measure. I remember very well the pleasure when I recollect, when I recollect the treasure and can we place that treasure, can we replace that treasure can we place that treasure, whether we can place that treasure. I have decided to be sunburnt.

Thank you so much.

Augustus Lyon.

Can you sit can you sit can you sit easily. How valiantly Florence says I find it astonishing.

And how often is there a republic. Very often and very tenderly. I feel the republican.

A honeymoon so soon again, when, why now.

Some have a honey moon with a husband too soon, some have a honeymoon with a husband soon enough. And we have a honeymoon at noon, every noon, we have a honey moon, a honey honey-moon at noon and in the afternoon and before noon and between the afternoon and the forenoon which is not noon. You understand me. I understand you very well.

I can sign myself sincerely yours.

And the old woman. The old woman is enjoying the best of health. She is annoyed with the American who detained her.

Brown thread and white thread, it is a pity that we do not find what we want and that I am such a nuisance to you. It is a great pity that I bother you but it is best so. How do you do I forgive you everything and there is nothing to forgive. How do you do I adore you.

Sincerely yours,

Augustus Merryweather.

Forty francs for a pencil. So Emil says. He says the pencil is worth forty francs. Please finish eating.

I gave seen something delightful. The cathedral rising to the stars the band practicing, the dark figures laughing and saying good night and we going away. I have seen something delightful. Sincerely yours,

Augustus Caesar.

How can you have been so thoughtless as to have brought this book and the melon. We have brought both. I have seen something really delightful, I have been mistaken for whom, for no one. I have just been mistaken. You have been mistaken for the benefit of flowers. That is exactly what I mean. And how often do we not mean we do not mean this.

Instead of that this. Tenderly little Miss, tenderly little Misses.

Instead of that this and we would miss the honey and the money but we do not because we have the money and the honey.

I do not astonish you at all, you are my ball and what do you do sitting, you sit there. And why are you not anxious to please because flowers come to you with ease and you are pleased with the flowers and all.

Thank you very much, Mrs. James Allen Augustus. Mrs. James Allen. Mrs. Augustus Allen. Thank you very much Mrs. Augustus Allen.

How can you cherish husbands. Husbands and husbands.

Thank you very much.

I am trying so hard to get to bed that is what she said that is what she said. I am trying so hard to get to bed is what she said.

We have been very wise to enjoy ourselves so much and we hope to enjoy ourselves very much more.

Thank you so very much.

Sincerely yours,

Augustus Ruine.

We have eaten heartily of food well salted and in consequence have found it necessary to eat a great deal of sweet to stimulate our thirst.

We have had all of these experiences in this climate and really the moon and the earth have reason to deal politely with one another. Columbus and the egg, Columbus or the egg or my darling with her eye glasses.

We have been nervous and now we are better, we pray every evening that we may the next day be a good husband.

When they are patriotic they do know the difference.

Kindly drink water again.

They have mentioned being Asiatic and Northern. They have mentioned having farmed their loving. They have mentioned being in earnest about sunshine and for moon-light. They have been in earnest more together. And did he buy a trailer. Did he buy their trailer. Did he buy their trailers.

I certainly think that automobiles suit cathedrals very well.

I am very much [in] earnest Mr. James Raymond.

And what became of their inhabitants.

I can do it from there by just pulling. How can you do it from there by just pulling.

There were a great many windows not broken and there were a great many windows not broken.

What do you say to gathering together a good woman and a strong man. What do you say to river scenery. What do you say to spending this day to spending a day to devoting a day to this journey. We have been mistaken and I have been mistaken. We have not mistaken one thing for another thing. Godiva speaks earnestly and says that. So does many another saint.

A honeymoon, so soon, again, yes it pleases when it comes

so soon and again. Yet or again, and some times when there is need of honey for the moon again.

Now let us say pussy. When did I say pussy. You are so full of a cow factory. You manufacture cows by vows. The cows produce reduce reduce they reduce the produce. Cows are necessary after feeding. We are needing what we have after feeding. After feeding we find cows out. How are cows multiplied. By proper treatment. Thank you so much for being so explicit.

She is gentle and considerate. She can do no more than be gentle and considerate and we find that to be quite enough to satisfy and not rebuff.

And now we hear her sentences. She says that as to inequality she is reminded of most things by their cautiousness. Do not be afraid to be of an early religion. And as to that dominion, what are dominion rights. Honey moons do not get startling information. And cows come out.

Little singing charm can never do no harm, little baby sweet can always be a treat. And are sonatinas in music boxes and do they follow one after the other and are music boxes grind organs yes or no. I believe it and I told her so and she believed it as I very well know. I tell her so so.

A belly band is made strand by strand a belly band can stand being knit by hand. And sewed together. And sewed together then. We know how to build a fire. Can tickle can tickle can tickle her for sin is said by writing on the wall with lead with lead penciling. We have two pen holders for which we have cared for which we have cared very much. We do not know this about these.

He ate she ate they ate there, she ate he ate and they are there, he ate she ate and they do care, they ate and we mate and we are there.

Oh no I love you so oh no.

I have often heard it said that a sky-lark never goes to bed. I have often heard it said that they sing. I have often heard it said that they are suddenly ahead and I have often heard it said that they sing.

When we were listening they were attending and when they

heard it said that they were frightening we wondered if they had heard.

I believe almost immediately in a soft egg. And so do I. I believe almost immediately in a pleasant surprise.

I see the moon and the moon sees me, God bless the moon and God bless me.

I did not know that the south wind brought the moon.

We are in their way I can see that plainly.

Yes now we will go.

When we say beg we say I beg you to do so. When I say beg I say I beg you to believe me. And when I say I beg you I beg it of you I mean I know you are all well and happy. This is the meaning of exclamation. He is led he is led he is gently led to morality. I understand the difference between bathing and bath tubs between elegance in a dentist's chair and elegance in a pair. I understand the difference between accounts and recounting and I understand the difference between rose and white. I also understand the difference between able and to be able. She is able she is said to be able, she is said to be able to receive me.

Sweet affection.

They say that they say woods are made that way. They are made altogether. And we gave them away. We gave them away to-day. So we say. Now can you tell me the rest.

This is the rest.

Thank you for the rest.

And now how earnestly we say it is the wrong color. But not this anyway.

And further flowers.

We sleep on the seat and we stay near the bench and we mount the electricity and we gather no indignation.

We sign what do we sign.

Fine fine.

I said it.

We said it.

We saw it.

And the choppers chop it.

And all alike we find the wood is woolen.

So is knitting.
I am not quitting.
Sitting.
I sit.
And you sat.
What does cover a hat.
Underneath it I have reason to need hawthorne.
Hawthorne for me.
A flower an open flower, a sensible extra flower, a seasonable and so-called flower.
I shall re-adjust my solution.
I solve, I resolve, I absolve, I fasten it with a tassel. I do know that church.
I suddenly see the scene. And the scene sees me. God bless the scene and God bless me.
Then we will go on so as not to get there too late.
Is there anything we hate.
I'll say so.
Then we'll go on.
In different countries ploughed fields are softer than in others. In different countries in different countries can you guess by the F.
Can you explain to me about the sparrows, the song sparrows and the Seine.
The Seine is a river which we can see.
It is very clear it is very clear when we hear and now shall we get ourselves ready. Yes.
We do not call a wind break a Robinson tree, nor do we call a hawthorne a thorn, we find it not at all useful when there are leaves on it. Useful enough for that much. Do you remember that a pump can pump other things than water. For this search the land. Yes tenderness grows and it grows where it grows. And do you like it. Yes you do. And does it fill a cow full of filling. Yes. And where does it come out of. It comes out of the way of the Caesars. Caesars are rich in thought and in deed. Indeed.
Coming in at the door.
Shut the door.
Yes.

What do you want to-day. Just the same as yesterday. Now do you. Yes I do.

Just a minute and you can have it. I don't want to wait. You are not waiting. I am not.

We read indeed and an Italian.

Would you drink with him for him or to him. Would you drink anything.

At her request I did suggest that the primroses were not all for the best. Oh no indeed, I have a creed. I have decreed that we consider speed. And what did we spend. We didn't spend any of it to-day.

We will call it so we will call it a celebration, because we had them and we have them and we will have them and we handled them and we handle them and we will handle them. I call it a celebration because we handled them and we will handle. I call it a substantial celebration because we increased hearing them and we settled them and we settled for them. I call it a celebration and so do they. She says she is really full of tenderness.

LAST PART

ONE SONATINA FOLLOWED BY ANOTHER DIVIDED BY A PLAY

Distinguished by there being no moat there at all. We have settled this by asking again and again about it.

The Black hand of the Porte Maillot. She says that a summer day can come in early spring. What is the difference between an early spring and a late spring.

The Black Hand of the Porte Maillot.

A PLAY

Those prominent in what is necessary to the automobile and dreaming in dusting.

She dreams of me in not that capacity. This is said to be erroneously referred to by themselves.

Allan and the best.

She with her mind attuned to cows.

They undertaking elements of pears. And he well he was the

third tenant of a large and really friendly house but it was not taken in his name.

Windows are prominently open and there are a great many monetary advantages. Do you know that Ripolin is the name of a certain kind of paint. I take a deep interest in invented names for universal industries. There is Kodak, there is Ripolin there is the recitative and there is the fact that a Lord Derby can not count.

Now we plunge into that play. I play you play and they play. Play and play and play away. I have already said this. Now I said this is the way I make a play. Play it if you please play it, I say play it, I say if you please play it and do you know I am perplexed and respected for having had an indicator of the slant of roads twice smashed in the same town and once when it was guarded.

A PLAY

Not the dears.

But dears.

Dears are the dears.

I look at my own and I see them.

We gain on them.

The first black hand dining.

We stayed home to sit and we did.

How can you think for money how can you think for me how can you think my honey how can you my busy bee. When I have time I will blow my nose.

What was a nice idea, to have my wife hear, hear what. It was a nice idea to have my wife here. Hear me. It was a nice idea to have my wife hear hear what. It was a nice idea to have my wifey hear. Hear. Hear.

A PLAY

I play for baby I play she is baby and I play that baby and Vincent Astor builds a home. Do you believe what I say.

I often say it so that you can know it, when this you see remember me and now I am a poet and I know it and I say to the Caesars all the four shut the door. Caesars all the four open the door and I adore not only a treasure but now I find that a cow is a treasure it is a treasure and loved without measure as it comes out through the door. And the floor. Yes and the floor. It comes out behind and the door before the door there are four four Caesars and I will show them the door. They know of the door. And the cow comes out of the door. Do you adore me. When this you see remember me.

Y.D.

Are you resting nicely. Oh charmingly. Are you pleased with everything. Oh so very pleased. Do you feel satisfied. Oh so satisfied. Have you pleasure in your point of view! Oh a great deal of pleasure.

There where they were pleased there where they were longer, there where they were there. Where. Everywhere. You please me you do please me.

Instance in this instance that flattery succeeds with Caesars but they do not really feel it because it is not flattery it is adequate representation.

I have thanked them privately, I now thank them publicly and to-morrow we will gratify them with fruit.

Middle man. Middle man. Middle of middle woman, middle of middle man, middle man when you can middle woman middle of middle woman. Caesars do not stray they stay.

Caesars stay they do not stray.

Caesars stay they do not stray. Stretch away not into the distance but close to and successfully separating they permit indeed they insist indeed they cause indeed they aid they do not pause they cause and we register with a smile and a nod that there is no need of a prod indeed we register that satisfaction has been obtained.

We have been told that telegrams are sold and we do not buy them. We have been told that rooms can be sold but we do not buy them. We have been told that chairs can be sold but we do not buy them.

What we buy is this and with it we satisfy the longing for a solitude à deux.

When we see women we say do you inhabit this hotel. When they see us they say we can very easily tell all that we wish to state.

I would indeed wish to wed. Would you indeed. When all is said it is very pleasant to be wedded.

Yes indeed and it is a pleasure that we can enjoy.

When we say did they we say they did. When we say did they we say they didn't. When we say they did, they did. When we say they didn't, they didn't. I think the thing to do is to telephone to the hotel if we can on Sundays to the hotel this evening.

I smoke a little pipe.

And who has given it to me.

We were we were.

They applaud. And them the electricity disappointed them. This was so unnecessary.

A beauty is known to be beautiful. How beautiful you are I see.

A reason why I see this is this.

Prettily prettily me she is all the world prettily.

They knew all that you know.

In this way I mention what she will say. In this way I will say what she will say. In this way. I take it literally.

Pleasure for her and pleasure for him it is a pleasure to her and it is a pleasure to him.

Pleasure.

Please.

To please.

He pleases me pleasurably. She pleases me pleasurably.

Pleasurably.

Eyes please

Yes.

Eyes please.

Bright at night not too bright at night.

I read to you and you read to me and we both read intently. And I waited for you and you waited for me and we both waited attentively.

I find knitting to be a continuous occupation and I am full of gratitude because I realise how much I am indebted to the hands that wield the needles.

I have been most pleasantly engaged in saying so.

I practice caution.

And delight in his treasure. And then we will measure our ears and their ears and we will know that we told them so and so and so we know and we feel about a fountain of joy and a well and all well. Very well.

Very well indeed very well indeed. And how are you. Very well indeed.

I have been pleased to hear that you have been pleased to hear what has pleased you to hear.

What do you hear.

I hear you say what you say.

Well you can hear it all day. Good day.

And what is his reward. His reward is the reward of the ages. A cow. All of us worship a cow. How. By introducing and producing and extension.

How.

You know about pipes. A shepherd has pipes. So he has. And so have I.

I do mention this and that, it is true of a pussy and a cat, that this is that and that is this and you are sleepy with a kiss. Who miss, us.

Why misses us, who dismisses us.

We kiss us.

Very well.

She is very well.

And as to cow which is mentioned anyhow. A cow is mentioned anyhow.

Thank you Romans Caesars and all.

I say it to you and I say it to you I say it to you how I love my little jew. I say it to you and I say it to you. I say it to you and I say it to you. I say it to you.

How I can I have the air of here and there and I say it to you I say it to you I love my own little jew. How can I have the air and I do care I care for her hair and there for the rest of her too my little jew. I love her too my little jew. And she will have endured the cold that is cured, it is cured it is cured and a cow how can a cow follow now a cow can follow now because I have a cow. I had a cow you have a cow, you have a cow now.

She is that kind of a wife. She can see.

And a credit to me.

And a credit to me she is sleepily a credit to me and what do I credit her with I credit her with a kiss.

     1. Always sweet.

     2. Always right.

     3. Always welcome.

     4. Always wife.

     5. Always blessed.

     6. Always a successful druggist of the second class and we know what that means. Who credits her with all this a husband with a kiss and what is he to be always more lovingly his missus' help and hero. And when is he heroic, well we know when.

Win on a foul pretty as an owl pretty as an owl win on a fowl. And the fowl is me and she is pretty as an owl. Battling Siki and Capridinks capridinks is pretty and winks, winks of sleep and winks of love. Capridinks. Capridinks is my love and my Coney.

PART I

Stanza I

I caught a bird which made a ball
And they thought better of it.
But it is all of which they taught
That they were in a hurry yet
In a kind of a way they meant it best
That they should change in and on account
But they must not stare when they manage
Whatever they are occasionally liable to do
It is often easy to pursue them once in a while
And in a way there is no repose
They like it as well as they ever did
But it is very often just by the time
That they are able to separate
In which case in effect they could
Not only be very often present perfectly
In each way which ever they chose.
All of this never matters in authority
But this which they need as they are alike
Or in an especial case they will fulfill
Not only what they have at their instigation
Made for it as a decision in its entirety
Made that they minded as well as blinded
Lengthened for them welcome in repose
But which they open as a chance
But made it be perfectly their allowance
All which they antagonise as once for all
Kindly have it joined as they mind

Stanza II

It is not with them that they come
Or rather gather for it as not known

They could have pleasure as they change
Or leave it all for it as they can be
Not only left to them as restless
For which it is not only left and left alone
They will stop it as they like
Because they call it further mutinously
Coming as it did at one time only
For which they made it rather now
Coming as well as when they come and can
For which they like it always
Or rather best so when they can be alert
Not only needed in nodding
But not only not very nervous
As they will willingly pass when they are restless
Just as they like it called for them
All who have been left in their sense
All should boisterous make it an attachment
For which they will not like what there is
More than enough and they can be thought
Always alike and mind do they come
Or should they care which it would be strange.
Just as they thought away.
It is well known that they eat again
As much as any way which it can come
Liking it as they will
It is not only not an easy explanation
Once at a time they will
Nearly often after there is a pleasure
In liking it now
Who can be thought perilous in their account.
They have not known that they will be in thought
Just as rich now or not known
Coming through with this as their plan
Always in arises.
Liking it fairly and fairly well
Which meant they do
Mine often comes amiss
Or liking strife awhile

Often as evening is as light
As once for all
Think of how many often
And they like it here.

Stanza III

It is not now that they could answer
Yes and come how often
As often as it is the custom
To which they are accustom
Or whether accustomed like it
In their bought just as they all
Please then
What must they make as any difference
Not that it matters
That they have it to do
Not only for themselves but then as well
Coming for this.
He came early in the morning.
He thought they needed comfort
Which they did
And he gave them an assurance
That it would be all as well
As indeed were it
Not to have it needed at any time
Just as alike and like
It did make it a way
Of not only having more come
She refused to go
Not refused but really said
And do I have to go
Or do I go
Not any more than so
She is here when she is not better

When she is not better she is here
In their and on their account
All may remember three months longer
Or not at all or not in with it
Four leaf clovers make a Sunday
And that is gone

Stanza IV

Just when they ask their questions they will always go away
Or by this time with carefulness they must be meant to stay
For which they mind what they will need
Which is where none is left
They may do right for them in time but never with it lost
It is at most what they can mean by not at all for them
Or likeness in excellent ways of feeling that it is
Not only better than they miss for which they ask it more
Nearly what they can like at the best time
For which they need their devotion to be obtained
In liking what they can establish as their influence
All can be sold for which they have more seeds than theirs
All can be as completely added not only by themselves.
For which they do attack not only what they need
They must be always very ready to know.
That they have heard not only all but little.
In their account on their account can they
Why need they be so adequately known as much
For them to think it is in much accord
In no way do they cover that it can matter
That they will clear for them in their plight
Should they sustain outwardly no more than for their own
All like what all have told.
For him and to him to him for me.
It is as much for me that I met which
They can call it a regular following met before.

It will be never their own useless that they call
It is made that they change in once in a while.
While they can think did they all win or ever
Should it be made a pleasant arrangement yet
For them once in a while one two or gather well
For which they could like evening of it all.
Not at all tall not any one is tall
No not any one is tall and very likely
If it is that little less than medium sized is all
Like it or not they win they won they win
It is not only not a misdemeanor
But it is I that put a cloak on him
A cloak is a little coat make grey with black and white
And she likes capes oh very well she does.
She said she knew we were the two who could
Did we who did and were and not a sound
We learned we met we saw we conquered most
After all who makes any other small or tall
They will wish that they must be seen to come.
After at most she needs be kind to some
Just to like that.
Once every day there is a coming where cows are

Stanza V

Why can pansies be their aid or paths.
He said paths she had said paths
All like to do their best with half of the time
A sweeter sweetner come and come in time
Tell him what happened then only to go
Be nervous as you add only not only as they angry were
Be kind to half the time that they shall say
It is undoubtedly of them for them for every one any one
    They thought quietly that Sunday any day she might
not come

In half a way of coming that they wish it
Let it be only known as please which they can underrate
They try once to destroy once to destroy as often
Better have it changed to progress now if the room smokes
Not only if it does but happens to happens to have the room
smoke all the time
In their way not in their way it can be all arranged
Not now we are waiting
I have read that they wish if land is there
Land is there if they wish land is there
Yes hardly if they wish land is there
It is no thought of enterprise there buying
Might they claim as well as reclaim.
Did she mean that she had nothing.
We say he and I that we do not cry
Because we have just seen him and called him back
He meant to go away
Once now I will tell all which they tell lightly.
How were we when we met.
All of which nobody not we know
But it is so. They cannot be allied
They can be close and chosen.
Once in a while they wait.
He likes it that there is no chance to misunderstand pansies.

Stanza VI

I have not heard from him but they ask more
If with all which they merit with as well
If it is not an ounce of which they measure
He has increased in weight by losing two
Namely they name as much.
Often they are obliged as it is by their way
Left more than they can add acknowledge
Come with the person that they do attach

They like neither best by them altogether
For which it is no virtue fortune all
Ours on account theirs with the best of all
Made it be in no sense other than exchange
By which they cause me to think the same
In finally alighting where they may have at one time
Made it best for themselves in their behalf.
Let me think well of a great many
But not express two so.
It is just neither why they like it
Because it is by them in as they like
They do not see for which they refuse names
Articles which they like and once they hope
Hope and hop can be as neatly known
Theirs in delight or rather can they not
Ever if shone guessing in which they have
All can be glory can be can be glory
For not as ladling marguerites out.
It is best to know their share.
Just why they joined for which they knelt
They can call that they were fortunate.
They can be after it is all given away.
They can. Have it in mine.
And so it is a better chance to come
With which they know theirs to undo
Getting it better more than once alike
For which fortune favors me.
It is the day when we remember two.
We two remember two two who are thin
Who are fat with glory too with two
With it with which I have thought twenty fair
If I name names if I name names with them,
I have not hesitated to ask a likely block
Of which they are attributed in all security
As not only why but also where they can
Not be unclouded just as yes to-day
They call peas beans and raspberries strawberries or two
They forget well and change it as a last

That they could like all that they ever get
As many fancies for which they have asked no one.
Might any one be what they liked before
Just can they come to be not only fastened
It should be should be just what they like
This day in unison
All out of cloud. Come hither. Neither
Aimless and with a pointedly rested displeasure
She can be glad to be either in their resigning
That they have this plan I remember.
Well welcome in fancy.
Or just need to better that they call
All have been known in name as call
They will call this day one for all
I know it can be shared by Tuesday
Gathered and gathered yes.
All who come will will come or come to be
Come to be coming that is in and see
See elegantly not without enjoin
See there there where there is no share
Shall we be there I wonder now

Stanza VII

Make a place made where they need land
It is a curious spot that they are alike
For them to have hold of which in need of plainly
Can be suddenly hot with and without these or either
For themselves they can change no one in any way
They can be often placid as they mean they can force it
Or wilder than without having thought Frank Wilder was
a name
They knew without a thought that they could tell not then
Not known they were known then that is to say although
They were just as famous as in when in eloquence shortly

Every one knowing this could know then of this pleased
She can be thought in when in which it is in mine a pleasure.
Now let me think when.
There should not be this use in uselessness.
It is easier to know better when they are quite young
Over five and under fourteen that they will be famous.
Famous for this and then in a little while which it is lost.
It is lost.
By the time that they can think to sing in mountains.
Or much of which or meadows or a sunset hush or rather
By this time they could which they could think as selfish.
No one can know one can now or able.
They may be thought to be with or to be without now.
And so it happens that at that time they knew
Or it happens that as at that time they knew
Which made pages no delight they will be felt not well
Not as ours hours are polite.
Or they think well or violent or weeding
Or maybe they be spared or if they can be wanted finishing
Or better not prepared.
It is not ordinary standing or standard or which.
Might they be mostly not be called renown.
Should they finish better with batches.
Or why are theirs alright.

Stanza VIII

I ought not to have known that they came well
Came here to want it to be given to them
As if as much as they were ever anxious to be not
Only having seen me they could be nearly all polite.
It was difficult to know how they felt then.
Now I know everything of which it is that there is no
difference
Between then and now but very much the same

As of course then it was not only here.
There they came well
Here they come well
Often make it be believed that they marry
It is not only that there was no doubt.
Indicated why they left in fear
Just as the same just is the same
They will be ought and autocratic
Come when they call.
They are called that they see this
They which is made in any violence
That they mean please forgive a mess
They can be often polite in languages.
Nobody thinks a thing.
They will welcome all shawled
I like a noon which has been well prepared
Well prepared never the less.
Hours of a tree growing. He said it injured walls.
We said the owner and the one then here preferred it.
Imagine what to say he changed his mind.
He said it would not matter until ten years or five.
She can be not unusual.
Or she can be taught most in exaggeration.
Or she can be moved once to balance all
Or she can be just unkind.
It is hoped that they feel as well
Oh yes it is hoped that they feel as well.
Argued with what they like or where they went.
Which they must have in any case
For accidentally they do not mean this.
Will there be any difference with how much they know
Or better than on account of which they much and wish
arranged
Can we call ours a whole.
Out from the whole wide world I chose thee
They can be as useful as necessity
More than they called which they could ask combined

Or made of welsh a treasure.
They mean me when they mean me

Stanza IX

With which they can be only made to brush
Brush it without a favor because they had called for it
She can be never playing to be settled
Or praying to be settled once and for all
To come again and to commence again or which
They will be frequently enjoyed
Which they never do as much as they know
That they like where they happen to have learnt
That seeds are tall and better rather than they will
It is much chosen.
Every year dahlias double or they froze

Stanza X

Might they remember that he did not dislike
Even if there was a reason that he did not choose
Nor rather as it happened which when he did not go away
They might which they not alone as nearly selfish
They will have placed in their own winning.
I know how much I would not have liked that.
They may be taken which is not the same as told
Made in which time they will frankly share
Might it be often not as well that they will change
Or in a way or principally in place
Made which they may which they made made unkind
It is not why they asked them would they like it

It is managed when they are able to agree
I come back to think well at once of most
Not only that I like it that they like it
But which in which way
That they chose
It is for instance not at all a necessity.
That once or twice or agreeable
Might they be very often very welcome
By which they mean will they come.
I have thought that the bird makes the same noise differently
Just as I said how will you do it if you like it
And they will not stretch well from here to there
If they know that in the full moon they should not plant it
Just before.
All might all mean that is the way to do
Not better than they have lost
But which they manage in their requital
I have known that sound and this as known
Which they will interlace with not only there
But the pale sky with the pale green leaves
Or which they will as they belong to trees
In this in their amount.
I come back to remember they will pay
Which they may do which they may say
Or which they may do whatever they do say
Always as often as they mention this
Which might annoy them does annoy them
As they call a pail a pail and make a mountain cover
Not only their clouds but their own authority
For having been here then as it is better to be
Which is an arrangement better made for them
Than not alone for them for which they will be wetting.
It came very closely but no one was just yet
Not to be frightened as they meant at all
I do not care that he should make threads so
Threads are tenderly heads are tenderly so and so
Very well merited
I should judge just inclined

Neither as disturbance or better yet
Might it be changed but once before
Left them to gather it wherever they can and will
Just the same.
It might be very well that lilies of the valley have a fragrance
And that they ripen soon
And that they are gathered in great abundance
And that they will not be refreshing but only
Very lovely with green leaves
Or managed just the same when payed or offered
Even if they do.
They will never be careless with their having stayed away.
I know just how they feel with hope
And their wishes after all will we come
No we will not come.
In any absent way we will not only not be there
But when will we be here in one way
Any mixing of which it is in their presence
They or renowned or will they be made there
Will they be made there could be a question
Any answer could not be a question to their arrangement.
After all if it came out it meant it came again
Of course any one always is an answer.
Once in a while one or two
They could count now with any obstruction
As much as they advance.
Will or well a price.
In looking up I have managed to see four things.

Stanza XI

But which it is not by that they are rich
But only for it not only when they may count
Or by the opening that they will go round
As having value for which they may plan more

In which they can attract a celebration
Of their own cause not only just as well as all absurd
Can they be well awakened because they have not heard
Or can they come to account as much as not abandon
By the time that they caused them not to blame
Just as much as they could as they fasten
Linking it not only as absurd but fairly often
Be they as well aware as not only not only fasten
But which they can wish as not only opening
Or very carelessly arrange by the time they will go
Finally not only why they try but which they try
In case of joining.
Why should nobody wait when they come there
They have met one who likes it by and by
He will learn more than it is often read
That they could always please
More than just by their count
After all why can they liken it to this
Or not only add very much more
Or not be any one known as politeness
It is not at all like or alike
An invitation suffices for the present
In the middle of their exchange
They can cease moderation
Or embellish no one at a time
But then to wonder if they will be more
Or if there will be more which follows by
They will be not at all leaving it
Any way do they differ as to excitement
Or stopping hastily with while in ambush.
They do delight that it was any bird
Made to be near than they could like to plan
Should be thought successor to their own
Without in pleasure may they like may now.
Just as soon as ever if they come
By that in trial that they manage
It is for this for which for them for her
Coming to think it only as they knew

Known makes it plain I shall
Think birds and ways and frogs and grass and now
That they call meadows more
I have seen what they knew.

Stanza XII

She was disappointed not alone or only
Not by what they wish but even by not which
Or should they silence in convincing
Made more than they stand for them with which
But they can be more alike than they find finely
In not only ordinary care but while they care
It is by no means why they arrange
All of which which they frustrate
Not only gleaning but if they lie down
One watching it not be left allowed to happen
Or in their often just the same as occasionally
They do not usually use that they might have mention
That often they are often there to happen.
Could call meditation often in their willing
Just why they can count how many are mistaken.
In not quite correctly not asking will they come.
It is now here that I have forgotten three.

Stanza XIII

She may count three little daisies very well
By multiplying to either six nine or fourteen
Or she can be well mentioned as twelve
Which they may like which they can like soon
Or more than ever which they wish as a button

Just as much as they arrange which they wish
Or they can attire where they need as which say
Can they call a hat or a hat a day
Made merry because it is so.

Stanza XIV

She need not be selfish but he can add
They like my way it is partly mine
In which case for them to foil or not please
Come which they can they can in June.
Not having all made plenty by their wish
In their array all which they plan
Should they be called covered by which
It is fortunately their stay that they can
In which and because it suits them to fan
Not only not with clover but with can it matter
That not only at a distance and with nearly
That they ran for which they will not only plan
But can be rain can be caught by the hills
Just as well as they can with what they have
And they can have it not only because of this
But because they can be here.
Or is it at all likely that they arrange what they like.
Nobody knows just why they are or are not anxious
While they sit and watch the horse which rests
Not because he is tired but because they are waiting
To say will they wait with them in their way
Only to say it relieves them that they go away
This is what they feel when they like it
Most of them do or which
It is very often their need not to be either
Just why they are after all made quickly faster
Just as they might do.
It is what they did say when they mentioned it

Or this.
It is very well to go up and down and look more
Than they could please that they see where
It is better that they are there

Stanza XV

Should they can be they might if they delight
In why they must see it be there not only necessarily
But which they might in which they might
For which they might delight if they look there
And they see there that they look there
To see it be there which it is if it is
Which may be where where it is
If they do not occasion it to be different
From what it is.
In one direction there is the sun and the moon
In the other direction there are cumulous clouds and the sky
In the other direction there is why
They look at what they see
They look very long while they talk along
And they can be said to see that at which they look
Whenever there is no chance of its not being warmer
Than if they wish which they were.
They see that they have what is there can there
Be there also what is to be there if they can care
They care for it of course they care for it.
Now only think three times roses green and blue
And vegetables and pumpkins and pansies too
She knew she grew all these through to you
And she can be there did he mind learning how now
All this cannot be mixed.
Once again I think I am reflecting
And they can be patient in not why now
And more than if which they are reflecting

That if they with which they will be near now
Or not at all in the same better
Not for which they will be all called
By which they will can be as much as if wishing
But which each one has seen each one
Not at all now
Nor if they like as if with them well or ordinarily
Should they be more enjoined of which they like
It is very well to have seen what they have seen
But which they will not only be alike.
They are very evenly tired with more of this
For they will happen to be in which resolve
Always made by which they prepare that no one
Is more able to be sure of which
They will not will they compel
Not only where they see which they see
But will they be willing for needing
Only which they could call not by it
If they have come again to do it not at all
As very much made in once by their own saying
Yes of course which they will not be at all
Not only not for them in which they like
I lead all may be caught by fattening
Or not either sent all which can positively say so
In their own pleasure neither which they like
It is mine when they need to accept add me
For which they mind one at a time
It is at one time no different between how many hills
And they look like that caught in I mean
For which they will add not when I look
Or they make it plain by their own time.
This which they see by
They turn not their back to the scenery
What does it amount to.
Not only with or better most and best
For I think well of meaning.
It is not only why they might stare to change
Or feel crops well as he has promised, he said.

That there would be several days not of rain
And there would then be plenty of good weather
Probably the crops would be good.
Alright they think in wishes
And some superstitions and some
Beginning and fortunately with places of ditches
And also formidably of which when
When they find the clouds white and the sky blue
The hills green and different in shape too
And the next to what followed when the other bird flew
And what he did when he dug out what he was told to
And which way they will differ if they tell them too
And what they do if they do not cover the vine too
They do it by hand and they carry it all too
Up the way they did still have it to do
And so they think well of well-wishers.
I have my well-wishers thank you.

PART II

Stanza I

Full well I know that she is there
Much as she will she can be there
But which I know which I know when
Which is my way to be there then
Which she will know as I know here
That it is now that it is there
That rain is there and it is here
That it is here that they are there
They have been here to leave it now
But how foolish to ask them if they like it
Most certainly they like it because they like what they have
But they might easily like something else
And very probably just as well they will have it
Which they like as they are very likely not to be

Reminded that it is more than ever necessary
That they should never be surprised at any one time
At just what they have been given by taking what they have
Which they are very careful not to add with
As they can easily indulge in the fragrance
Not only of which but by which they know
That they tell them so.

Stanza II

It is very often that they like to care
That they have it there that the window is open
If the fire which is lit and burning well
Is not open to the air.
Think well of that is open to the air
Not only which but also nearly patiently there
It is very often why they are nearly
Not only with but also with the natural wine
Of the country which does not impoverish
Not only that but healthily with which they mean
That they may be often with them long.
Think of anything that is said
How many times have they been in it
How will they like what they have
And will they invite you to partake of it
And if they offer you something and you accept
Will they give it to you and will it give you pleasure
And if after a while they give you more
Will you be pleased to have more
Which in a way is not even a question
Because after all they like it very much.
It is very often very strange
How hands smell of woods
And hair smells of tobacco
And leaves smell of tea and flowers
Also very strange that we are satisfied
Which may not be really more than generous
Or more than careful or more than most.
This always reminds me of will they win

Or must they go or must they be there
They may be often led to change.
He came and when he went he said he was coming
And they can not be more in agreement
Than cakes are virtuous and theirs is a pleasure
And so they either or a splendid as a chance
Not to be seen to be not impervious
Or which they were not often as a chance
To be plainly met not only as anxious.
Will they come here I wonder why
If not will they try if they wonder why
Or not at all favorably
Just as can as in a way
A cow is and little cows are
He said it so and they meant more
Which it is for this an occasion or not
Just as they please
Can they be just as careful as if they have a chance
To be not only without any trouble
Or can be they came

Stanza III

They can lightly send it away to say
That they will not change it if they can
Nor indeed by the time that it is made
They can indeed not be careful that they were thankful
That they should distinguish which and whenever
They were not unlikely to mean it more
Than enough not to decide that they would not
Or well indeed if it is not better
That they are not cautious if she is sleepy
And well prepared to be close to the fire
Where it is as if outside it did resemble
Or can be they will relinquish.
I think I know that they will send an answer.
It can be sensibly more than they could
That one sheep has one lamb and one sheep has two lambs
Or they can be caught as if when they had been

Not only as they like but she can say
He can say too two can be more that is to say
Three can be more than one more
And only after they have five nobody
Has quarreled not only for them but after a while
She knows that they know that they
Are not remarkable.
It is often more which they use that they
Knowing that there is a month to-day
In which often they use or can they use
Which they knew it could be in no venture
That they will use he will carefully await
And leave it like that to be carefully watching
Will we come and will we come then
They can to which can they be to which they use
Or not at all as in a fashion
More than kind.
It is often so that they will call them
Or can be there for which they will not see them
Nor can they us what they will like
In for instance will they change this for them.
Coming by themselves for them in no matter
Could one ask it is not usual
That if they are polite they are politer
Or either of them not to be one for them
Which they can call on their account for them.
It is all all of which they could be generous
If no one gave more to them
They could be with them all who are with them
For them can they be more than many
Not only but righteous and she would be
Not angry now not often for them
With not as told not by them
It is very well to have no thorough wishes
Wish well and they will call
That they were remarkable
And it is well to state that rain makes hills green
And the sky blue and the clouds dark

And the water water by them
As they will not like what they do not have
As nobody has been indifferent
Not only will she regret
But they will say one two three
Much as they use.
It is very well to know.
More than to know
What they make us of
Although it is cold in the evening
Even if a fire is burning and
Summer is of use to them

Stanza IV

All who have hoped to think of them or wonder
Or can be they will like what they have had
More than they should if they went away freshly
And were very modest about not knowing why it was
That they were not denied their pleasure then
For which they can be more than not inclined
Which makes it plainly that in one way it made no difference
That they were always said to be just when they came
There where they liked and they were not allowed
Not only ordinarily but just now
They were agreeable which is why they are they
They hesitate they more they come where they are standing
They will take courage which they will not want
Nor will they worry very much as why they wait
They will not be often there
Think well of how very agreeable it is to meet them
To say yes we will go we know where we have been
We will say yes it is not without trouble that we came
Nor do we manage definitely to share.
But we must with one and all go there.
It will be often fortunately that strawberries need straw
Or can they yes indeed have marsh grass ready
It will support all who will have support
And she will kindly share hers with them

His with them
More than that they will stop this for them
Not only certainly but very surely
No one needs kindly any disappointment
Will they step in and out and can easily
One heel be well and one heel one be well
Or as an ever ready change for once in a while
There can be reasons too why there are reasons why
If they can be said as much
That they will stay behind not only here but there
For them in a way they stay

Stanza V

Be careful that it is not their way not to like that
Not only not to be careful but to be very much obliged
Also moreover not to be the cause of their going
But which they will endeavor not to change
Not only for this but by the time
That which they knew there they must remain
If for them not at all it is not only why they like
But which they may wish from foolishness
Once at a glance.
It is not only why they are careful to replace
Not only which they can as they disturb
Or any weakness of wishing they would come there
More often than they do or carefully not at all
As it is their care to bestow it at one time
Should they because or in or influence
Not only called but very likely called a sneeze
From first to last by them in this way introduces
Them one at one time.
It is at once after that they will be better than theirs
All alike or all alike as well or rather better not
It can only not do not do all of which
They prefer elaborate to why they while away
Their time as they can accidentally manage
As a chance in which provocation is what they can call
Or while they went they gathered more

In made in gain
And more than all of it called cold
Or why they should arrange carefulness
Not only is our neat but as our plan
Named called useful as it is understood
Just why they could they interpose
Just fortunately in around about
At all managed getting ready there
To be determined but not by themselves alone
As often as they are more there
Which interested them.
They could be bought necessarily two or taken
In place of when they were attached to whatever
It is left to be planned that they can call
For it in all the hope that they can go
Or stay away whichever it is made to like
As they may mean or mean to do
It is fortunately by all of them
Made not only with this but for this.
A change from rest or a change from the rest
Well and welcome as the day which when the sun shines
Makes water grow or covers others more
Than when they looked there where they saw
All of which when they had not wondered
Would they like it there best
Might I ask were they disappointed.

Stanza VI

When they were helped as every one can
Once when they do and once when it is
Not only their feeling but also their way
Not to suppose that they will wish
That they can receive nor more than suggest
From which they look as much as if ever they can
That they will oblige which will be for them
Not only theirs but nearly as much
As theirs not alone but which they can
Not only join but nearly so

Make their arrangement believe their own way
Come whichever they can in whatever way
That they conclude that they must use
It not only for them but without any doubt
As they will hear better or not so well
In which and on which occasion
They will not only call but let them know
Not only what they allow but whatever they wish
As not only theirs.
It is a chance that they will be left
Or be consoled by each with one as no mistake
But they attach themselves they do trouble
They come when they will
They allow. They can establish.
They can even agree not only to what they have
But should they be more than bereft
If they not only see but not only see
All or more than all because and because
Of which they are obliged
Being as they are to go there.
It is very kind of them to come.
As well as they can because and moreover
When they think well they think without that
Which moreover makes it yield
Because it is an instance of often now
Not only with it but without it
As even when and once in a while
As much as they change theirs in their own
As once allowed because they undertake can
As they can positively learn
Which it is mine to have then.
All that they can do is theirs not only then
They can often be thought all as at once
More often they will relish
At once they can change it
It is not only if at once that they are all
Or do they like it too
Or can they see it all

Or even might they not like it
If it is at once whatever they claim.
It is not only not a misfortune
It is wholly theirs to be believe me

Stanza VII

What do I care or how do I know
Which they prepare for them
Or more than they like which they continue
Or they can go there but which they mind
Because of often without care that they increase aloud
Or for them fortunately they manage this
But not only what they like but who they like.
There can be said to be all history in this.
They can be often opposite to not knowing him
Or they can be open to any impression
Or even if they are not often worried
They can be just bothered
By wondering do they often make it be alike afterward
Or to continue afterward as if they came
It is useless to introduce two words between one
And so they must conceal where they run
For they can claim nothing
Nor are they willing to change which they have
Oh yes I organise this. But not a victory
They will spend or spell space
For which they have no share
And so to succeed following.
This is what there is to say.
Once up a time they meant to go together
They were foolish not to think well of themselves
Which they did not were they willing
As they often were to go around
When they were asked as they were well aware
That they could think well of them
Remember this once they knew that the way to give
Was to go more than they went
For which they meant immediately faster

It is always what they will out loud
Can they like me oh can they like me.
No one can know who can like me.
This is their hope in wishing however
When they were not only laden with best wishes
But indeed not inclined for them to be careless
Might they be often more than ever especially
Made to be thought carelessly a vacation
That they will like this less.
Let me listen to me and not to them
Can I be very well and happy
Can I be whichever they can thrive
Or just can they not.
They do not think not only only
But always with prefer
And therefore I like what is mine
For which not only willing but willingly
Because which it matters.
They find it one in union.
In union there is strength

Stanza VIII

She can be thought to be accurate with acacia
Or by and by accustomed to be fairly
Just why they should in often as in or often
Could they call a partly necessary for them
Or why should anxiousness be anxiousness
Or their like that because more than they could
They will be named what do they do if the like
Or could they be troubled by it as a thought
Should they consider that they will gain
By not having it made for them to join
They will plainly state that only then only only there
More than if they will show all of it
Because please be plain for this time
And do not couple that they abandoned
Or which they abandoned because not only they
were not used

In better than whenever or wherever they will go
I think I do not sympathise with him.
It is often known how they are just how they are
And if they are often just as well as being here
It is not at all unlikely they will change
And this you know all of it which you know
Be only thought not to please.
I think that if I were faithful or as bought
Or should be checked or as thought
Or finally they can claim for it more
Or just why they are identified
Or pleading they will call it all they know
Or have it that they make it do
Not only as they have not only as they have
It is other than theirs that they think is worth while
But which they come frequently to separate
In advantageous or advantage by their time
That they will come at once or not
For which they will come way of nine
She may be thought better have it spared them
That they will cover other than allowance.
He will come to show well enough all there
Or better have it strange or come again
Night like or night like do.
It is very foolish to hesitate between do and dew.
Or not at all broadly on which account
They can favor or fulfill or never marry
It is while while they smell that all it came
It came to be very heavy with perfume
Just like it can only it was not more than just
Why they went back.
Back and forth.
I have often thought it to be just as well
Not to go only why not if they are going
But they will like why the look
They look for them and they are reminded.
That often any day all day
They will not go alike but keep it.

However much they say.
How many did you know
Or not say no.
Or no
Come to couple spelling with telling.

Stanza IX

Just why they could not ask them to come here
Or may they press them to relieve delight
Should they be planned or can they cause them then
To have it only lost they do not care to leave
Should they come when and will they forward it back
Or neither when they care just when they change
Can they not leave or will they not allow
More than they wish it is often that it is a disappointment
To find white turkeys white and little ones the same
Should they be pleased or should they rather not be pleased
Or more than they do should they rather keep it for them
Or more than this should they not infrequently
Or now when they see the difference between round
and about
Or not only why they change but what they change
One for one another.
It is often a very best need that they have
To come to see that after all
It was after all when they came back
Or need they not be provoked
By thinking that they will manage to please them.
How often very often do they go
Not which they wish or not which they wish
However it is better not to like it at all
I find it suddenly very warm and this can easily be
Because after all may be it is
In which case do they need any more explanation
Or indeed will they bother
Or after all can there be any difference
Between once in a while and very often
And not at all and why not and will they

Should they be pleased with everything just the same
So that they will think how well they like
What they will do which they do
For them at all.
It is often no matter and a difference
That they see this when they look here
And they can very well be ready
To see this when they look where they do
Nor or can they be there where they are
But not there where they are when
They are at once pleased with what they have
As they do not wish not only but also
To have it better where they like.
It is often no purpose not to have disgrace
Said that they will wait.
All often change all of it so.
It may be decided or not at all
That it is meant should they use
Or would they care to, think well long
Of what they think well.
And thank you
It is why they ask everything of them.
Should it be equally well planned
Made to carry or please it for them too
As they can often care or the difference
Between care and carry and recall
Should they find it theirs can they
Will they not be thought well of them.
Or not at all differently at once.
She can have no illusions
Nor be prepared not to be baffled
Or think well of them for which awhile
They chose.
It is for this that they come there and stay.
Should it be well done or should it be well done
Or can they be very likely or not at all
Not only known but well known.
I often think I would like this for that

Or not as likely
Not only this they do
But for which not for which for which
This they do.
Should it be mine as pause it is mine
That should be satisfying

Stanza X

It is not which they knew when they could tell
Not all of it of which they would know more
Not where they could be left to have it do
Just what they liked as they might say
The one that comes and says
Who will have which she knew
They could think all of which they knew as full
Not only of which they could they had as a delight
Or could it be occasionally just when they liked
It was not only theirs that they used as this
Not which they had with them not with them told
All have it not in any way in any anger
But they have it placed just when not there
For which they will allow could it or would it be told
That they shall not waste it to say to them
All of which after a while it is
As an arrangement
Not only theirs and only not at all.
They must be always careful to just be with them
Or they will not only not be but could be thought
To change which they will never know
Not only only all alike
But they will will be careful
It is not only this that antagonises that
Or they may be just as well in their refreshment
They will do always they will always do this
They could not relieve often which they do
They could be thought will it do
Once more come together does it matter
That it could be that they showed them this

But not this that they showed them that they showed
them that
    Or only once or not with not as only not once
    Could they come where they were
    Not only so much but also this much
    Just whenever they liked this much
    Which they were to declare
    That no one had had corroboration
    For which they will not only like
    Letting once make it spell which they do
    They can call it not be it as careless
    Not only to ask but neither rested for
    Which they will better can it have it
    Not only there around but this
    It is pleasantly felt for all
    Not only why they liked with which
    They came for it with their undertaking
    Made that they will or use or will they use
    By which they will know more than they incline
    Coming as it does coming as it does
    Are they allowed
    After all if it is so

Stanza XI

    I thought how could I very well think that
    But which they were a choice that now they know
    For which they could be always there and asking
    But made not more than which than they can like
    Not only why they came but which they knew
    For their own sake by the time that it is there
    They should be always rather liking it
    To have not any one exclaim at last
    It must be always just what they have done
    By which they know they can feel more than so
    As theirs they can recognise for which they place
    And more and moreover which they do
    It is not only to have all of it as more
    Which they can piece and better more than which

They may remain all or in part
Some can think once and find it once
Others for which for which they will
It is at no time that they joined
For which they joined as only
Not for which it is in partly measure
Having alike be once more obtained
They made no trouble as they come again
All which they could
But they will care
All for which it is at once thought
Just when they can surprise
No one in what they could there
Make without any pause a rest.
They will think why they
And they will come
In response.
Should they be well enough.
Otherwise they can consider that
Whatever they have missed.
I think I know I like I mean to do
For which they could they will place
He will place there where
It is finally thought out best
No means no means in inquietude
Just when they give and claim a reward
Not for which they go and get this
They have been with the place their place
Why is there not why is there not with doubt.
Not able to be with mine.

Stanza XII

One fortunate with roses is fortunate with two
And she will be so nearly right
That they think it is right
That she is now well aware
That they would have been named
Had not their labels been taken away

To make room for placing there
The more it needs if not only it needs more so
Than which they came

Stanza XIII

But it was only which was all the same

Stanza XIV

It is not only early that they make no mistake
A nightingale and a robin.
Or rather that which can which
Can which he which they can choose which
They know or not like that
They make this be once or not alike
Not by this time only when they like
To have been very much absorbed.
And so they find it so
And so they are
There
There which is not only here but here as well as there.
They like whatever I like.

Stanza XV

It is very much like it.

Stanza XVI

Could I think will they think that they will
Or can they be standing as seated still
For which they will leave it make it be still
That they will reach it for which they will until
They should be said to be planned for which they will
Not which they need not plan not more than will
It is an estimate of ferocity which they would not know
Not with surprise nor from the wish
That they would come at all
Can they be mentioned
For which they can not be only lost
For which they will can they can they come in

For which they will not but very likely
But they can not be there with which they will
For they can be with that kind that is what is
When they can like it as they do
But which they can not be for them
All made as they are not without it
Often left to them to come to arrange this
More than they can at most.
It was not only that they liked it
It is very kind of them to like it.

Stanza XVII

Come which they are alike
For which they do consider her
Make it that they will not belie
For which they will call it all
Make them be after not at least ready
Should they be settled strangely
Coming when they like an allowance
Naming it that they change more for them
With which which is certainly why they waited
They can be more regularly advised
In their case they will be able
Not only which they know but why they know
It is often that do their best
Not only as it is but which in change
They can be as readily which it is alike
Theirs as they better leave
All which they like at once
Which nearly often leave
This is the time in which to have it fasten
That they like all they like
More than which they can redeem.
It is often very well to if they prey
Should they could should they
They will not be imagined fairer
If they next from then on
Have it as not diminished

They can place aisle to exile
And not nearly there
Once in a while they stammer but stand still
In as well as exchange.
Once in a while very likely.
It is often their choice to feel it
As they could if they left it all
A ball fall.
Not two will give
Not one will give one two
Which they can add to change.
They will change what they like
Just what they do.
One two three or two

Stanza XVIII

She can be kind to all
If she wishes chickens to share
Her love and care
But they will think well of this
Which can not be amiss
If they like.
Two dogs for one or some one.
It is a happy wish
For some one.

Stanza XIX

She can think the thought that they will wish
And they will hold that they will spell anguish
And they will not be thought perverse
If they angle and the will for which they wish as verse
And so may be they can be asked
That they will answer this.
Let me see let me go let me be not only determined
But for which they will mind
That they are often as inclined
To have them add more than they could
She will be certainly seen if not as much

They will be left to be determined
As much as if they pleased they pleased
Not only theirs but only theirs
For them as much as known and not only
Not repeated because they will be seen
Partly and for less for which they are not very clearly
Made to be better than often as serviceable
Is it as much as why they like
For which they are often as much mistaken
Anything astonishes a mother or any other.
A stanza in between shows restlessly that any queen
Any not a stanza in between for which before which
Any stanza for which in between
They will be for which in between
Any stanza in between as like and they are likely
To have no use in cherishing.
They could be not alone consoled
They could be they can can they
Finally relieve.
It is often eight that they relinquish a stanza
Just when they feel that they are nearly
That they can could and do color
For which they will not only be inconvenient
For which they all for a forest
Come in as soon as our allowed
They prepare nor do they double
Or do they add prefer to before and call
She can be ours in allusion not only to
But why they will as much encourage
Readily for instance or can for instance
Come with not only as much as they tell
They tell it because if not why not
Such should be called their glory or their make
Of angling with and for around
Can it be wading for which they wade
Theirs once again the same
All which they said it said it in and answered
May be they like

Might it be uncontained likely
That they should as much joined with ease
But not by this for once once is not only one
They presume once alike not by their own present.
They present well. It followed once more
Only theirs in case. For which.
They add conditionally to not previously adding
More than they gave to one.
One is not one for one but two
Two two three one and any one.
Why they out tired Byron.

PART III

Stanza I

For which can they it which
That they can then or there either
By means of it for which they could
Recognise it is more than in going
They can come will they come until
The exactingly which they in exact
For which they will in and
They need not be for which they go
Theirs is all but not which it is in a chance
That they could incline to be inclined
For them or not or more inclined
Now not at all deserting
Nor not at all deserting
For which they finish English
Can they make cake or better
For which when did he like
Theirs or not at all theirs
They will not leave a well alone
Or not because now the water comes
Just as they could.

They are always just not even
He is at least tired by the heat
Or he will
Just not join not just join
All that they like to do.
It is why I see when I look out at it
That it is just like when I see it
And it is fortunately not a bit of it
By this for which they please come out
Of there.
Can they call one forty might
Or it is not might it
If it is not only they did
But which will they if they do
Not only this or which but can or can
Should more not any more
Any day make raspberries ripe
As they can do make what they do there
In leaving having had which
Not only while they do not but while they do
In often not at all now I am sure
Not sure not only how
But can it be at once.
Now to suppose it was like that.
Every time he went he went
And so it was not that they went
Not not at all.
And when he came back not when he went
He came back not when he came back
When he went.
One not to come to go when not to be
Not only not from here not here from there
Just as they used as usual
For which it it is not that that it
Must not do go
They leave it there is no there they do do
They do not do one two
As all round any arranged is not in at best

Once they he did once he they did or not
At all at any time.
It is so much that there is no difference in so much.
One one and two two one.

Stanza II

I think very well of Susan but I do not know her name
I think very well of Ellen but which is not the same
I think very well of Paul I tell him not to do so
I think very well of Francis Charles but do I do so
I think very well of Thomas but I do not not do so
I think very well of not very well of William
I think very well of any very well of him
I think very well of him.
It is remarkable how quickly they learn
But if they learn and it is very remarkable how quickly
they learn
It makes not only but by and by
And they can not only be not here
But not there
Which after all makes no difference
After all this does not make any does not make any difference
I add added it to it.
I could rather be rather be here.

Stanza II

It was not which they knew
But they think will it be though
The like of which they drew
Through.
It which may be that it is they did
For which they will be never be killed
By which they knew
And yet it is strange when they say
Who.
And so not only not here
May be they will be not in their place there
For which they will what will they may be there

For them for which not only very much
As is what they like there.
Now three things beside.
Add which not which to which
They wish which they divide.
If a fisherman fishes
Or else a well
Very well does an attack
Look back.
For that in use an extra make a moment
Further in use which they can be there when
In open use of which they like each one
Where they have been to have been come from.
It is often that they do regularly not having been
Before.
As much as and alike and because
Once before always before afraid in a dog fight
But not now.
Not at all now not when they not only wish to do
Can they be ours and very pretty too.
And you.
Once more I think about a lake for her
I do not think about a lake for them
And I can be not only there not in the rain
But when it is with them this it is soon seen
So much comes so many come.
Comfortably if they like what they come.
From.
Tables of tables and frames of frames.
For which they ask many permissions.
I do know that now I do know why they went
When they came
To be
And interested to be which name.
Who comes to easily not know
How many days they do know
Or whether better either and or
Before.

She can be eight in wishes
I said the difference is complicated
And she said yes is it it is
Or she said it is is it.
There seems so much to do
With one or two with six not seven
Either or.
Or believe.
That not only red at night can deceive.
Might they we hope better things of this.
Or of this.
Is.
When they are once or twice and deceive.
But leave
She can be called either or or before
Not only with but also with
With which they wish this
That they will like to give rain for rain
Or not.
It is just like it sounds.
I could not like it then nor now
Out now
Remained to how.
However they are careful.
Having forgotten it for them
Just how much they like
All potatoes are even when they have flowers
All adding is even
If they asked them
Would they ask them.
It would not be like alike for which
They did.
They had and did.
But which they had which they had which they is and did.
Gotten and gotten a row
Not to in did not and in said so
It is not only that I have not described
A lake in trees only there are no trees

Just not there where they do not like not having these
Trees.
It is a lake so and so or oh
Which if it is could it does it for it
Not make any do or do or it
By this it is a chance inclined.
They did not come from there to stay they were hired
They will originally will do
It is not only mine but also
They will three often do it.
Not now.
Do I mind
Went one.
I wish to remain to remember that stanzas go on

Stanza III

Not while they do better than adjust it
It can feeling a door before and to let
Not to be with it now not for or
Should they ask it to be let
Can they be sent as yet
For can they can they need met
Way and away in adding regret to set
And he looks at all for his ball.
I thought that I could think that they
Would either rather more which can
For this is and antedated a door can be
Which after all they change.
He would look in the way
Of looking.
Now added in again.
It is a way having asked in when
Should they come to be not only not adding some.
I think it is all very well to do without that
But it is why they could be with without that
For which they called a time
Not having finished to say that nearly there
They would be neither there as box wood grows

And so if it were they could be as easily found
As if they were bound.
Very nearly as much a there
That is one thing not to be made anything
For that but just for that they will add evening to anything

Stanza IV

Not which they know for which they like
They must be last to be not at it only with
It can for which they could with an a
Many can not come in this for nor without them
Some of which will they for them awhile
For which it is not only at an attempt
They can find that they can retouch
Not only what should be cared for
So they make this seem theirs
And only integrally shared as much as fine
They will out and out confer
That they will always can be so
As what they like.
Be mine prepared
What can it be not for their add it to
Can and delight for which not why they neglect
Just when or just when
For which not more than
Or by nearly
It is not their coat.
They must care for their furniture
Not but as one
For could and forfeit too
Coming and one.
It is not only that they could be here
When they are often made just can
It is my own that no one adds for it
Not only is it added well
She can only cloud go around
By that in awoken
Could and clad

Can they be eaten glad
Should not only should not under known
Say any way
A way
Equal to any stanzas are all three
They must be spared to share
Should it not only this and all around
They will have will appointed
Not only why they look not that
They call meadows are or all
For it is not only only their name
But which is a plain and a plain plaintive
Too or more.
I can not be indifferent to a little while
By which all tall at all
They could be not only any in any case
What does he mean by that
Not only not only not any interest not interested
But they will a valley.
Once every day they ate to a day
Not obliging not at not to obliging
But she will have meant
Or they will but they maintain
Ease by a minute.
It is not only their four in amount
Or while or a while
Or going
Or just as soon by which ought
Will they not have any as presence
They could be ought they be manage
Not only she thinks which
Just as never which many which
Made or manage they thrust.
It is often all they order or in order
But which they endanger
Do or not do.
However can be in account of whatever they do.

Stanza V

It is not a range of a mountain
Of average of a range of a average mountain
Nor can they of which of which of arrange
To have been not which they which
Can add a mountain to this.
Upper an add it then maintain
That if they were busy so to speak
Add it to and
It not only why they could not add ask
Or when just when more each other
There is no each other as they like
They add why then emerge an add in
It is of absolutely no importance how often they add it.

Stanza VI

By which are which add which a mounting
They need a leaf to leave a settling
They do not place a rein for resting
They do not all doubt can be a call
They can do which when ever they name
Their little hope of not knowing it.
Their little hope of not knowing it.

Stanza VII

By it by which by it
As not which not which by it
For it it is in an accessible with it
But which will but which will not it
Come to be not made not made one of it
By that all can tell all call for in it
That they can better call add
Can in add none add it.
It is not why she asked that anger
In an anger can they be frightened
Because for it they will be which in not

Not now.
Who only is not now.
I can look at a landscape without describing it.

Stanza VIII

That is why a like in it with it
Which they gay which they gay
But not only just the same.
Now who are now
Our who are now
It is not first not they are
But being touching all the same
Not and neither or the name.
It is very anxious not to know the name of them
But they know not theirs but mine.
Not theirs but mine.

Stanza IX

Tell me darling tell me true
Am I all the world to you
And the world of what does it consist
Can they be a chance to can they be desist
This come to a difference in confusion
Or do they measure this with resist with
Not more which.
Than a conclusion.
Can they come with can they in with
For which they can need needing
It is often by the time that not only
Which waiting as an considerable
And not only is it in importance
That they could for an instance
Of made not engaged in rebound
They could indeed care
For which they can not only
Be very often rested in as much
Would they count when they do
Is which which when they do

Making it do.
For this all made because of near
No name is nearly here
Gathering it.
Or gathering it.
Might it in no way be a ruse
For it which in it they an obligation
Fell nearly well.

Stanza X

Now Howard now.
Only righteous in a double day
It is ought frown
They could however collaborate
As only in the way
Of not only not renowned.
What is it often
Oh what is it often
Or should
Should as any little while.
Think more what they mean
Oh think more what they mean
Now I know why he said so
Oh no.
It is if it is.
What is the difference.
What is the difference both between for it and it
And also more also before not it.
It can be an absence better than not before.
It is just why they tried.

Stanza XI

I only know a daisy date for me
Which is in wishes can forget for it
Not which not that that is
And is that that not be that with
It is not any one can think
Why be without any one one can

Be favored flavored not which
It is not only not only neither without
But this is only so.
I cannot often be without my name.
Not at all
They will not wonder which at a time
And can it be alright.
They can lead any one away.
Now look not at that.
Having heard now hearing it
Should just engage those
Not always connected
Readily express
For them forget
It is very easy to be afraid to hear one come in.
All like all to go
There is often when they do not mention running
Or walking or not going
Or not why they do not find it in for him.
Just why they should or just why
Ate or bate or better or not sigh
He she can sigh and try why
They seize sigh or my.
It is often when it is not stated
That at it two or to
That it is better added stated
That they are to
I often like it not before
They do not or do not listen one to one another
Or by guess.
It is just as much as allowed
Why they carry or
All would or wood or wooden
Or all owed
Or not vestiges or very sight
Of water owned or own
Or not well velvet
Or not aligned

Or all or gone
Or capitally
Or do or comforting
Or not
Renown.
They will say pages of ages.
I like anything I do
Stanza two.

Stanza XII

Stanza ten make a hen
Stanza third make a bird
Stanza white make a dog
Stanza first make it heard
That I will not not only go there
But here

Stanza XIII

In changing it inside out nobody is stout
In changing it for them nobody went
In not changing it then.
They will gradually lengthen
It.

Stanza XIV

I could carry no one in between

Stanza XV

Can thinking will or well or now a well.
Wells are not used any more now
It is not only just why this is much
That not one can add it to adding main
For never or to never.
Suppose I add I like to
I can should show choose go or not any more not so
This is how any one could be in no hope
Of which no hope they did or did not
There is no difference between having in or not only not this

Could it be thought did would
By it a name.
I think I could say what nobody thought
Nobody thought I went there
This is however that they add sufficiently
Because it is not better allowed
All will come too.
Just joined how to houses
But they will like an only name
They could be thought why they had a weakness
To be sure.
Now this is only how they thought.
Let no one leave leaves here.
Leaves are useful and to be sure
Who can or could be can be sure
I could think add one add one advantage
That is how they like it.

Stanza XVI

She does not who does not it does not like it
Our our guess yes
But it does not it does not who does guess it
But they will place it or not place it yes
They could in insistence have nobody blamed
Which they do ours on account
Can they or can they can they blame this
This that they will wail when not in resting
But which they for which they could date and wait
Will they do what they are careful to do too
Or like this will they like this where they go
When it is not only not certain where they went
they were here
At all as likely as not up and down up and down to go
Not because before by which they attracted
They were with an on account which they knew
This not only not which they need blessing
Which or not which when they do not or which way
They do go

It is not inadvertent that they oblige
It is waiting they gather what do they like
Cherries not only not better not ripe
It was a mistake not to make not only a mistake with this
In not only in all noon after noon that they like
It is always arbitrary to come with bliss
For them to join it to come with it
They could manage just what they did
But did they not feel that
They could be not only not allowed but not clouded
It was very different again
Just when they join that they look.
They refer to a little that is a little trunk
A very little trunk once.
How very sorry they are for not for placing
Well place well
Just once to join and not too alike
That they go
Or will they not only in place of which to happen to be last
not to save it to say so
Or go.
And so they went carefully together.
As they like it which
They mean that for when
It is not mine
Fine

Stanza XVI

It is not which they will not like or leave it as a wish which
they compare
All of most all for that did they if not as it is
Should they dare or compare
Could it have been found all round
Or would they take pleasure in this
Or can they not be often whichever
As they told theirs in any day.
Does it make any difference if they ask
Or indeed does it make any difference

If they ask.
Would they be different if nobody added it all
Or looking just alike do they mind any extra
Can they or should they combine
Or should they not easily feel
That if they could they can or should
We ask.
Be not only without in any of their sense
Careful
Or should they grow careless with remonstrance
Or be careful just as easily not at all
As when they felt.
They could or would would they grow always
By which not only as more as they like.
They cannot please conceal
Nor need they find need they a wish
They could in either case they could in either case
Not by only for a considerable use.
Now let only it be once when they went
It is of no importance to please most
One of them as it is as it is now
It is not only for which they cause
That it is not only not why they like
Them.
They could often be a relish if it had not been thought
That they should write.
They will be only not more a choice
For which alone they remain.
Proclaim.
I wondered why they mentioned what they like.
All of which only what they knew
Just why they yearn
Or not rest more.
A counter and not a counterpane
They could be relished.
Just why they called wait wait.
What is it when there is a chance
Why should they like whatever they do

Not only if they will but if they will
Not only
It is not more than this shame.
Shame should not be for fountains.
Not even not yet.
But just when the mountains are covered
And yet they will please of course they will please
You which it is.
Not any not on any account
Can it not only be why they want.
It is always which they like.
It is a thought give a thought to Cuba
She could in cooking
And only not let owls frighten not birds
Not only not
Because in only ending birds
Who ends birds where.
Now I have said it.
It is of no use one year
A toad one year
A bird a little very little as little bird one year
And if one year
Not only not at all one year.
It came very difficultly.
Just not in not in not in not as in him.
And so on account on account of reproach.
Could they if not she would be startled.
But they cost neither here nor there.
Just as I think.
Once when they should they if indifferently would
When to look again
Pinny Pinny pop in show give me a pin and I'll let you know
If a pin is precious so is more.
And if a floor is precious so is not a door.
A door is not bought twice.
I do think so earnestly of what.
She had no chagrin in beauty
Nor in delight nor in settled sweetness

Nor in silkiness alright.
But why often does she say yes as they can say
She finds that if one is careful one has to be very much
Awake to what they do all need.
Now often I think again of any english.
English is his name sir.
That much is not only not only not a disadvantage
Over them.
Once more I wish italian had been wiser.
But will they wish
They wish to help.
And their wish succeeded.
And added.
Once more I return to why I went.
I went often and I was not mistaken.
And why was I not mistaken
Because I went often.

Stanza XVII

Not only this one now

Stanza XVIII

How can no one be very nearly or just then
Obliged to manage that they need this now
She will commence in search not only of their account
But also on their account as arranged in this way
She will begin she will state
She will not elucidate but as late
She will employ she will place adding
Not with it without it with their account
Supposing they can say the land stretches
Or also can be they will say it is all told
Or perhaps also they will say
Or perhaps also they will say that they went from
here to there
Or not only just then but when just then
Also perhaps not only might they not try
Can be not only what they wish but will they wish

Perhaps after a while it is not why they went
Not only which it is but after it is
They might be thought to have it not known
Only which they are obliged
To feel it at all not which they can know
They could call colors all or not
Incomplete roses.
They find fish an ornament
And not at all jealously at any and all resemblance
They have been warned to try and be called all
For which they plan a favor
Should they be thought to be caught all around
By that time it is well to think it all
Not only can they be
It is a pleasure that twice is neglected
In which amount.
They anticipate in place.
Could no one try of fancies.
However how is it if it is right and left.
Or rather should it did it happen to be more
They can allowed or stranger
They have not then once cost
But which in theirs and on which occasion
Can they be minded.
Now how can I think softly of safety
Which which they do
It is not only their only hindrance
But not well won not with it.
In intermittence can they remind sees.
She can fortunately not count
If she says but which if they say
But which they find.
Now only this when they all think.
How can she manage our places.
It is for this they could recall
Better than all do.
It was not often that I could not join them
Which they did.

Now how could you disguise joins
By which it is in ate and dishes
They could be only they could be only worried
By what they remain with what they will
Or not unkind.
This is what I think I think I often did the same
When they should be all there as known
After all I am known
Alone
And she calls it their pair.
They could be cut at noon
Even in the rain they cut the hay
Hay and straw are not synonymous
Or even useful with them
Or even useful with them
Or as a hope that they did
Which after all they did not.
In this way any one or did add not a precaution.
Think how well they differ caution and precaution
Or not.
Or should they allow ours in a glass
For them they carry
Better not be strange in walking
They do or do not walk as they walk as they part.
Will they mean mine or not theirs
They will they will like what they entitle
Should they be theirs.
He asked did they that is it
That is did it mean it was with them
There with them
They could not be ought not be in mind
So then
All of which reminds no one
Having said.
Do which or they can be kind.
She says some or summer could be.
Not only not again for when.
I can think exactly how I found that out.

Just when they say or do
Once and before.
It is not only that they like
In the meantime.
If even stanzas do.

Stanza XIX

Not what they do with not
Not only will they wish what
What they do with what they like
But they will also very well state
Not only which they prefer by themselves
And now add it in aging ingenuity
And which they will as soon as ever they can
But which they tell indeed can they or can they not proudly
Not only theirs in eight but which they meant
They will all old declare
That believing it as a patent pleasure in their care
Nor where where will they go older than not
Nor will they furnish not only which they had but when
they went
In reason.
It is often that they allow a cloud to be white
Or not only patently white but also just as green
Not only theirs in pleasure but theirs in case
Not only however but not only however
Or not at all in wishes that they had chickens
Which can be alternately well or ducks
Or will they spread for them alone
Go be not only their care.
This which and whatever I think
I not only do but make it be my care
To endanger no one by hearing how often I place
Theirs not only why they are best not
Not by it as they like.
I have thought while I was awakening
That I might address them
And then I thought not at all

Not while I am feeling that I will give it to them
For them
Not at all only in collision not at all only in mistaken
But which will not at all.
I thought that I would welcome
And so I could be seen.
I then thought would I think one and welcome
Or would I not.
I then concluded that I might be deceived
And it was a white butterfly
Which flew not only not but also
The white dog which ran
And they they were accomplished
And once in a while I would rather gather
Mushrooms even than roses if they were edible
Or at least what not.
I do not wish to say what I think
I concluded I would not name those.
Very often I could feel that a change in cares
Is a change in chairs and not only can and cares
But places
I felt that I could welcome in anticipation wishes
Not only which they do but where they do
How are our changes.
When they could fix titles or affix titles.
When this you see hear clearly what you hear.
Now just like that not just like that
Or they will enjoin and endanger
Damage or delight but which they crow
They have threatened us with crowing
Oh yes not yet.
I cannot think with indifference
Nor will they not want me
Do will they add but which is not
Where they could add would or they would or not
For which they for which fortunately
Make it be mine.
I have often thought of make it be mine.

Now I ask any one to hear me.
This is what I say.
A poem is torn in two
And a broom grows as well
And which came first
Grows as well or a broom
Of course any one can know which of two
This makes it no accident to be taught
And either taught and either fight or fought
Or either not either which either
Can they be either one not one only alone.
Should it be thought gracious to be a dish
Of little only as they might mean curiously
That we heard them too
And this I mean by this I mean.
When I thought this morning to keep them so they
will not tell
How many which went well
Not as a conclusion to anxious
Anxious to please not only why but when
So then anxious to mean. I will not now

Stanza XX

Now I recount how I felt when I dwelt upon it.
I meant all of it to be not rather yes I went
It is not that now they do not care that I do
But which one will
They can not be thought nervous if they are left alone
Now then I will think of which went swimming.
It does make a difference how often they go
Or will they prepare that I know
I know this I know that I shall say so
Or can they choose an anagram
This one said this one.
If one we hurried for this one
Just when they did wish that it should be settled then
They could think let us go
Just when they will they can

All my dear or but which they can
Having been long ago not knowing what I felt
And now
It does make a difference that well enough a cow
Can be recognised now so then
If not twenty as ten
Or one enough without it then.
This that I can
I repeat I do not know what I felt then
Which they do which they do
Nor will they track it if they follow then
How are it is to do
A kite is a delight this I can do then
But not with then for which they allow them
This is the way not to end but to see when the beginning.
I like a moth in love and months
But they will always say the same thing when
They sing singing
I wish I could repeat as new just what they do
Or alike as they hear when they do not listen to every one
So she said it they but which they
She said the nest was empty but not so
The nest was empty that is to say not there
It was as if she looked alike
By which no one mean startled
Like that
I think I will begin and say everything not something
But not again and only again alike
Thank you for the touch of which they leave
He easily destroys my interest in may be they do
but I doubt it
But not at all with which by nearly which time
But just as well heard
Why should he not say he did say that
And it was amusing.
And by and by not which they do
I now I do not know what I feel
So in extra inclusion.

What do I think when I feel.
I feel I feel they feel they feel which they feel
And so borrowed or closed they will they will win
How can any one know the difference between
worry and win.
This is not the only time they think which they know
Or better not alright.
How can they eager either or and mend
She can mend it not very well between.
Of course he knows at what he does not only hear
Oblige me. I also oblige him. And think then.
Do I repeat I do not know what I do not see to feel which
they hear
Oh yes

Stanza XXI

When she meant they sent or a grievance
Was she meant that he went or a need of it henceforward
Was it with it that they meant that he sent or he thought
That they should not plainly have not bought
Or which they went to be naturally there
It is a pause in mistaken.
They could know that they would call
Or they would prefer it to before
On their account.
I should look if I saw
But she would send if she would intend to prefer
That they might cause it best and most.
It is not only which they go but when they go
Or if not said to send or say so
Now think how palpably it is known
That all she knows which when she goes
They look for him in place of that
Of which they are used or to be used
In preference
And so they halt more to partly do
Do or due or only dew or did you do it.
I could not favor leaves of trees to in any case

Place me to mine.
This is not what they care or for poetry.

PART IV

Stanza I

Who should she would or would be he
Now think of the difference of not yet.
It was I could not know
That any day or either so that they were
Not more than if they could which they made be
It is like this
I never knew which they can date when they say
Hurry not hurry I could not only not do it
But they prepare.
Let me think how many times I wished it.
It flattered me it flattered me it flattered me
And I was all prepared which they sent
Not only not why but where if they did not enjoy
Their place where they meant with them
And so they can be fitly retired.
This is what I saw when they went with them.
I could have been interested not only in what they said but in
what I said.
I was interested not interested in what I said only in what
I said.
I say this I change this I change this and this.
Who hated who hated what.
What was it that announced they will not mind it.
I do think often that they will remember me.
Now who remembers whom what not a room
No not a room.
And who did prepare which which vegetable very well
And might I not only feel it to be right to leave them to say
Yes any day it is because after which way

They shell peas and of the pea shell they make a soup to eat
and drink
    And they might not amount to calls upon them.
    They were in place of only where they went
    Nobody notices need I be not there only
    But which they send it.
    Not to think but to think that they thought well of them.
    Here I only know that pumpkins and peas do not grow
    Well in wet weather.
    And they think kindly of places as well as people.
    I should think it makes no difference
    That so few people are me.
    That is to say in each generation there are so few geniuses
    And why should I be one which I am
    This is one way of saying how do you do
    There is this difference
    I forgive you everything and there is nothing to forgive.
    No one will pardon an indication of an interruption
    Nor will they be kindly meant will be too or as a sound.
    I am interested not only in what I hear but as if
    They would hear
    Or she can be plainly anxious.
    How are ours not now or not as kind.
    They could be plainly as she is anxious
    Or for their however they do
    Just as well and just as well not at all
    How can you slowly be dulled reading it.
    It is not which they went for there were dishes
    It is not why they were here not with their wishes
    Or accidentally on account of clover
    I never manage to hammer but I did
    In with all investigation
    And now I now I now have a brow
    Or call it wet as wet as it is by and by
    I feel very likely that they met with it
    Which in no way troubles them
    Or is it like to.
    It did it a great deal of good to rub it

Stanza II

I come back to think everything of one
One and one
Or not which they were won
I won.
They will be called I win I won
Nor which they call not which one or one
I won.
I will be winning I won.
Nor not which one won for this is one.
I will not think one and one remember not.
Not I won I won to win win I one won
And so they declare or they declare
To declare I declare I declare I win I won one
I win in which way they manage they manage to win I won
In I one won in which I win which won I won
And so they might come to a stanza three
One or two or one two or one or two or one
Or one two three all out but one two three
One of one two three or three of one two and one

Stanza III

Secretly they met again
All which is changed in made they can be merry
For which they could in any regulation
Manage which they can have in any case a trial
Of when they do or sing sisters
And so much is taken for granted
In which appointment they color me
Or leave it as not in a glass or on the grass
They pass.
Not at all
For which no one is met in winning
They will be very well pleased with how they stand
Or which or to which or whither they repair
To change it to change it fairly
Or can they like all that they have

Let us think well of which is theirs.
Why do they not count
Count how do you count
There is no counting on that account
Because if there is which is not what I say
I will make it do any day to-day
Or not why
They allow me to apply for it
The call will they call by which they plan
I will not gain gain easier easily
One which one which not now.
Why do they like which they like or why not
It is often many or as much which they have seen
Seen is often very well said
I think I have no wish that they will come
With their welcome
Nor which they try not to do
In any case for which they formerly
Were not repaid.
They are readily not here.
Once more no one not one begins
This is the difference
Not it or argument
But which and when
They enfold not in unfold
Beware aware deny declare
Or and as much in told
They cannot be thought restless when they do come and go
Either one either say so.
I say I felt like that.
Once they came twice they went which one will do
Or which they like for them or will they do
What they ask them to do
I manage to think twice about everything
Why will they like me as they do
Or not as they do
Why will they praise me as they do
Or praise me not not as they do

Why will they like me and I like what they do
Why will they disturb me to disturb not me as they do
Why will they have me for mine and do they
Why will I be mine or which can they
For which can they leave it
Or is it not
I have thought or will they let
Them know the difference if they tell them so
Between let us not be reckless or restless
Or by word of mouth
Can they please theirs fairly for me.
Just why they lay with the land up.
Coming to see it so.
It was not once when they went away that they came to stay.
Why should all which they add be each
Each is a peach
Why can they be different and try to beside
Be all as all as lost
They do not hide in which way
Better call it mine.
Our ours in or made between alike
With which cakes bake cakes
And it makes cake or cakes polite
But if they all call not when they do
Who ought they try to be alike
Which or for which which they can do too.
I refuse I I refuse or do
I do I do I refer to refuse
Or what what do I do
This is just how they like what they send
Or how to refuse what is that
That they need to sound sound lend
Can you question the difference between lend.
Or not lend
Or not send
Or not leant
Or not sent
But neither is a neighbor.

A neighbor to be here
She can be he can be useful or not useful
When they did not come why did they not come here.
Believe me it is not for pleasure that I do it
Not only for pleasure for pleasure in it that I do it.
I feel the necessity to do it
Partly from need
Partly from pride
And partly from ambition.
And all of it which is why
I literally try not only not why
But why I try to do it and not to do it.
But if it well-known it is well-known

Stanza IV

Mama loves you best because you are Spanish
Mama loves you best because you are Spanish
Spanish or which or a day.
But whether or which or is languish
Which or which is not Spanish
Which or which not a way
They will be manage or Spanish
They will be which or which manage
Which will they or which to say
That they will which which they manage
They need they plead they will indeed
Refer to which which they will need
Which is which is not Spanish
Fifty which vanish which which is not Spanish.

Stanza V

I think very well of my way.

Stanza VI

May be I do but I doubt it.

Stanza VII

Can be can be men.

Stanza VIII

A weight a hate a plate or a date
They will cause me to be one of three
Which they can or can be
Can be I do but do I doubt it
Can be how about it
I will not can be I do but I doubt it.
Can be will can be.

Stanza IX

How nine
Nine is not mine
Mine is not nine
Ten is not nine
Mine is not ten
Nor when
Nor which one then
Can be not then
Not only mine for ten
But any ten for which one then
I am not nine
Can be mine
Mine one at a time
Not one from nine
Nor eight at one time
For which they can be mine.
Mine is one time
As much as they know they like
I like it too to be one of one two
One two or one or two
One and one
One mine
Not one mine
And so they ask me what do I do
Can they but if they too
One is mine too
Which is one for you
Can be they like me

I like it for which they can
Not pay but say
She is not mine with not
But will they rather
Oh yes not rather not
In won in one in mine in three
In one two three
All out but me.
I find I like what I have
Very much.

Stanza X

That is why I begin as much

Stanza XI

Oh yes they do.
It comes to this I wish I knew
Why water is not made of waters
Which from which they well
Can they be kind if they are so inclined.
This leads me to want to wonder about which they do
I feel that they shall be spared this
They will agree for which they know
They do not do or describe
Their own use of which they are not tried
Or most or mostly named to be where
They will not as willingly not declare
That they appeal but do not prefer a share
Of plainly when they will
It is this I wish any minute
Oh yes I wish do I I do wish any minute
For them for fortune or forlorn or well
Well what do you do either what do you do
But like it or not
This that they can think just think
She has put her hair up with hairpins
Or do or do not only just do not only think
Finally than this.

It might be worth any cost to be lost.
They like that which they did
He did he remembered not only that he did
Oh why should any one repine one at a time.
Curiously.
This one which they think I think alone
Two follow
I think when they think
Two think I think I think they will be too
Two and one make two for you
And so they need a share of happiness
How are ours about to be one two or not three.
This that I think is this.
It is natural to think in numerals
If you do not mean to think
Or think or leave or bless or guess
Not either no or yes once.
This is how hours stand still
Or they will believe it less
For it is not a distress yes
Which they can free to build
Not by a house but by a picture of a house
But no distress to guess.
For this they are reconciled.
I wish that they were known.
This which they permit they please.
Please can they not delight and reconcile
Could anybody continue to be
Made openly one to see
That it is very pleasant to have been
With them
When this you see.
Once when they were very busy
They went with me.
I feel that it is no trouble
To tell them what to do
Nor either is it at all a trouble
To wish that they would do what I do.

This is well and welcome to mean
I mean I mean.
Think however they will be ready
To believe me.
Think well of me when this you see.
I have begun by thinking that it is mine
It is mine many often one at a time
In rhyme.
Of course in rhyme which is often mine
In time one at one time
And so I wish they knew I knew
Two and one is two.
This is any day one for you.
This which I explain is where any one will remain
Because I am always what I knew
Oh yes or no or so
Once when they went to stay
Not which not only once or twice yesterday.
This introduces a new thought as is taught.
I wish I exchanged will they exchange me
Not at all.
This is why they bought a ball.
To give it to them to be all
All which they keep and lose if they choose.
Think how can you be and beware
And constantly take care
And not remember love and shove
By design.
It is well to be well and be well and be welcome
Of course not to made to be
Honorably four to three which they do.
This is how they think well of believing all of theirs
To have been known.
It is singular that they can not only succeed
But be successful.
How should they not speedily try
If they could or could not know
That I did it.

Which is why they are so quiet with applause
Or can be the cause
Of their waiting there
For their meal
If they had it.
It is very beautiful to be eight and late.
Why should any one be ready too
As well as not for and with you
Which they do.
See how one thing can mean another.
Not another one no not any not another one.
Or not any means not or can not might three to one.
That is what they say to play.
And which is white if they might
They will call that they spoke to her

Stanza XII

Just why they mean or if they mean
Once more they mean to be not only not seen
But why this beside why they died
And for which they wish a pleasure.

Stanza XIII

But which it is fresh as much
As when they were willing to have it not only
But also famous as they went
Not to complain but to name
This understanding confined on their account
Which in the midst of can and at bay
Which they could be for it as once in a while
Please can they come there.
This is an autobiography in two instances.

Stanza XIV

When she came she knew it not only
Not by name but where they came with them.
She knew that they would be while they went.
And let us think.

She knew that she could know
That a genius was a genius
Because just so she could know
She did know three or so
So she says and what she says
No one can deny or try
What if she says.
Many can be unkind but welcome to be kind
Which they agree to agree to follow behind.
Her here.
Not clearly not as no mistake
Those who are not mistaken can make no mistake.
This is her autobiography one of two
But which it is no one which it is can know
Although there is no need
To waste seed because it will not do
To keep it though perhaps it is as well
Not to belie a change of when they care
They mean I like it if she will do it
But they could not complain again.
Let me remember now when I read it through
Just what it is that we will do for you.
This is how they asked in a minute when
They had changed a pencil for a pen
Just as I did.
Often of course they were not welcomed there
When they meant to give it all they liked
Made many more beside beside
Which when they tried or cried
He could not have his way
Or care to please please
And prepare to share wealth and honors
Which if they or if they or if they
Had not had mine too.
More can they gain or complain
Of which announce pronounce a name
When they call this they feel
Or not at all a heel she changed all that

For them fair or at once they will change hair
For there or at once more than all at once
Whenever they can.
This makes no allowance
Now this is how they managed to be late or not.
When once in a while they saw angrily
Or impatiently yesterday
Or beguiling February
They could so easily be thought to feel
That they would count or place all or kneel
For which they had been frightened not to do
They felt the same.
In which on no account might they have tried
To be remained to try why
Shall they be careful at all or not.
This is why they like me if they think they do
Or not which they the time they care I care
Or when where will they name me.
However tried however not or cried
She will be me when this you see.
And steadily or whether will they compel
Which is what I tell now.
This is a beginning of how they went at once
When I came there cannot they compare
No they cannot compare nor share
Not at all not in iniquity much which they engage
As once in a while perfectly.
All many so or say
But this or which they can
Believe me I say so.
I have not said I could not change my mind if I tried.
More than just once they were there.
All this is to be for me.

Stanza XV

I have thought that I would not mind if they came
But I do.
I also thought that it made no difference if they came
But it does

I also was willing to be found that I was here
Which I am
I am not only destined by not destined to doubt
Which I do.
Leave me to tell exactly well that which I tell.
This is what is known.
I felt well and now I do too
That they could not wish to do
What they could do if
They were not only there where they were to care
If they did as they said
Which I meant I could engage to have
Not only am I mine in time
Of course when all is said.
May be I do but I doubt it.
This is how it should begin
If one were to announce it as begun
One and one.
Let any little one be right.
At least to move.

Stanza XVI

Should they call me what they call me
When they come to call on me
And should I be satisfied with all three
When all three are with me
Or should I say can they stay
Or will they stay with me
On no account must they cry out
About which one went where they went
In time to stay away may be they do
But I doubt it
As they were very much able to stay there.
However can they go if they say so.

Stanza XVII

How I wish I were able to say what I think
In the meantime I can not doubt
Round about because I have found out

Just how loudly difficulty they do
They will they care they place
Or they do allow or do not bow now.
For which they claim no claim.
It is however that they find
That I mind
What they do when they do or when they do not do
It.
It is not only not kind not to mind
But I do do it.
This is how they say I share I care
I care for which share.
Any share is my share as any share is my share
Of course not not only not.
Of course I do which I of course do.
Once I said of course often
And now I say not of course often
It is not necessary any more.

Stanza XVIII

She asked could I be taught to be allowed
And I said yes oh yes I had forgotten him
And she said does any or do any change
And if not I said when could they count.
And they can be not only all of three
But she can establish their feeling for entertainment
She can also cause them to bless yes
Or can be or can they be not
Made to amount to more than can they.
This is what they do when they say can they
It is often that it is by this that they wish this
When they will value where they went when they did
They will also allow that they could account for it
Or might they not only not choose
It is often whichever they were fortunate and not fortunate
To be for which they can in all they like
This is what they use
I have thought I have been not only like this

Or they can please or not please
Which for instance and forsaken and beside which
They will oh please they will
Not only when they can as if allowed
It is all of it which they knew they did.
This is what I say two to belie
One to date and decry and no one to care
And she made as rashly careful as not
When they could think twice just the same.
This is at any time when they do not often see them
Theirs when they went away
Not only not included but why not included
Only they will not agree to permanence
Not more than twice as much.
Very much as they say aloud
Will you be back in a minute or not.
Let me think carefully not think carefully enough
By which I mean that they will not please them so
Not even if they know that they went too
So it is gracious once gracious to be well as well
As when they like liked it.
This is what it is made to be able
To need whichever they could be well-furnished
All the same three now.
This could if it could lead it if it did
To a cow. Think of it.
This is what I return to say
If I never do nor I ever do
How can it be so if it is true
Or just true as through or you
Made which they like as much.
Now commence again to be used to their
Saying that their cousin was one
Who felt that it was not a name
To which they meant to think well of them.
This is however how they do not deny
That they will not try to care
To leave it there from time to time

At once
It is very well-known that they are indifferent not to wishes.
Can she be sought out.
I wish to say that any case of a failure
Is what they were spared.
I wish to think that they will place
Much as more than they wish
As their changing it not only for them.
Could any one influence any one
One and one.
Or not.
If not why not.
Or if not would they not be more than
If they were changing which way any one
In which way any one would not need one
If not one and one.
Or not by them.
It is made why they do if they call them.
They could recognise the sun if there was another one
Or not at all by me
When this you see.
Or not in an exchange there might
Be only why they should.
Be this as it might
She could be pleased to
Be not only with them but by them
As well as for them
Which makes it at a meaning
And their equal to delight and plight.
Which of which one.
I had many things to think about quite often
They will call me to say I am displeased to-day
Which they can in adding often.
It is not why they knew that it is
Not only why they went but if they went when they went.
By this time they are as often with us
But we think of leaving them with others.

We wonder about it.
And they will not know if we go.

Stanza XIX

I could go on with this.

Stanza XX

Should however they be satisfied to address me
For which they know they like.
Or not by which they know that they are fortunate
To have been thought to which they do they might
Or in delight that they manage less
For which they call it all.
This is what I say fortunately
I think I will welcome very well in a minute
There nicely know for which they take
That it is mine alone which can mean
I am surely which they can suggest
Not told alone but can as is alone
Made as likely for which no matter
As more than which is lost
Recommend me to sit still.
As more often they could not see him
Have it to be or not as not
It not made it not not having it
Should they fancy worshipping
Worshipping me is what they easily can
If they come to think still that they think it still
Just why not if not
I have changed forty-nine for fifty
And can she be meant.
Or would it be a nuisance to like no one
Or better not if not only not to change
Change it should stop with not
Do you feel how often they do go
Go and so and which and met and if
And they are riding

There are so many things to ride.
And water and butter
And can they be no chief to me
I am not only not chiefly but only
Not with care.
And so much as they ever think
Remain to remain and not remain if not remain mine.
I have abused not leaving it not following it out
I also have not which can they not which they plan.
All of which is in why they used
To use me and I use them for this.
This too we too or not to go.
I often think do they sound alike
Who hates that or a hat not I.
Now I will readily say not I
But which they read to ready
Or say not I can day or say
Not blindly for caution or which or what
What about.
This is how I however remain
Retain is considered whatever they gain
I gain if in the main they make plain
Just what I maintain if I use a fruit.
Should just when this be any chance.
Better why often.
I have thought why she went and if she went he went.
No one knows the use of him and her
And might they be often just tried
Can they mean then fiercely
Should it chance to cover them not enough
I mean a hat or head
And also what a chair
And beside what beside pride
And all at once tried to believe me
Coming as if it could be entitled
One which they won.
One two.
I often think one two as one and one.

One one she counted one one and this made
Economy not only which but of which
They will not kneel of which they do.
I could be just as well obliged.
Finally I move from which
You can deduce the sun shone
By this time
Out loud
All of which can be able to be
Do I make a mistake
And if I do do you not at all either or
This time it should not have followed
Or not either to do it.
Little by little they engage not to change
Or different as it is they might if they should
But they will manage to indifferently relieve
More of which they could alight and aloud.
It is very foolish to know that they might alight
Not only do.
This which they feel they must discourage
And everything I say.
I will tell how once in a while

Stanza XXI

I know that twenty-seven had been had
For which they know no name
But our equality can indubitably spell well
For it or for which or for might it be
That it is a change to think well
Of not only when but might they be just where
They will care
Now fancy how I need you.
I have thought which they meant as willing
It is often a disappointment to dispense without
They will cool not which but very most
Well as welcome without.
She said she knew what I meant too
He too.

Although although allowed out loud.
As if they could remember where there
And there where.
Should she join robust or not
Or fortunately for it as they are not without
It is easily eaten hot and lukewarm and cold
But not without it.
Could it be thought that I could once be here
Which if they will can they not
I have heard it well enough to know
That he has not only not been mistaken yet again.
While will they now.
Oh yes while will they now
You should never be pleased with anything
If so they will crowd
But if they crowd or yes if they crowd
Which is it which if they can seat them.
I often feel well when I am seated seating them or not so
I go to remain to walk and what
Always when when is it.
It is often however they are bright.
She could often say however they can say
You always have to remember say and not so.
It is always not only not foolish
To think how birds spell and do not spell well
And how could it do birds and words
I often say so not at all amount.
All who should think season did not mean what
What is it.
I have been and have been amounted to it.
When they come in and come in and out.
Naturally it is not.
Or however not a difference between like and liked.

Stanza XXII

I should not know why they said so.

Stanza XXIII

I cannot hope again if they could mean which they liked.

Stanza XXIV

It is easy to grow ours more.
Or for which they will need a place to be
They could thank if not think that they arrange
In a way would they be angry in a way
If they could more which when they gather peas
They feel that it is not right to pay
Nor which if they nor which if they stay there.
Who need share stay there with stay away
Who will decline publicly
What is it if they will wish
Or be for which they beguile when they wish
Or can be not for which they can be spoken
It does not bother me to not delight them
They should fancy or approve fancy
They could call or can they for which will they might
But not only be the time but if which they manage.
It is in partly a reason that they feel well
Nor might they be more enclosed.
Fortunately they feel that it is right
To not give it giving it
As they do them for curls.
It is not often that they are always right
It is not often that they are always right
But which aggression or a guess
Or please addition or please a question.
Or please or please or please
Or and a foil of near and place and which nature
Will they plan to fit it to not in a point.
I wish no one the difference between a point and place
Oh yes you do oh do you.
This which I do or for intend to know
They could or call or if it is a place
In this place the sun which is not all
Is not so warm as told if it is not cold
But very warm which if favorably it is.
I could if I knew refuse to do it.
Or just when they feel like it they try

Beside which if they surround my home
They come to stay and leave it as they like
Not only not because.
Wish if vegetables need the sun
Or wish if not only not the sun but none
Also wish if they wish that they will size alike
And only if which if a wish which they will oblige
Not only necessary but they think it best.
This which I reflect is what they like to do
They like me to do
Or but or well or do be well to do
For them to like to do if I like what I do
Enormously.
Fancy what you please you need not tell me so
I wish to go or if I do I wish to go
I have often been interested in how they forget to go
Also I have been interested in if they wish to go
I have been better able to determine.
Not only however but whichever they would like
If it were partly told
That she Madame Roux is never yet quite through
But which cannot annoy because I like to try
To see why will she be here
It makes a change in faces
Her face always can change seen near or far
Or not at all or partly far.
It is not partly as they can share
Why should it be like whom.
I think I know the share
Share and share alike is alone
And not when in integrally in a way.
She could often be made sympathetic in a way a day.
It might however be she seen to be all
They feel more than they could
In point of sympathy of expression.
Now when I should think of them of this.
He comes again they come in she can come to come in.
All this is why they like but remember that for me

I am to tell not only well but very well
Why I shall easily be for all to me.
This is the reason.
I have been not only not forgetting but not only.
They will call it a chance.
Because of this can be because of this.
Which not only be how do you like not only not be
They will be satisfied to be satisfactory
Now not only not but will it be their appointment
To come when they said they would.
I said I would tell
Very well what is it that they plan to carry
Of course they plan to carry
How should it be better to put not any blue but that
Not any blue but that and change the mind
The ear and always any obligation.
Once more think twice of that.
It is very difficult to plan to write four pages.
Four pages depend upon how many more you use.
You must be careful not to be wasteful.
That is one way of advancing being wasteful
It uses up the pages two at a time for four
And if they come to and fro and pass the door
They do so.
This is my idea of how they play
Play what play which or say they plan to play which
Which is in union with whichever
They could be thought to be caught
Or planned next to next nearly next to one time
At one time it was very favorably considered
That they would oblige them to go anywhere.
Remember how we could not disturb them
It is very important not to disturb him
It is also important to remember this
Not if they disturb him
But really will they disturb him
I often do I not often think it is time to follow to begin
They could establish eight or arrange

This is not why they please or add as carelessly
They will have no use for what they said.
Now I wish all possibly to be in their shuddering
As to why if they came in and out
If they came in and out
What is the use of union between this with this.
They will add any word at most.
If she said very much or little or not at all
If she said very much or not at all
If she said a little very much or not at all
Who is winning why the answer of course is she is.
When I say that I know all of the might she be mine
She is it is particularly to care
To make it do she offers it as a compromise
To have been needed about I have not only
Not changed my mind.
Now let us think not carelessly
Not all about not allowed to change or mind.
Mind what you say.
I say I will not be careful if I do
I also say I should say what I do
I also do have a place in any antedated rose.
A rose which grows. Will they like that.
She will like that.
We have decided that only one dahlia is beautiful
That salads are not necessary
And that she has been very kind about pansies.
How can you change your mind.
This is what they know as collection.
A collection is why they place it here.
I often think how celebrated I am.
It is difficult not to think how celebrated I am.
And if I think how celebrated I am
They know who know that I am new
That is I knew I know how celebrated I am
And after all it astonishes even me.

PART V

Stanza I

If I liked what it is to choose and choose
It would be did it matter if they chose and choose
But they must consider that they mean which they can
If to-day if they find that it went every day to stay
And what next.
What is it when they wonder if they know
That it means that they are careful if they do what they show
And needless and needless if they like
That they care to be meant
Not only why they wonder whether they went
And so they might in no time manage to change
For which which fortune they went or meant
Not only why they like when they sent
What they mean to love meant.
It is this why they know what they like.
I like to have been remembered as to remember
That it meant that they thought when they were alike
As if they meant which they will undergo to choose
In which they can remain as little as they claim
In which not is it you
But which it is it is not without you
That they knew you and so forth.
This can be mine at night
Which does it mean to care.
Not only why they liked but just as if they liked
Not only what they meant but why they will not.
This is what there is not or yet.
Not to continue to do their best yet.
Think however I came to know it all.
I often offer them the ball at all
This which they like when this I say
Can they be called to play once in a way of weight

Or either our roses or their cake
I wish I had not mentioned which
It is that they could consider as their part.
Now then I had forgotten how then
Nor made it please away a weight
Oh yes you like it
Or if not for what if now and then
Without them it is often meant to be mine.
Let me say how they changed apart alike.

Stanza II

If you knew how do you very well I thank you
Or if you knew how do you do how do you
Or if not that changes more to many
And may be they do or not if not why.
This is how it is that it does not make any difference
To please them or not or not
Or not to not please them or oh yes yes.
They could should they under any circumstance
Understand differ or differs.
It is why they wondered if they liked
What indeed makes no difference
As they manage
To relieve plunders and blunders
Any one is often thought susceptible.
Or which one wishes.
Now I have wandered very far.
From my own fireside.
But which they knew in a wonder.
It is a wonder that they like it.
I have often thought that she meant what I said.
Or how do you this about that.
Or if at any time.
It had been not only not remembered
I depend upon him I depend upon them.
Of or how they like.
This what I say makes me remember that.
That if it did

Which can just as you said
Or which can be
If they managed it
Or by the time they did.
This is however just how many are alike.
Once upon a time who will be left to rain
Or like it as much as ever
Or even more than that if they like it.
They must be often thought to be just as careful
As not to give them give anything away.
However how many do like to.
This is not what I meant by what I said.
It should be that I think that it might do
If I made it do
I also think that I should not say
That they know which way
They could arrange to go and say
That they will not stay if not
If not what do they like alike
Or as much as just yet.
I could often be caught liking it
Oh yes I could
And then it can not only if they say so.
Oh yes only not yes.
In just this way they went as they can
I have refused went and went as much.
I also have refused whatever they went.
But if wherever they went.
Not one in any two
Or just arise or if not only not to like.
It can not be alright.
When they thought how often about a wall.
When they thought how often about a wall.

Stanza III

Just when they wish wish
Or will they or must they be selfish
To not do you should not do not do

Not as if not to to to do
There that is better.

Stanza IV

I like any two numbers more than any two numbers before
Or not.
But if it had been alright to be bright.
Could I have been bright before or not.
I wonder if I could have been bright before or not
Not only why they do but if they do what I like
If I do what I like.
I could not nor can I remember
Whether if they were there if they were there to care
May be they could be wondering if it were like
If it were like it as it is
As it is if they meant only which
Whenever it is by this time
Of course no difference makes no difference at all.
I wish to think about everything anything if I do.
Or by the time easily
Or not only why they should.
Or please believe.
That they mean what they mean by that.
If not why should no one mind what they say.

Stanza V

Please believe that I remember just what to do
Oh please believe that I remember just what to do
Or please believe that I do remember just what to do
And if I remember just what to do
There will not only be that reason but others
Which at one time.
I like what I have not prepared before of course not.
As fast as not so fast
Not that it does not make any difference.
This is what they like what I say.

Stanza VI

This one will be just as long
As let it be no mistake to know
That in any case they like what they do
If I do what I do I do too
That is to say this conclusion is not with which.
It can be just as well known
Do you change about mutton and onions or not.
This is why they sleep with a ball in the mouth
If not what is there to doubt.
I have forgotten what I meant to have said ahead.
Not at all forgotten not what.
It is not whatever not is said
Which they can presume to like
If at no time they take any pains
Not to like it.
This is how I remember however.
Anybody not anybody can remember however but it does.
Not make any difference in any way.
This is what I wish to kindly write.
How very well I will at night
As well as in the day-light.
I could just as well remember what I saw
Or if not I could just as well remember
What I saw when I could.
The thing I wish to tell
Is that it makes no difference as well
As when there is this not this not to tell
To tell well or as well.
I have not thought why I should wish beside
Coming again as coming again.
They could write three to one
Or not two to one but which is not which
If they ask more than any fourteen.
Fourteen is however they like but not for me.
I am very capable of saying what I do.

I wish that they could not wish which nor do they.
I know what I say often so one tells me
Or if not I could not look again.
Might it be whichever it is
It is not my custom not only to think of a whole thing.
Does it make any difference which one they decide
Of course it does of course it does.
Alright let us think everything.
I have begun again to think everything.

Stanza VII

Now should or should not if they call with it
That I could not not only hear but see
Say when with spitting cavalry
She tears all where with what can be not now
They could be called to hurry call or hear or hair
Or there
Not only with nor welcome
Can they come and climb a vine
In place of chairs in place of chairs in place of chairs.
I could have thought I would think what with
What not not with only that
It is just as much noise as said
Or if not only which I cannot come again to combine
Not only fairly well but mounted.
I do not need the word amounted
Oh not at all
He knows when she came here
For which they can in all which all which called
Perhaps enchain perhaps not any name
For theirs will come as used
By this it is not only I mean
I mean I mean is always said again.
Remember what I said it is not just the same
Or not with only stretched.
In a little while he meant to perceive
For which they can or can not do
Do believe that I will say it used to be like that.

I wish to well assure it did not use to be like that
Not only that it did I did I did and did or do
Which can they come to for which they knew you
They knew who knew you
Every little while I often smile
And all which can come which they will approve
And not only not soften
But just as fairly often
Can they not come to say what they can do
I do very much regret to keep you awake
Because you should be asleep
But even so it is better to stay
And hear me say that is right here
What not only which they care
This can be made a reason why
They will be welcome to arrive and cry
They could do which they care.
Now to come back to how it is not all alike
Since after all they first
Since after all they were first
Best and most.
Now listen often cautiously
Best and most is seen to sweeten
Often often it is eaten
Much which much which much they do
Come and do and come for you
Did I not tell you I would tell
How well how well how very well
I love you
Now come to think about how it would do
To come to come and wish it
Wish it to be well to do and you
They will do well what will they well and tell
For which they will as they will tell well
What we do if we do what if we do
Now think how I have been happy to think again
That it is not only which they wish
It is as I have said a resemblance

To have forgotten as many times they came
That is to say we said
This which I said which I said this.
I said that it did not make any difference
And it did make this difference
As it made it made it do.
This which I mentioned made not only why but often
Now I have lost the thread of how they came to be alike.
Not only why if not but with their cause
Of course their cause of course because they do
I had been certain I would a little explain
Which can they do.
When I look down a vista I see not roses but a faun
That is to say the fields after hay
Are ploughed after hay
Not on the day
But just after the day
Like alike when it is chosen.
I wish never to say choose I choose
Oh not at all not while they like
Not while I like alike but do they
They may be often not declared as mine
For which I can not very well think well
Because just now I do not think well
Of at all.
She can be right to think that the sun
Not only does not fade but makes it less faded.
She can be right she often is always
This is what I said I would say
I say it as well as ever naturally
Because with which they would investigate
That they could not take a chance
Not to not to not to make no mistake
Not which at once to do.
It is often however they like
That they make it do.
I refuse ever to number ducks.
Because I know by weight how eight are eight.

Oh yes I do.
And a stanza too or a stanza two.
How do you do very well I thank you

Stanza VIII

I wish now to wish now that it is now
That I will tell very well
What I think not now but now
Oh yes oh yes now.
What do I think now
I think very well of what now
What is it now it is this now
How do you do how do you do
And now how do you do now.
This which I think now is this.

Stanza IX

A stanza nine is a stanza mine.
My stanza is three of nine.

Stanza X

I have tried earnestly to express
Just what I guess will not distress
Nor even oppress or yet caress
Beside which tried which well beside
They will not only will not be tried.
It is not trying not to know what they mean
By which they come to be welcome as they heard
I have been interrupted by myself by this.
This can be which is not an occasion
To compel this to feel that that is so
I do not dearly love to liven it as much
As when they meant to either change it or not
I do not change it either or not.
This is how they like to do what they like to do.
I have thought often of how however our change
That is to say the sun is warm to-day because
Yesterday it was also warm

And the day before it was not warm
The sun as it shone was not warm
And so moreover as when the sun shone it was not warm
So yesterday as well as to-day
The sun when it shone was warm
And so they do not include our a cloud
Not at all it had nothing to do with a cloud
It had not to do with the wind
It had not to do with the sun
Nor had it to do with the pleasure of the weather either.
It had to do with that this is what there had been.
It is very pleasant that it is this that it should have been
And now that it is not only that it is warmer
Now very well there is often that they will
Have what they look when they look there or there
To make a mistake and change to make a mistake and change
To have not changed a mistake and to make a mistake and
change.
Change the prophecy to the weather
Change the care to their whether they will
Nothing now to allow
It is very strange that very often
The beginning makes it truly be
That they will rather have it be
So that to return to be will they be
There will they be there with them.
I should often know that it makes a difference not to look
about
Because if to do they that is is it
Not which it makes any difference or.
But just what with containing
They need or made so surrounded
In spite of in a delay of delayed
It is often very changed to churn
Now no one churns butter any more.
That is why that is where they are here.
I wish I had not mentioned it either.

This whole stanza is to be about how it does not make any
difference.
    I have meant this.
    Might it be yes yes will it
    Might it not be as much as once having it
    Might it not only be allowed
    And if not does not it bring back
    Or bring back what is it
    If they bring it back not for me
    And if it brings it back for me
    Or if it brings it back for me
    So and so further than if.
    It is easy to be often told and moved
    Moved can be made of sun and sun of rain
    Or if not not at all.
    Just when they should be thought of so forth.
    What they say and what they do
    One is one and two is two
    Or if not two who.

Stanza XI

I feel that this stanza has been well-known.

Stanza XII

    Once when they do not come she does not come
    Why does she not come.
    She does not come because if she does not come
    Not only this.
    They can be thought and sought
    But really truly if she need to
    But which they make in which and further more.
    It is not by the time that they could be alone.
    What is the difference if he comes again to come here
    Or to come here to go there to them
    Or which they do which they do well
    Or which they do not do well
    Or more than which they do not do well

Stanza XIII

There can be pink with white or white with rose
Or there can be white with rose and pink with mauve
Or even there can be white with yellow and yellow with blue
Or even if even it is rose with white and blue
And so there is no yellow there but by accident.

Stanza XIV

Which would it be that they liked best
But to return to that it makes no difference.
Which would make no difference
Of course it makes a difference
But of course it makes a difference
And not only just now.
Whenever I return to this it is dull
And not by what I do
Or if by what I do
It is this that they like that I like.
I have wished to think about what to do
I do not have to wish to think about what I do
Nor do I wish to have to think about what they do not do
Because they are about out loud.
After all what is a garden.
A garden is a place in which
They must be in which
They are there and these.
This is not what to say to-day.
I have wished to be as this.
And I have and am as so I said I wished.
What could they use they could use
What could they either use
They could either use or use
If it is usual or is it usual
To be usually there.
It does not make any difference
That which they like they knew
Nor could it make any difference to use two.

After it was known to be is it as they knew
Think well of think of a difference
Or think well of think well of a difference.
They can be they can be there can be hours of light.
Light alright the little birds are audacious
They cannot kill large barn yard fowl.
How often have I seen them and they were right
How often have I seen them and they were not able to delight
In which they do.
It is not often necessary to look to see.
Not often necessary to look to see.
How easily she can can be there
Or how easily easily declare
Which they can be able to share
That they can can they bear this.
Or can they bear that.
I wish I could be rich in ways to say how do you do
And I am.
Or not only when they can venture to not remember
to prepare
Not only when they do
If not as not in which arrangement they concur
It is might it be easily mine.
I will not be often betrayed by delayed
Not often
Nor when they cherish which not often
They will come come will they come
Not only by their name
They could however much if however much
Not only which they come and cause because
Because of all the rest.
It is not only that they manage mine.
Will they be mine if not only when
Do they cover to color when
If they color when with then
Or color cover with whether clover
Can cover a color with clover then.
It is not safe to use clover as a name

When thinking of balsam and balsam is not only not the same
But not now the same.
In spite of which they tell well
That they were right.

Stanza XV

I have not come to mean
I mean I mean
Or if not I do not know
If not I know or know
This which if they did go
Not only now but as much so
As if when they did which
If not when they did which they know
Which if they go this as they go
They will go which if they did know
Not which if they which if they do go
As much as if they go
I do not think a change.
I do think they will change.
But will I change
If I change
I can change.
Yes certainly if I can change.
It is very foolish to go on
Oh yes you are.
How could one extricate oneself from where one is
One is to be one is to extricate whichever
They can be not for this any for an occasion
Of which they are remarkable as a remembrance.

Stanza XVI

Be spared or can they justly say
That if that if they will after all it will
Be just as if they say
Not only not they might but they will do
This they will do or if this will they do if
They will not only if they will not only will

But if they will they will do this.
For this thing to think it a thing to think well.
Having found that not only theirs or rather that
That it did make a difference that they knew
Now they know but none only which now they know
They know this.
They did if they had known not only know this.
But which can they be known this which they wish.
I had no doubt that it a difference makes
If there is doubt if money is about
I also know but which I know or worry
If when they give and take they give in a hurry
But which of which of this there cannot be a doubt
That if that could if it could come to be about
That if they did know this just as they had
Will as they had will to be worried still
Or not only not necessary a necessity
I wish to say correctly this
I wish to say that any day the roads a roads
Will they be roads they say when if
In not only not obliged to leave it well
But which if they can be to recollect
Oh yes not only which to gather to collect
They do try so to have the wind to blow
Not only not here but also not there.
This which I wish to say is this
There is no difference which they do
Nor if there is not or a difference which
Now which as which we should not add to now
No not indeed
I wish to say that they could eat as well
As if when now they heard when now
They had it had it when now
This is what which I did do say
That certainly to-day to hear to get to-day
That which as yet to-day is a relief to-day
Oh yes it is a relief to-day but not
Not without further ought or ought.

Now they need mine as theirs
But when they heard refuse a difference
Not any one has ours now.
Not in that way oh no not in that way
Come thought come thought of me.
I am always thinking that if in their way
If in their way it is if in their way
Insist if in their way
So could in of course shine but not wires shine
They can complete this time will will this time
There or they could in no doubt think.
This which I do I know or only only say say so.
This which has happened is my sand my sand my said
Of course my said why will they manage this wish.
Now I wish to tell quite easily well
Just what all there is of which to tell
Immediately increases hold as told
Or can they better be better be known
I have thought in thinking that is walking
That the way to be often more than told in walking
Is after all as much as told in walking
That they as well will be just not to have
Theirs be theirs now. It is not only this a change
But theirs might be
I have lost the thread of my discourse.
This is it it makes no difference if we find it
If we found it
Or which they will be brought if they worry or not
Without which if they begin or yet began
Can they be equalled or equal in amount
When there is a doubt but most of course
Of course there is no doubt.
I have said that if a cuckoo calls
When moneys in a purse in my own pocket
It means wealth
Moreover if the cuckoo to make sure
Comes near then there can be no doubt if doubt there be
But not by this to see but worry left for me

Makes no doubt more.

Does it can be it does but I doubt it.

After this I think it makes no difference what their
characters are

What you have oh yes I thank you
What I have is made to be me for mine
I should not please to share oh no of course.
But not to go into that is not in question
Not when no bird flutters
Even if they yet can be yet here
This which I think is of this kind around
They will be called to tall
No one is tall who has not all
They have not only all
Which is which they can
They say August is not April
But how say so if in the middle they can not know.
Think how well to like everything.
I wish to say that I made no mistake in saying any day.

Stanza XVII

I feel that often in a way they link
Not if they should and shouted
But can they mind if which they call they went
Or not only not of course
But not only welcome more.
There is no doubt that often no alone
There has been a waste who quiets a waste
But which they will they wish
I say yes readily steadily do either do
But which they will in theirs to theirs deny
Not to have been ruffled by success
Or either or they can not be inclined
To gather more than give giving is foolish
Spending is a pleasure gathering is making
Bettering is no delight they like to light
Of course they like to light it.
They like not to explain but add a day.

Very likely to take away if to take away
Before it was of importance not to go now
But not now.
I wish to think to refuse wishes
Also not to refuse trees or please
Not to refuse bells or wells
Not to refuse does or could
Not refuse made to be with which to go
Made to be minding others leave it so
What I have said is this I am satisfied
I have pride I am satisfied
I have been worried I will be worried again
And if again is again is it
Not to be interested in how they think
Oh yes not to be interested in how they think
Oh oh yes not to be interested in how they think.

Stanza XVIII

I could make at it most or most at it.

Stanza XIX

I felt that I could not have been surprised
Or very much as they do
If it is that I remember what
What do they if they never dot
But which is not warranted by what
What will they have as is if not to mean
It is not difficult to either stand
Which on account if without flavor
Shall they be shamed with generation
They can leave it half as well.
I wish to remind everybody nobody hears me
That it makes no difference how they do
What they do
Either by our or either by at all
This is why no doubt it followed better
To have no one eight or eat before.
This which I think is this.

I think I could do not without at night
Not only not a moon
Can they be told as well
This what is what I do can come
Not to prevent which when they mean they come
Or not only for it.
All this is of no interest
If indeed there is no right
No right to keep it well away
Just when they do or either not delight
Can they collect or recollect their way
Not only which but whether they can plan
I wish to say I do not not remember every day
Not I
Not even when I try or why
Not even well not even very well
Not even not without which not even more
Should or just yet recollect
That they that is not there
Even not there much as it is much allowed
For them to come for them to come.

Stanza XX

I wish to say that who could
Or just as well as welcome
This which I know now I know followed how
How did it follow of course it followed how did it follow
Not only no tide is perplexed
But they will perplex less in usefulness
Useful or noon can well be kept to right
Should they not care for
What will they care for
I like to think how every one thought less
Of what is this when even is it know
Mine is what is it mine is
Shall they not often be not only made a way
Make and made made stayed.
This which I have remembered is made known

Shall they should always know
Or less the same
They can be often thought made quite well.
She could in which instance for instance
Leave love alone.
They could call dears early years
Or not only their care but with their care
Can she be well to manage more or less
However much it is however much alike
This which I know is what I know
What I know is not what I say so
Because I wish to draw drawers and drawing
Or can they even call and talk well and welcome.
Think how often it does not change and mind
They are not glad to sit and find
Find it nearly out.
It is not nearly nearly so
It is not fairly nearly nearly so.
For which it is not often not only better that they like
In which is reason.
In reading a long book which I look
In reading and reading a long gay book
I look
This is what I see with my eyes.
I see that I could have been made the same
By which by in which name the same
They can include in tries and tires
And feel or felt can it not it inspire or inspires
They could in no doubt know.
I cannot well remember whether it was yesterday that I wrote
Or if yes of course naturally I should
Wait another day.
Or have waited another day.

Stanza XXI

I wish always to go on with when
When they meant then

Stanza XXII

Not only by their hope I feel so
Can they be not with all a wish to know
That they will well declare to do so
But which they will as much as all delight
For this in their way one way one way to know
That it is never gladly to be so
In which it is in often which it is
As they will not be made with them
To be here with them
A stanza can be bought and taught
If not why if not will they or can he will they not
It is not often that they narrowly rejoin
Or as the way or as their way
They will be finally as their way
Can they be finally as their way.
This which I know I know that I can do
Or not if not if I can do if not
If not at all they were not only not to wait awhile
Or which if which is better than only not better
It is possible that only if they did and could know
They would happen to arrange that they could not be
Which they had thought and taught
Or meant to teach or meant
Happily it is sent.
This makes no hope of better than it should
They were pleased that they were well well meant
Or left to have no other as it were
Left finally for it.
I wish to announce stanzas at once.
What is a stanza
When I say that often as a day
I feel that it is best to know the way
That if upon the road where if I went
I meant to feel that is if as if sent
She if I came and went

Or well what is it if it makes it do
Not only which if not only all or not alike
But it is it is just like Italy
And if it is just like Italy
Then it is as if I am just like it
That is make it be.
There is no necessity to make it be if it is
Or there is not any real making it do too
Because if which it is or just to know
To know and feel and may be tell
Is all very well if no one stealing past
Is stealing me for me.
Oh why oh why can they count most
If most and best is all
Of course it is all or all at all
Most and best met from there to here
And this is what I change.
Of course I change a change
Better than not.
This that I must not think I do
Which is to do but met and well
Well when I like when they like.
There is no hope or use in all.
Once again to try which of a choice.
Theirs is no sacreder in sacrament
For finally in disposes
When they plan
This which I can do.
I wish once more to begin that it is done
That they will fasten done to done
Or more nearly care to have to care
That they shall will and can be thought
To need most when
When whenever they need to mean
I mean I mean.
This which I do or say is this.
It is pleasant that a summer in a summer

Is as in a summer and so
It is what after all in feeling felt
Can they not gain.
Once again I went once or more often than once
And felt how much it came to come
That if at once of one or two or one.
If not only if not one or one
One of one one of one which is what
What it is to win and find it won
This is not what I thought and said
I thought that the summer made it what it is
Which if I said I said I said it
And they were using used to as a chance
Not only to be which if none it was
It was used for which for which they used for it.
I wish I could say exactly that it is the same
I will try again to say it if not then
Then not alike there is no then alike
There is no then not like alike and not alike
But that.
This which I mean to do again.

Stanza XXIII

Often as I walk I think

Stanza XXIV

But this does not mean that I think again.

Stanza XXV

Which can be which if there
This which I find I like
Not if which if I like.
This which if I like.
I have felt this which I like.
It is more then.
I wish to say that I take pleasure in it

Stanza XXVI

A stanza can make wait be not only where they went
But which they made in theirs as once awhile
Can they be close to wishing or as once
Can they not be for which they will
As wish can be more reconciled for them
In which respect they will or so
Or better so or can they not be meant
All which they plan as theirs in theirs and joined
Or not be left to rather wish
But which they will in no way
Or not in any or rather in any way
Theirs which they leave as much
Or better not or better not all alone
Not if they call in early or to care
Or manage or arrange or value
Or relieve or better like
Or not at all as nearly once compared
Or made it to be gained
Or finally as lost
Or by them not detained
Or valued as equally
Or just as much established by their lost
Or finally as well prepared
Or can they not without them which they cherish
Not only by them but by the time
Not only will they but it is one to like
Or manage just as well as if
As if they planned theirs which they know
Or in as well as do
Would they be more contained
To leave it not for them
By the time that all of it is better
Once more to have it do it now
As moon-light
Naturally if they do not look or go
They will be always there or not at all

Not why they went to manage as it is
Felt which they like or as a place to go
They could feel well they went
They could not partly show
Just which or why it is
Not only as it is more than they thought.
They will arrange to claim
It is not only which they will or know
Or changing for it partly as they if.
If it is only made to be no delight
Not only as they finish which as well as they began
Or either not to on account
Not only why they will
Or often not often not often not
It is of more than will they come and can
Can they be here if after joining
They will partly in at once declare
Now in no haste if not now in no haste
As just when well supported they need it
Not only if they use but do they use
And might they not be well not be well inclined
To have not which they manage or amuse
Not which they fragrantly and always now
If when they know mint can they not know
Not often will they better have than either or
Not only when they share
But even when they share
There is no mending when they delight
When they delight to have or can they share
It is partly this which is not only mine
Or not not only mine
Or will they not
Or will it be meant to attend
Or follow rather than not follow now
Just and in that way or rather not to say
They will not happen to be often disturbed
Or rather not to have or love it so
They should not can or will not do their way

Of better not to like or indeed can it matter
Not even not at all
And so marking it as once and only once
In which in which ease
Can they be mine in mine.

Stanza XXVII

It is not easy to turn away from delight in moon-light.
Nor indeed to deny that some heat comes
But only now they know that in each way
Not whether better or either to like
Or plan whichever whether they will plan to share
Theirs which indeed which can they care
Or rather whether well and whether.
Can it not be after all their share.
This which is why they will be better than before
Makes it most readily more than readily mine.
I wish not only when they went

Stanza XXVIII

To come back to a preparation
Or fairly well know when
It is as much as if I thought or taught.
Taught could be teaching
Made in which is strange if strange
That they will otherwise know
That if indeed in vanishes
Theirs where they do not even do
What after all can be which can they call
They can call me.

Stanza XXIX

A stanza should be thought
And if which can they do
Very well for very well
And very well for you.

Stanza XXX

This is when there are wishes

Stanza XXXI

Of course he does of course he likes what he did
But would he mind if he liked what he did
Would he like it better if it did not matter
Not only if he liked what he did
But often just as well
If he did not share in seeing it there
And so might they not only be so
But which if once more they were readily
But which they like.
In there as only as a chance
They could control not only which they liked.
I think very well of changing
I do think very well of changing this for that.
I not only would not choose
But I would even couple it
With whatever I had chosen.
Not only can they gain
But might they gain
They should as they manage
They should share as they manage
They should be often as they manage
Or can or mean disturb
Or as they like
Or leaving it fairly well
Much as they wish or will
Fairly nearly or alike.
I could if I wished have spoken
Or rather not not only
I could arrange and amount
Or for which they would keep
They could have all or could they have all
But in the adding of a place

They will commence intend amuse
I would rather not come again.
It was often so much better than I thought
I could not manage with anguish
I felt that there was partly as a share
To prepare
Liking and liking it.
It is of no importance
Not a chance than which they will
For which they know in no renown
Ordered and colored there
They will not only reach it but pleasantly reach it.
Which is why they will add it as they call.
They could be left to mean
Or rather might they rather be left to mean
Not only why they like but often when
All of it has been shortened by being told
At least once at a time
For them they will know variously
That is not only meant as meaning
But most of all as most of all
Are there not only adding theirs as when
When could they call to shorten
Shorten whatever they are likely as very likely
To have not where they planned
But just as much as place
A place is made to mean mischief
Or to join plan with added reasoning
They could without without which
Might it be without which
All of it which they place to call
Not only made differently indifferently.
I could do what I liked
I could also do whatever I liked
I could also as much
I could be there and where
Where can that be
Where can that be

As not only when but always
Always is not however why they like
There are often opportunities to be chosen
More as they like if they at once they like
Not only as not only used to use
Should they in every little while remain
Not only as much as if they cause
They never need cause distress
This which I have I add to liking
There is no necessity to decide an amount
Of whether as they do they might do this
Because whenever and if why they like
All which or which is strange
Need not in the meantime mean any end of when
Not only for the wish but as the wish
I manage whatever I do I manage
I could not only like hers but mine
Mine can be or if whether they could do this
Might they not only be in season as a reason
Should they have found it or rather not found it again.
This which is what can be what they need not only for them
They will be plainly a chance
Plainly a chance
Could they not only like it
Can they not only like it
Or if they can not only like it
However can they even be with or without it
For which as better or a just alike
As planned.
Once when they could be choose as a choice
They will feel that which as moreover
It is an opportunity
Not only in exile.
What is exile or oh yes what is exile.
Exile is this they could come again
They will be felt as well in reason
As which if which they planned
I could be ought I be without

Without doubt.
Now a little measure of me
I am as well addressed as always told
Not in their cause but which can be they need
After which can it be
That this which I have gathered
Can gather must will change to most
Most and best.

Stanza XXXII

Could so much hope be satisfied at last
Can they be lost as lost
Can they be carried where as found
Or can they not be easily met as met
By which they use or very much they like
Made while they please
Or as much.
When very often all which can they call
Or further happen can they not call
Can they not be without which help
Or much or much alone
It can be not only why they wished they had
Finally funnily or as funnily at one time
It is more than they relieve caution
But which they might.
Might they be thought very often to have come.
Neither in mean nor meaning
They will be presently be spared
They will all feel all which they please
They will not either share as they manage
No plan which can they like
Often which more than for which
Can they like
I feel very carefully that they can be there
Or in no pretence that they change the time
Time which they change.
It troubles me often which can or can it not be
Not only which in and because their share.

Let me listen do when they mount
Or if not as they did.
Did or call.
Rest or restless or added rest
Or which or which might they
Made to be arranged for which
Might they be pleased if after often
They could not share tried
Or even places.
They can not acknowledge or add it.
Fortunately to rest.
They can be well enough known
Or by the time they wished
I can not often add add to welcome
Please be not only welcome to our home
Can they call a terrace terrace
And also pleasure in a place or garden
Or does which can does it please
Can they please if they must
But which which is that it
So very often is not only left and right
But can they add to which whichever
Can they not only please.
It might be called all hills or nationality
Or not be even always
Being placed as can they wish
It could be often helped
Help or it is as more
This is the story.
A head should be a chimney
That is well or welcome
It might be made in forty years or two
One for a man and one or one a woman
And either having neither there.
Each one is not at all in their replacing
Alas a birthday can be squandered
And she will always please
Or call it well alone

Can they never try to otherwise attain obtain
Or feel it as they must or best.
Best and lest they change for all.
I regret that it is one to two
Or rather yet as change maintain.
Or please or rather certain a mountain.
Not nearly dangerously.
It can be often thought to be helpful
She can not change what she can not change it for.
It is why wondering do they or lilies fail.
Growing each day more pale that is the leaves do.
Otherwise there is a pleasure in adding
A doubling of their plan.
They will add adding to their tender care
And often as if much as if
More of which as if
They would be well pleased well pleased as if
They could in their hope be carefully.
I wish now to state it clearly.

Stanza XXXIII

They can please pears and easily
They can easily please all easily
For which they please

Stanza XXXIV

There is no custom to know yes and no
They could be easily meant to be fairly well meant
To have in which and can they try
But which and which they carefully rely
Upon it.
In no mean happening will they call
They will never differing from will refuse
And remain meant to please
And so remain meant to please and delight
All of which they meet
All meant in adding mine to mine.
In which case most and best is readily read

Nor do they mean to find and please
As they mean which they add to adding
Or better still add which to add and apples
And to add bless and caress
Not only ought but bought and taught
In kindness.
Therefore I see the way

Stanza XXXV

Not which they gather.
Very fairly it is often
Which they have as is their way
They will rather gather either
Either or which they can
For instance.
It is a curious thing.
That now.
As I feel that I like
That it is as much as
It is exactly like
When I found it easily easily to try
And it is as if it were
As very much alike
As when I found it very much
I did then not wonder but wander
And now it is not a surprise as eyes
Nor indeed not if I wonder
Could it be exactly alike.
This I wish to know.
If you look at it if you look at it like it
It is very simple it is just as alike
By this it is more not only this.
Little by little it comes again.
For which no one need more need like it
It is like it not only here but there
They could which ever they
What I wish to do to say
It is as much as if like it.

This I can like as not dislike.
It has often been said in landscape historically
That they can tell.
What if they wish they can tell.
As I am wandering around without does it matter
Or whether they oblige that they see other
They can if they manage or at best
Either a color
I think well of landscape as a proof of another
I wish well of having brought to think
Which is why well at first.
At first I did not know why well
Why quite well as much as well
Why it could be just as well
That it is like or if and like
This landscape this color.
What is a landscape
A landscape is what when they that is I
See and look.
Or wonder if or wander if not which
They come slowly not to look.
I think so well
Of when I do
Which I consider
Which they do I do
Or if not if at all
When I see over there
There where they color do not call or color
Not if water not if not if water
Not if they could be a part
Think well of gather well
I come to wish which if I add or wish
It is now that however it is now
This which I think which it is the same
When unknown to fame I needed which I did not claim
For them or further made for them
In which they added claim to blame
I wish to say that not only will I try

I will try to tell very well
How I felt then and how I feel now.

Stanza XXXVI

What is strange is this.
As I come up and down easily
I have been looking down and looking up easily
And I look down easily
And I look up and down not easily
Because
It is this which I know
It is alike that is.
I have seen it or before.

Stanza XXXVII

That feels fortunately alike.

Stanza XXXVIII

Which I wish to say is this
There is no beginning to an end
But there is a beginning and an end
To beginning.
Why yes of course.
Any one can learn that north of course
Is not only north but north as north
Why were they worried.
What I wish to say is this.
Yes of course

Stanza XXXIX

What I wish to say is this of course
It is the same of course
Not yet of course
But which they will not only yet
Of course.
This brings me back to this of course.
It is the same of course it is the same
Now even not the name

But which is it when they gathered which
A broad black butterfly is white with this.
Which is which which of course
Did which of course
Why I wish to say in reason is this.
When they begin I did begin and win
Win which of course.
It is easy to say easily.
That this is the same in which I do not do not like the name
Which wind of course.
This which I say is this
Which it is.
It is a difference in which I send alike
In which instance which.
I wish to say this.
That here now it is like
Exactly like this.
I know how exactly like this is.
I cannot think how they can say this
This is better than I know if I do
That I if I say this.
Now there is an interference in this.
I interfere in I interfere in which this.
They do not count alike.
One two three.

Stanza XL

I wish simply to say that I remember now.

Stanza XLI

I am trying to say something but I have not said it.
Why.
Because I add my my I.
I will be called my dear here.
Which will not be why I try
This which I say is this.
I know I have been remiss
Not with a kiss

But gather bliss
For which this
Is why this
Is nearly this
I add this.
Do not be often obliged to try.
To come back to wondering why they began
Of course they began.

Stanza XLII

I see no difference between how alike.
They make reasons share.
Of which they care to prepare
Reasons which
I will begin again yesterday.

Stanza XLIII

If they are not all through

Stanza XLIV

Why have they thought I sold what I bought.
Why have they either wished that they will when they wish
Why have they made it of use
Why have they called me to come where they met
Why indeed will they change if no one feels as I do.
Why can they carry please and change a choice
Why will they often think they quiver too
Why will they be when they are very much further
Why will they fortunately why will they be
It is of no consequence that they conclude this
For which it is in no degree a violation
Of whether they will wish
All can see why they see
Will they see me
I do I think I will will I be will I be
Fortunately for it is well well to be welcome
It is having left it now
They mean three to change.

I will include I will allow.
They could having see making it do
She can arrange our a cloud
But they think well of even
I wish to remember that there was a time
When they saw shapes in clouds
Also as much.
And now why why will they if they will
See shapes in clouds but do not
Do not draw the attention of any other one to it.
They can be even used to it.
What I wish to remember is not often whether theirs
They can be living what there is
Or rather why they are inclined
To leave hills without clouds
To be covered with haze
And to be transparent not in mist
But finely finally well
They could be such as there
Will they or will they not share
They might be thought to be well caught.
I feel that I have given this away.
I wish now to think of possession.
When ownership is due who says you and you.
This as they feel this.
They will accomplish willows with a kiss
Because willows border rivers.
Little rivers are in a marsh
Having forgotten marshes and trees
Very much or very well who sees.

Stanza XLV

I could join if I change.
If I could see which left it that
Can they call where they will as left.
But which they like.
Oh yes they do oh yes which they do like
They need any stanzas any stanzas there.

They could be seen as much.
Leave it as much.
Can they be fairly fancied.
Can they be as much as fairly fancied.
No one knowing how knows how.
I feel.
I feel that they will call it tell well.
If not in joined can they release.
Or yes not as to please.
I wish once more to think of when a wagon
Can they not yet be drawn.
Of which of whether if they need.
Of whether yet they share.
Can they be seen to care.
Colored as oxen.
It is not only here that they know oxen.
Oh yes oh no it is not only so.
It is that they will leave and leave.
And might they can they leave.
If they can leave to have to come to leave
They will come which can they come
I will not think some come.

Stanza XLVI

Why are ours filled with what it is
That they reach mine.
They do and if they do will they be theirs as mine.
And if it is night they could just they share
Might they be one I won
Or can they be which if they could.
I must say all which is as if they had met.
Often adding had makes leaves as well
If gathered when they fell they usefully are used
It is not why they like they readily grow.
She chose one to two.
Heliotropes are through through the air.
And yet I saw her choose
Find it for him

I saw her choose.
She could be thought to be.
They like alike.
I wish to notice that they are at all.
To arrange to choose.
As much as for which use.
I will mention it.
She has been very well known to like it.
I can say that it is a pleasure to see the bouquet.

Stanza XLVII

I will can I request.
That they should offer this.
I have not felt to which can be true
That they will yield if either if they wish
Will they to you

Stanza XLVIII

I have been astonished that black on white
This I have been astonished that it thickens
But why should black on white
Why should it thicken.

Stanza XLIX

I wish moreover that I think again.
Will you follow me as much as thought
How could when any know.
What could I do if when I felt I left.
Left it to her to do.
Not much which I can know
In which I know.
I can be often or rather awfully doubtful
If I can be seen to have been wished
Wished well as while.
For all which all that while
Can it be not alone not liked.
They can be no occasion to leave roses
On bushes.

But if not only why I sit
But can be not only if only why I sit
I can be often as much as ever
More can they like.
I think that if I feel we know
We cannot doubt that it is so
They cannot with which they change
Once more they see that it is I
Brown is as green as brown is green for me.
This makes me think hardly of how I learn.

Stanza L

Can you please please me.
Can he be not only why I like.
Which they shall never refuse to hear
I refuse to hear her.

Stanza LI

Now this a long stanza
Even though even so it has not well begun
Because whichever way they can contrive
To think well will it be
Need I remember what I carry
Can I plan this as strangely
Can I can I not even marry
May I come further than with which I came
Can I completely feel can I complain
Can I be for them here.
Can I change sides
Can I not rather wish
Can I not rather wish.

Stanza LII

There has been a beginning of begun.
They can be caused.
They can be caused to share.
Or they can be caused to share.
Should no one have thought well or well

For which no one can change frighten.
Or plainly play as much.
Or nearly why they need to share
Or can they just be mine
He has come to say I come again.
They could really leaving really leaving mine.
I could not only wish
I could not only wish for that.
I could not only wish for that here.
It is very rarely that there is a difference known
Between wood and a bone.
I have only felt that I could never exchange
They will be thought to welcome me.
I am coming.
They will not be annoyed that I am coming
They will be glad
They will have often had it.
I have often admired her courage
In having ordered three
But she was right.
Of course she was right.
About this there can be no manner of doubt.
It gave me pleasure and fear
But we are here
And so far further
It has just come to me now to mention this
And I do it.
It is to be remarked that the sun sets
When the sun sets
And that the moon rises
When the moon rises.
And so forth.
But which they meddle or they will as much
They have asked me to predict the weather
To tell them will it rain
And often I have been a comfort to them.
They are not a simple people
They the two of them.

And now they go just as well
As if they were used to it.
Which they are.
They go into the fields.
There can be things to do
Which there are
Which there are in the fields
And so they have not sought to change the noon or the moon.
But will they ask a question
Most certainly they are not divided.
It is often thought that they know
That it is as well to know years apart.
Ask quietly how they like it.

Stanza LIII

By which I know
Can they like me
Not only which they know
But they will wish
They will wish which they know
And now and ours not at all
Can they be once with which they will declare
And place and ours know
They can with better which they even well declare
That they can change or is it in a union.
They can be finally to find that they
Can see and since as one can come.
Come one as one can add to come
Come which they have
Once more to add feeling to feeling.

Stanza LIV

Could she not have it as they made an impulse
He will not feel that it is made to change
They will conclude that parts are partly mine.
They will have will.
Will they come when they will

Or will they wait until.
If when if not when will they.

Stanza LV

I have been thought to not respect myself
To have been sold as wishes
To wonder why and if and will they mind
To have it as it is and clearly
To not replace which if they as they do
Can they content can they be as content
For which they will if even be it mine
Mine will be or will not be mine
Rather than mine and mine.
I wish to say
That it is her day
That it might be well
To think well of it
It is not often led or left
But whichever and whenever
Can they not only be
All mine.
I often think will I be thought to know
Oh yes of course I will be known to know
I will be here I will be here and here
It may not be that it is I am here.
I will not add it more and not
Not change which is a chance to leave it.
I can be often very much my own
I wonder why
Is it that is it here.
Can I but not to try
I can cradle not infancy but really
What I can.
They can collect me.
They can recollect me
They can if mine is mine.
Not even mine is mine.
Mine which is mine.

Nobody knows a name for shame.
Shame shame fie for shame
Everybody knows her name.

Stanza LVI

I could be thoroughly known to come again.
Often if I do
I come again.
As often if I do.
I could not change often for often.
Which I do.
Often for often which I do.

Stanza LVII

I have often been doubtful if yes or no
Annoys him.
Or is it only the setting sun
Or the chairs softening
Or the direction changing
In which they see why I do.
Might it not be only what they like.
I like what I like.
Can they not like what they like.
But very often he means nothing.

Stanza LVIII

By which they might.
I have often thought that it is right
That they come if they might
But which they change from their right
To imagine which they might
If they tried.
Not only why they wish but if they wish for us
It can be not only that only that is gone
But which they might not only
But which they might if not only
Once when they went to go
But which if they might

I think might they if they might.
I wish would wish that they might
If they might they would not if they wish.
Would they if they not only would they
But which if they would if they might.
Now then how strangely does it happen
If better not not only now and then.
This which I wish to say is this.
It has happened which I wish
Now and then.
This which I wish is to happen
Now and then.
This which is if I wish.
Which is to happen now and then.
The way to change this to that
That is now this now this to that
Or that to is it this to that
Or no not indeed that.
Because of this or is it this to that.
By which I mean to say dozens to-day
Yesterday or dozens also
Or more over more alike and unlike.
This which I wish to say once which I wish to say
I wish to say it makes no difference if I say
That this is this not this which I wish to say.
But not not any more as clear clearly
Which I wish to say is this.
She has left roses and the rose trees.
By which I mean to say is this.
If it had happened not only were they not remembered
But if at all not even if at all
Not even if at all if if they were not remembered.
I could have not only which if which if whenever.
I can choose what I choose that is to say not chosen.
Not only if they were not having been where.
No one can partly go if I say so
However much they could
Did if they would.

But which they much as if they were
To add more he comes here
As if he came here from there.
I wish to say I could not remember better
Nor at once
By which I mean
Could they come here I mean.
They have come here.
Each one has come here once or twice as that.
Make it three times and they will remember better.
Not only that but will I will I be
Partly with it partly for it
Partly for three
Not three but three times.
And not three times three but any three times.
This can be wrong it can have happened well
Very well it can have happened.
That if they came four times
They had come three.
It can not even not be better yet
Not as yet
Should they be thought to be.
By which no one means what I do.
I do not partly do not.
Or if not partly do if not
I come back just to think is three not more than four.
Or is three not enough if four are not more.
This can they try.
This that they can come here
Of course this that they can come here
Of course no more no more of course no more.
Can we know that there is this difference.
No more not any feel it known as well
This which I tell this which I tell.
Do you delight in ever after knowing.
But which they mind that always as they come
Not only heard it once but twice but not again.
They could they could if not their ground

They could if they could not stand their ground
They will be shelves of shelves
Rather be only rather with their shells of shells
Or best or needed needed in their praise
Of course we speak very well of them
They have been able too.
Able to be able not only ours abound
But which could which tell if no one.
No one adds palpably to their amount.
There there they read amount account
Cover better a wasp came sitting gently
To tell of a coincidence in parting
And to be well kept in which after which
In doubt in no doubt now
But they feel grapes of course they do or show
Show that grapes ripen ripen if they do
Not always do if not if not that they often do
But which if which
There is no advantage.
I wish to say again I like their name
If I had not liked their name
Or rather if I had not liked their name.
It is of no importance that I liked their name.
There can be this difference.
It can be one number that is written
To mean that it is another number which is to follow
Or it can be that the number which is to follow
Is the number that is written.
The only thing that helps one with that
Is memory.
And sometimes I remember and sometimes I do not
And if I remember can I be right.
Or is it best to look back to be sure.
After all they could not know which I said.
And they are not forgotten but dismissed.
Why should one forget and dismiss which one of this.
This which they add that I do.
I could never believe that I could not happily deceive.

Stanza LIX

Some one thinks well of mine.
Some how some think well of mine.
Well as well but not as well as mine.

Stanza LX

Next to next to and does.
Does it join.
Does it mean does it join.
Does it mean does it mean does it join.
If after all they know
That I say so.

Stanza LXI

I wish once more to mention
That I like what I see.

Stanza LXII

By which I might if by which I might.
There can be only which if once I might.
If once I might delight.
If if not once if not I might delight.
Either is other other is order
Or if they ordered that no one is to wish
Not only wish but which
Not only not not only
Not if they not if they wish.
They not only had they been
But they had been as much as disappeared
They could candles water-falls if they liked
They could call bread easily bread
They could even do as they wish
They might even do that
Not only as they like but when they find
Not easily when they find
Not more not easily when they find
They carry which they carry

They add not only not that which they add
But they must not add will they
If they need no one to force them
To declare
That they will not add if they change.
They should not easily delight.
Not only theirs.
Should they increase if they could like it.
And can they call for them.
I wish moreover to say
That I was not surprised.
I could remember how many times there was an interval
In not only which way but in any way
They can nearly not be known
Not more than once at all.
After which can they lead.
I need no one to rest well
They will call a light delight.
They like sun-light day-light and night as a light
They also like day-light
They also need their light.
They also will show it as their light to-night.
They also will remain if they remain and leave it.
As they might.
This which I say has meant this.
I cannot call it that there is no doubt.
Is there if I say what I do say
And say this.
Moreover if they stretch as not only will they do it.
But can they not only not do it
But not have done it.
Not at all.
She can be appointed.
It can be an appointment
They will not nearly know
Which they can care to share.
I wish I wish a loan can they
Can they not know not alone

Not know why they can
As it is of no use
That they sat as they say
In a way as they did not sit
In a way to stay.
This which has been as this.
They have been with them there.
Can they not care to spare
That they were if they were there.
This which I remember
I do not remind them to say.
Of all of them one of them.
Which can birds lay.
They like to be as tall as more anymore.

Stanza LXIII

I wish that I had spoken only of it all.

Stanza LXIV

So far he has been right
Who did alight
And say that money would be plenty.

Stanza LXV

They did not know
That it would be so
That there would be a moon
And the moon would be so
Eclipsed

Stanza LXVI

Once in a while as they did not go again
They felt that it would be plain
A plain would be a plain
And in between
There would be that would be plain
That there would be as plain
It would be as it would be plain

Plain it is and it is a plain
And addition to as plain
Plainly not only not a plain
But well a plain.
A plain is a mountain not made round
And so a plain is a plain as found
Which they can which they might
Which they tell which they fill
Could they make might it be right
Or could they would they will
If they might as if they will
Not only with a will but will it
Indeed it will who can be caught
As sought
For which they will in once
Will they they will
Might they not will they will
Much which they had they will
It is of ever ready pleasure
To add treasure to a treasure
And they make mine be mine
If once when once
Once when they went once
In time
They can be used to prove
They can be well they have been
Shove
Shove is a proof of love
This which they have been
And now they add this which
In which and well they wish
They add a little pink
To three which were as well
For which they do not add
A wish to sell
They will add will they well
Well if they wish to sell
Well well if they wish to sell
Who adds well well to a wish to sell

Who adds well to a wish
Who adds a wish to well
We do.
We had been as well
And we do.

Stanza LXVII

I come to gather that they mean
I do.
I come not only well away
From hound
A hound is a dog and he has known his name
Another dog and not a dog
Not a dog in his name
I wish not wish not will
Will they be well as well
And for it no one need a moon
A moon at noon
What was it that she said
A sun and moon and all that loss
Divide division from a horse.
She said I would she said I did
Not only which not only why.
Why will be well as well reject
Not to neglect
Not if they wish alike to try
Can they as well be well
Will they as by and by.
Which I can say
Which I can to-day
To say
Could they come as they go
More than which whether it is best
Do do so.

Stanza LXVIII

I need not hope to sing a wish
Nor need I help to help to sing
Nor need I welcome welcome with a wind

That will not help them to be long.
Might they not be there waiting
To wish this
Welcome as waiting and not waiting more
I do not often ask I do not wish
Do not you wish
Do not you either wish
Or ask for all or more.
There is no hesitation to replace
Which when they will and can they will
By and by he asks it not to be there.

Stanza LXIX

Be made to ask my name.
If I think well of him be made to ask my name.

Stanza LXX

I cannot leave what they will ask of it
Of course of course surely of course
I could if I could know
Does if does it seem so
Can we if I am certain to be sure
That it is as I do
It should be changed to place
They can if will they care
They can if as it could
Be not more added.
I cannot if I ask be doubtful
Certainly not
Nor could I welcome change as neither change
Nor added well enough to have it known
That I am I
And that no one beside
Has my pride
And for an excellent reason
Because I am not only
All alone
But also

The best of all
Now that I have written it twice
It is not as alike as once.

Stanza LXXI

There was once upon a time a place where they went from
time to time.
I think better of this than of that.
They met just as they should.
This is my could I be excited.
And well he wished that she wished.
All of which I know is this.
Once often as I say yes all of it a day.
This is not a day to be away.
Oh dear no.
I have found it why will he.
This which I wish to say is this.
Something that satisfies refuses.
I refuse to be ought or caught.
I like it to be caught or ought.
Or not if I like it to be ought or caught.
This is whatever is that they could be not there.
This is an introduction to Picabia.
When I first knew him I said
Which was it that I did not say I said.
I said what I said which was not in him.
Now who wishes that said is said.
Not him or women.
Or sigh or said.
I did not say I wished it was in him.
Not at all I said forget men and women.
Oh yes I said forget men and women.
Oh yes I said I said to forget men and women.
And I was not melancholy when I thought of everything.
Nor why I thought.
Of course nor why I thought.
That is enough not to have given.
And now if why might I.

The thing I wish to say is this.
It might have been.
There are two things that are different.
One and one.
And two and two.
Three and three are not in winning.
Three and three if not in winning.
I see this.
I would have liked to be the only one.
One is one.
If I am would I have liked to be the only one.
Yes just this.
If I am one I would have liked to be the only one
Which I am.
But we know that I know.
That if this has come
To be one
Of this too
This one
Not only now but how
This I know now.

Stanza LXXII

I think I said I could not leave it here.
I can be all which when whenever either or
Can they be which they like for.
Or will they worry if they lose their dogs.

Stanza LXXIII

Can she be mine oh can she can she be
If they could welcome wish or welcome
But they will be surprised if they call me
Yes can they gather or they gather me.

Stanza LXXIV

It is not what they did which they ask me
Or for which if they could they give to me
Not ducks of Barbary

Because if ducks there be
They will be eating ate or would be
Better known than if not.
Will they leave me.
Of course if rather gather.
Can they be inestimably together.
It is as very long to be indefinable
As not for which not if for which
They wish.
Thank them for gathering all of it together.

Stanza LXXV

I like that I like.
Oh yes not if not I like
Can they be a credit a credit to him
I like
If when if I like
Not if in choosing chosen.
Better which pronounced which
If which plus which
Can they be I like.
I need no one to prefer refer
Or rather mainly used.
More which they change.
Let us be thoughtful
Let us know that if they could be known
They would be gathered if at known
Say so
Manage not only not to say so.
Saying no
I wish to think that I had thought.
I had not only loved but thought
I had not only even called and taught
I had meant will or well of fishes
I had thought could they call me well of wishes
Can they be only once allowed
But which they frame.
Having not had a picture

Which to frame
Now I do know a name
Why when they like a man called Susan
He will regret allowed for Susan
Or just why why if they can not try.
It is to gather other than he knows
When once is often
Who will begin again.
Ours are ours all ours are hours
We had a pleasant visit with not mine
Would they have been would they have been in time.
Should they if they.
They will gather love is mine.
Butter is mine.
Walls are not only mine
Will they or if they had rather
Been when they were to find mine.
They will not either leave it all to chance
Or yet no one knows movements which having fallen
He fell to seat it where they could be all
No one imagines all for either all
Red or not red
I do dislike to hear
That red is here.
Thank you kindly for the thought
That either we are bought.
Or really not to be bought
By either caught or ought.
Should shell fish be well baked.
Or either will they all in origin.
Remain remained tall.

Stanza LXXVI

I could not be in doubt
About.
The beauty of San Remy.
That is to say
The hills small hills

Beside or rather really all behind.
Where the Roman arches stay
One of the Roman arches
Is not an arch
But a monument
To which they mean
Yes I mean I mean.
Not only when but before.
I can often remember to be surprised
By what I see and saw.
It is not only wonderfully
But like before.

Stanza LXXVII

Now I wish to say I am uncertain if I will if I were every day
of any day.

Stanza LXXVIII

It is by no means strange to arrange
That I will not know
Not if I go or stay because that is of no importance
No what I wish to say is this.
Fifty percent of the roses should be cut
The rest should bloom upon their branch
By this means no one will mean what they pleased
And even if they are occupied they are content
To believe mind and wind, wind as to winding
Not as to rain and wind.
Because because there is very little wind here
Enough of rain sometimes too much
But even so it is a pleasure that whether
Will they remain or will they go even so.
I wish to know if they only mean to know
By me by you they will as readily maintain
That not by me by me as well remain
I wish to know if it is well to be by now to know
That they will remain if they might mean I know
If once if once if I might mean I know

That not which only if which only now to know
Know not in mean known if it is not only now
They could in gather mean if they meant mean
I mean.
This which I wish to add I wish to wish to add.
Can I can I be added which is not any wish.
To add.
I which I wish to add why should add not rhyme with
sad and glad
And not to talk to-day of wondering why away
Comes more than called to add obey to stay
I wish I had not thought that a white dog and a black dog
Can each be irritably found to find
That they will call us if if when if added once to call
Can they be kind.
We are kind.
Can they be kind.
I wish no one were one and one and one.
Need they think it is best.
Best and most sweetly sweetness is not only sweet.
But could if any could be all be all which sweet it is
In not withstanding sweet but which in sweet
Can which be added sweet.
I can I wish I do love none but you

Stanza LXXIX

It is all that they do know
Or hours are crowded if not hours then days.
Thank you.

Stanza LXXX

Can she be not often without which they could want.
All which can be which.
I wish once more to say that I know the difference
between two.

Stanza LXXXI

The whole of this last end is to say which of two.

Stanza LXXXII

Thank you for hurrying through.

Stanza LXXXIII

Why am I if I am uncertain reasons may inclose.
Remain remain propose repose chose.
I call carelessly that the door is open
Which if they can refuse to open
No one can rush to close.
Let them be mine therefor.
Everybody knows that I chose.
Therefor if therefor before I close.
I will therefor offer therefor I offer this.
Which if I refuse to miss can be miss is mine.
I will be well welcome when I come.
Because I am coming.
Certainly I come having come.

These stanzas are done.